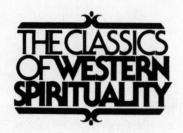

D1261074

THE CLASSICS OF WESTERN SPIRITUALITY
A Library of the Great Spiritual Masters

NATIVE MESOAMERICAN SPIRITUALITY

ANCIENT MYTHS, DISCOURSES, STORIES, DOCTRINES, HYMNS, POEMS FROM THE AZTEC, YUCATEC, QUICHE-MAYA AND OTHER SACRED TRADITIONS

EDITED WITH A FOREWORD, INTRODUCTION AND NOTES
BY
MIGUEL LÉON-PORTILLA

TRANSLATIONS
BY
MIGUEL LÉON-PORTILLA,
J. O. ARTHUR ANDERSON, CHARLES E. DIBBLE
AND MUNRO S. EDMONSON

PREFACE
BY
FERNANDO HORCASITAS

PAULIST PRESS
NEW YORK • RAMSEY • TORONTO

Cover Art
The artist, Gloria Ortíz, is a native of Cali, Colombia. Currently a free lance designer and artist in Manhattan, Ms. Ortíz studied art at Marymount College in Tarrytown, New York and has shown her paintings in Bogotá and New York. Mythological images from her Latin American roots were the inspiration for Ms. Ortíz' cover art.

Design: Barbini, Pesce & Noble, Inc.

Library of Congress
Catalog Card Number: 80-80821

ISBN: 0-8091-2231-6
      0-8091-0293-5

Published by Paulist Press
Editorial Office: 1865 Broadway, New York, N.Y. 10023
Business Office: 545 Island Road, Ramsey, N.J. 07446

Printed and bound in the
United States of America

Contents

Editor of this Volume

MIGUEL LEON-PORTILLA was born in 1926 in Mexico City. After receiving an M.A. degree in philosophy at Loyola University of Los Angeles, Cal., he studied history at the National University of Mexico from which he holds a Ph.D. in pre-Columbian literature and history. He was a student of the well-known Nahuatl scholar Dr. Angel M. Garibay. He has taught courses in Mesoamerican cultures, languages and literatures at the National University of Mexico and, as a visiting professor, at various universities of the United States and Europe. He is at present a member of the Institute of Historical Research at the National University where he served as Director from 1963 to 1975. He has worked among Nahuatl speaking Indians in various parts of Mexico. The study, analysis, paleography and translation of the pre-Columbian literature in Nahuatl has constituted his main field of interest. He has published numerous articles in such journals as *Estudios de Cultura Nahuatl, Historia Mexicana, Bulletin de l'Association Gillaume Budé, American Anthropologist, Current Anthropology, Hispanic American Historical Review* and *The Americas.*

The list of his books, originally written in Spanish or English, includes *Aztec Thought and Culture* (Univ. of Oklahoma Press), *Pre-Columbian Literatures of Mexico* (Univ. of Oklahoma Press), *The Broken Spears* (Beacon Press), *Time and Reality in the Thought of the Maya* (Beacon Press), as well as several volumes of texts in bilingual editions, Nahuatl-Spanish, published by the National University of Mexico Press. Translations of several of his books have appeared in French, German, Italian, Russian, Polish, Swedish and Hebrew. Professor León-Portilla, who is a member of many learned societies, has received the Sourasky Prize, the Serra Award and has delivered the Distinguished Lecture 1974, at the Annual Meeting of the American Anthropological Association. He resides in Coyoacan, in the outskirts of Mexico City, with his wife Ascensión, also a historian, and their daughter Marisa.

Author of the Preface

FERNANDO HORCASITAS received an M.A. degree in Anthropology from the University of the Americas, Mexico, in 1953. He has taught courses in Ethnology, Nahuatl Language, Mesoamerican Codices and Chronicles, and Ethnohistory of Mesoamerica at the Colegio de México, University of the Americas, National University of Mexico and Escuela Nacional de Antropología. He has contributed numerous articles to Mexican, American and European scholarly journals and received a Guggenheim fellowship to prepare a work on the Colonial drama in Nahuatl, published by the National University of Mexico in 1974 as *El teatro náhuatl.* His bilingual (Nahuatl and English) *Life and Death in Milpa Alta* was issued by the University of Oklahoma Press in 1972. At present he is coeditor with Miguel León-Portilla of *Tlalocan,* a journal dedicated to the publication of Mesoamerican sources, often in Indian languages, and a research professor at the Instituto de Investigaciones Antropológicas of the National University of Mexico where his work lies mainly in the ethnography of the modern Nahuatl speaking peoples of Mexico and Central America.

Foreword

The ancient Mesoamericans, the peoples who inhabited nuclear and southern Mexico, and adjacent parts of Central America before the Spanish arrival, included among their cultural achievements rich literatures which give testimony of their spiritual concerns. Some texts belonging to such literatures in various indigenous languages escaped destruction and have reached us. The aim of this book is to present relevant examples of them.

For the most part these testimonies were originally expressed in Nahuatl (also known as Aztec or Mexican) and in Yucatec and Quiche-Maya. Although we are not able to establish precise dates of composition, we can assert that the majority of the texts we offer in translation were conceived in the post-classic period of Mesoamerica (950–1521 A.D.). Their authors were the sages, priests and members of the ancient nobility. Most of them remain anonymous to us but we know at least the names and something about the lives of a few. Thus we will include here the extant compositions of the sage Nezahualcoyotl (1402–1472), and of some of his contemporaries.

Our book encompasses examples of the Mesoamerican creation myths, discourses known as "the ancient word", the story of Quetzalcoatl, doctrines about the afterlife, numerous hymns, poems, and a series of compositions of philosophic reflection about realities human and divine.

Various questions will be discussed in the Introduction to facilitate the understanding of these Mesoamerican classics. Among them stand out the following: How these testimonies were expressed and preserved? Which was the cultural background of their authors? In what sense these texts can be described as examples of spirituality? How such a literature escaped the destruction which followed the Spanish conquest and, in our days, has become a subject of research?

FOREWORD

The present publication of this literature has become possible to a great extent thanks to various colleagues and friends. In particular I want to express my gratitude to professors Arthur J. O. Anderson, Charles E. Dibble, and Munro S. Edmonson for their generosity in permitting me to take advantage of parts of their translation into English of some texts of the *Florentine Codex*, and *The Popol Vuh, The Book of Counsel.* I should like to express also my appreciation to the staff of the Paulist Press for their careful work in editing and publishing my own text and the translations I have prepared for this book.

Preface

During the first two generations after the conquest of Mexico by Cortes in 1521, Christian missionaries and their native converts succeeded in setting down, on paper and in the European alphabet, a multi-faceted body of pre-Columbian Indian literature. These myths, epics, and poems, centuries old by the time of the European invasion, had been preserved by memorization and in the pages of the native books we call codices.

The present work is a collection dedicated to literary production in various indigenous languages of Mexico and Central America, with particular emphasis on that in Nahuatl, the tongue of the Aztecs. It contains the most engrossing examples of said literature, translated directly into English by modern scholars from the resonant phrases of the ancient Mexicans.

The post-Conquest recording of the texts lasted a period of some 70 years (1530–1600) and the material comprised poetry, mythology, song, oratory, fragments of plays, temple hymns, sagas, and folklore. Toward the year 1600, however, the vitality of the early period of missionary and Indian intellectuality was waning, and as there loomed that great century of consolidation—the seventeenth—scant attention was paid to the manuscripts lying in the dusty monastic libraries of Mexico and Central America. Millions of people still spoke the aboriginal languages but the pre-Hispanic ways of life and ideological patterns had paled to the point that the deeper meanings of the texts, often of a mystical nature, had become almost unintelligible to all. Most of the words could be translated with the aid of Indian-Spanish dictionaries but after attempting to interpret the ancient texts, the few scholars still interested in pre-Columbian literature were not much wiser than before beginning their task.

In spite of the research of a few exceptional men—a handful of Jesuits in the eighteenth century and a scattering of historians in the nineteenth—Indian literature was lost to the world. Scholar and lay-man alike remained ignorant, though in many cases curious, of how the native peoples, by then maligned or grotesquely romanticized, had really viewed the cosmos and mankind. The key to the door of "a world that had never heard of Caesar", separated from the Old by tens of thousands of years, seemed to have vanished forever.

The story of the re-discovery of pre-Columbian literature is not unlike that of the decipherment of Egyptian hieroglyphs. The last priests and scribes who could read the ancient texts died around the sixth century A.D. and the books of Manetho and Herodotus, con-fused and contradictory, were not enough to unravel the mystery. During some 1300 years travellers from distant parts of the world journeyed to temples such as that of Karnak to gaze upon immense walls and obelisks, profusely covered with carved signs, and won-dered what the enigmatic inscriptions concealed. After 1821, thanks to Champollion and Young, who based their research largely on contemporary linguistic materials, the decipherment of the hiero-glyphs enabled the world to realize that the Egyptians had produced more than sphinxes, pyramids and tombs. The discovery of the meaning of the hieroglyphs revealed the flesh and blood of ancient Egypt, the spirit of its people emerging in a thousand hitherto unex-pected ways.

But in the Mexico of the 1890's the visitor was still led by force through the halls of the National Museum to view what seemed to him, and to the world at large, a forest of stone death heads and idols decorated with writhing serpents. If he was curious enough, and could read Spanish, a few of the missionary chronicles were avail-able in print, but his perspective of ancient Indian life and thought remained even more muddled than that of visitors to Egypt before the age of Champollion.

Nevertheless, between 1890 and 1910, quietly, known only through scholarly publications, a few students of the Indian lan-guages, especially Nahuatl, were working on the ancient texts: Eduard Seler in Germany and Francisco del Paso y Troncoso in Mexico, to mention only two. A systematic, scientific interpretation of the past through its written sources was being launched on a small scale. The exploration and interpretation of ancient Indian mentality through its literature did not evolve in one moment.

In this century a Mexican priest, Angel Maria Garibay, well

PREFACE

versed in humanistic studies, began to learn the language of the Aztecs in the 1920's and his first translations of Nahuatl poetry were published in the next decade. In 1940 he produced *Llave del náhuatl*, a grammar with an appendix containing many ancient texts. Since then a school of translators—Mexican, American and European— have labored painstakingly, slowly opening the door to which the key had been lost. Our knowledge of Nahuatl literature, consequently, dates back only a little more than half a century and the present book, the work of Garibay's most distinguished successor, is the only comprehensive anthology in English today.

The struggle to re-discover Aztec literature was well worth the toil it involved. What a fresh, multi-colored world lay behind the door that had been sealed for 300 years! Instead of a savage tribe of plumed warriors and grim priests dancing around a sacrificial stone to the woeful beating of a tom-tom, the Aztecs now unfold before us as a puzzled, meditative people, ridden with questions about the essence of human and divine, perplexed by the real meanings of life and death. Their literature expresses these concerns in refined cadences, exultant at times, wistful at others, extolling friendship and music and pleasure and beauty. Among these poetic "strings of flowers", sung to the plaintive notes of the flute, are interwoven the subtle doubts that mystified the poet-philosophers: preoccupations with this life and the hereafter, and the difficulties of finding truth on earth.

Understandably, a modern reader may wonder how a book on the literature of an ancient American civilization can be involved with Western culture, how it can be relevant to modern man.

But two peoples are involved here and in different senses both are heirs to Western civilization. The first is the modern Indian, and I have in mind especially the groups of Nahuatl speech. They are involved but will not be affected perceptibly by this book, in part because its contents are in English and in part because they have already inherited much of the material the work deals with. The second people are the non-Indians, direct heirs to European culture.

The modern Indian still preserves as oral literature a part of what this book contains. After the cataclysm of the Spanish conquest and the decline of his ancient culture, despite a short flowering under the missionaries, the native peoples became a mass of peasantry, in the long run largely incorporated in Western civiliza-

PREFACE

tion. Almost a million people still speak the Nahuatl language but more than half of them also know Spanish, wear Western clothing, profess Christianity, ride in buses, and occasionally go to the movies. To varying degrees, however, this collectivity retains its ancient psychology and some of its philosophical and literary patterns.

The Ancient Word or moral speech is still alive in many Indian communities and is expressed at marriage ceremonies in solemn sentences to strengthen the young couple in their new life. The cosmogonical myths are not dead: stories about the creation of man and the universe are still told, about how a youth jumped into a fire and blazed forth as the sun and how his younger brother emerged more faintly as the moon. The deluge myth is re-told in versions reminiscent of the pre-Hispanic stories, intertwined with the Biblical account. Even some of the details of the epic of Quetzalcoatl, the culture hero, have survived among the inhabitants of communities at the foot of the snowy peaks of Popocatepetl and Iztaccihuatl, scene of the Toltec mystic's departure from the country. The villagers point out traces of hands and feet on certain rocks and attribute these marks to the passing of a holy man in ages past.

The wistful laments over the withering of flower and song are not dead. In the mountains of northern Puebla, during a curing ceremony at the entrance of a cave, I have heard a Nahua woman in her cups, half tears, half laughter, sing:

Let there be violin playing,
Let there be guitar playing.
May I enjoy myself, may I laugh before the world!
I am only here for a while, I am only passing;
Tomorrow or day after I will be under the earth,
I will become dust.
Let us drink our liquor, let us enjoy it!
Today, this afternoon, we will rejoice,
We will laugh here.
Let those who are sour forget their sourness,
Let those who are angry forget their anger.
Not every day, not every afternoon,
Will we be here to enjoy life on earth.

Her song is an echo, altered as it may be, of the ancient lyric poems, many examples of which the reader will find in this book.

PREFACE

The pre-Columbian spirit and oral legacy undoubtedly aided the Indian to survive into our times. And he has survived, against the most crushing, overwhelming odds. Through the centuries the Ancient Word and the lyric songs have given heart and courage to the individual as they did 500 years ago.

The present collection should interest social anthropologists and ethnohistorians engaged in the study of Mexican and Central American peoples. Through these texts the researcher or field worker can acquire a deeper perspective into the value attitudes of the Indian community, often affected by the struggle between the traditional and the modern. A generation or two ago he did not possess this complementary but valuable material.

The science of archaeology is also affected by the re-discovery of Indian literature, as is the outlook of the art historian. The new National Museum of Anthropology of Mexico, inaugurated in 1964, exhibits inscribed verses taken from the Indian sources at the entrance of the different halls. And when a modern archaeologist unearths the figure of a goddess in his diggings he will no longer be forced to label it starkly as "Xochiquetzal, goddess of flowers". Today he has a host of richly worded texts amplifying his perspective and the meaning of his discovery.

And finally, of what value can this book be to the ordinary modern reader who is neither an ethnologist nor an archaeologist? He will find that this work presents human problems couched in exquisite literary forms. Often they are not necessarily Indian nor our own: they are simply human. A collection such as this cannot fail to be an invitation to those who are inclined to explore moral climates and are receptive to new ideas. The intellectual pursuits of the Indian worshippers of the gods Tlaloc and Huitzilopochtli will occasionally seem home ground to him. At other times he will be faced with ideas that will be totally new.

No society is in a perfect state of equilibrium and the Aztec was no exception. During the late fifteenth and the early sixteenth centuries, when many of these texts reached their present form, the ancient Mexicans seem to have been passing through a crisis not unlike that of our own modern world: militarism, state worship, insatiable desires of conquest, and unending warfare. The voices of those who created these conditions can be heard in this book, but so can those of the dissidents who sought less tangible realities. A school of art, that perhaps could be called "secular", came to portray naturalistic subjects such as images of the common man, fruits, and animals. It competed with the art that created hieratic "poems in stone" such as that of the Mother Goddess, Coatlicue, She of the Snaky Skirt. To many thinkers "He Who Is Near and Close" was perhaps not felt to be so near and close as He had been. "He Who Is as Invisible as the Night and Intangible as the Wind" may have seemed more invisible and intangible than ever. The perceptive reader will discover the poet's resources in facing these questions and expressing his unique *clamavi ad te* to the Giver of Life. When the reader turns to the mystics who wrote the Yucatec-Maya and Maya-Quiche parts of this book he will find situations and anxieties parallel to the Aztec, although the mode of expression will exhibit an intensity and color of its own.

Inevitably, much of what the modern reader will get out of this book, as in any reading, will depend upon the reader himself. Some may discard Indian literature as a product of a fantastically remote culture, alien to what he considers his own supremely enlightened and progressive civilization, and may dismiss its mythology and imagery as too exotic to transmit any direct message. Another type of reader, however, captured by the beauty of the lines, his mind perhaps less cluttered with stereotypes, will be able to bridge the gulf and find a breath of life in the texts. He may want to open the book at random and he may find verses here and there, composed "in the night, in the wind", that will bring ease to his heart as he walks "between the abyss on one side and the ravine on the other." And those who are weary of all the conflicting elements in our present realities, who long to shatter "this sorry state of things entire" will find heart if they can get a glimmering—even though it be faint—of the jade and turquoise the Indian poet sought and found in his songs.

Pronunciation Note

The alphabetic representation of the sound units of the words from the Mesoamerican languages in which our texts were composed follows the system introduced by the Spanish missionaries immediately after the Conquest. Although there are modern phonetic alphabets to write Nahuatl (Aztec), Yucatec-Maya, Quiche-Maya, and Mixtec, I have preferred to stay close to the traditional system that reflects the ways in which most of these testimonies were rescued and are thus preserved in the ancient manuscripts.

In general, all the letters have the same phonetic value as in Spanish. Nevertheless there are some exceptions and other points in particular that ought to be clarified for English-speaking readers.

Vowels:

- *a*   as in f*a*ther
- *e*   as in m*e*t
- *i*   as in f*ee*t
- *o*   as in *o*rgan
- *u*   as in f*oo*t

Consonants:

- *h*   with a soft aspiration as in *h*orse
- *tl*   very frequent in Nahuatl, represents a single sound and therefore should not be divided. Its pronunciation is similar to that of the *tl* in A*tl*antic
- *ts*   and *tz* also represent a single sound as in bi*ts*

u (or hu-) before *a, e, i* and *o* is pronounced as the English
w

x as the English *sh*

The Maya language has several explosive consonants: *b, k, p,
t, tz.*

While Nahuatl words are stressed on the next to last syllable,
Maya are often accented on the last.

Introduction

1. General Introduction

Compositions by poets, sages and priests of pre-Columbian Mexico comprise the bulk of this volume. Now, the mere fact that these texts are published here as part of *The Classics of Western Spirituality* poses several questions worthy of attention. In summary form they can be expressed as follows: Was there such a thing as a native literature in that part of the Americas before the Spanish arrival? If there was, and we know that some of its productions have come down to us, what sort of spirituality can we perceive in them? Finally, whatever may be the meaning we will discern in these texts, why are they set here side by side with the spiritual masters of Western civilization?

Although the whole answer to these and other related questions will be given precisely by the contents of this book, I consider it appropriate to bring them into focus now. Yes, pre-Columbian man in Mexico and in some adjacent places of Central America—in what is today described as Mesoamerica—actually attained the level of a civilization and high culture. He developed functional socioeconomic structures, lived in large towns and cities, was the creator of divers and often extraordinary forms of art, invented a calendar one ten-thousandth closer to the astronomic year than our own count after the Gregorian correction and, finally, was in possession of both oral tradition and writing by which he preserved the memory of his past and his own views on things human and divine.

Extremely important achievements of the Mesoamerican peoples were actually their discoveries of precise systems of measuring the passing of time and their various forms of writing. Such accomplishments, the result of long processes of cultural development, transformed the life of ancient Mexico. As was the case in other civilizations, mainly those that flourished in Egypt, Mesopotamia, the Indus River Valley, and China, to be in possession of a calendar and of legible characters or hieroglyphs opened enormous possibilities to the Mesoamericans. For with these agriculture as well as religious and social endeavors followed much better defined and more effective patterns. The sages also had the means of keeping precise records of significant events.

Oral tradition no doubt persisted and even became in various ways systematized in the native schools. But its effectiveness increased tremendously with the art of reducing to symbols the core of the religious beliefs, ancient wisdom, myths, and history that were recorded in the painted books. More ample consideration will be given here to oral tradition in the Mesoamerican centers of learning and to the specific forms of calendar and writing developed in this part of the New World. For the moment it is enough to recognize their existence as resources that permitted the preservation of native literatures in various languages of Mesoamerica. That some examples at least of said literatures have thus reached us is now a critically well established fact.

How these texts escaped the destructions that followed the Spanish conquest and were eventually rescued will be a subject of special consideration in this book. The fact is that more than fifteen of the pre-Columbian books or codices and numerous documents in different native languages, mostly transcriptions of ancient compositions made during the sixteenth century, are carefully preserved at present in various museums, archives, and libraries of Mexico, the United States, and several European countries.

As detailed information on the whereabouts of the compositions to be included here will be offered later, we will now turn our attention to the second question: What kind of classics of spirituality can be found among the extant Mesoamerican texts?

Native American Classics of Spirituality

To give a universally acceptable definition of spirituality is not an easy task. And if this holds true even in specific cases within the sphere of the Western world, the problem increases enormously in dealing with cultural traditions such as those of the ancient native Americans. A generic description shall be at least attempted since it is necessary to frame an answer to the question that has been raised. A valid description should include, as sine qua non elements and traits, the following: a sense of mystery, the awareness that beyond what is physically perceivable, beyond what appears as merely material, there are in the universe other sources of meaning, dynamic principles, supernatural beings, ultimate realities, with which man can communicate once he discovers the means of approaching them.

A capacity whose mere existence more than once has been denied appears to be at the core of the question. The belief in spirituality, as a human attribute related to a soul or a nonmaterial aspect of man, has been described, for instance, as a trait that characterized

INTRODUCTION

the early or primitive stages in mankind's cultural evolution. On the other hand, some contemporary philosophers and scientists, recognizing the existence of this attribute in man, underline the fact that the capacity to approach the realm of mystery and of ultimate realities may be trained and enriched, or, in opposite cases, dimmed.

People living at different times and places have discovered for themselves or learned from others how to conceive ideas such as those of the world as a realm of meaning, and, although a place of sorrows, the habitat of symbols where dialogue with ultimate realities, even a personal Supreme Being, is difficult but not impossible. Some of the discoverers or followers of this form of wisdom, enriched with it, have transformed their own and many others' lives. Some have exerted tremendous influence as prophets, saints, mystics, religious leaders, and so on. Others have restricted their concern to speculation or knowledge and, though they eventually have transformed the existence of their disciples and of large societies, their aim has not been a living approach to what can be described as sacred in the universe of ultimate reality. This has been the attitude of some philosophers and theologians.

And of course there is also the case of those who seem to have been born destitute of, or have completely lost, that sense of mystery, that awareness of a concealed beyond, those who restrict their interest to what is for them the only reality, the material universe. In the generic description I am trying to give, these last typify an extreme, the one that seems farthest removed from any sort of spirituality. However, it is ironical that so-called materialist thinkers or atheists often fall into assertions that, in a negative form, imply the absoluteness of the ultimate realities. Their unsociability with what is labeled a mere superstructure of material reality sounds thus apparent. The only exception perhaps is represented by those who seem to have been born without this human concern for ultimate meaning, those blind to mystery and to any possible beyond.

Now an answer can probably be attempted to the question about what kind of classics of spirituality can be found among the ancient native texts of Mexico and adjacent parts of Central America. Some of these compositions convey the myths and ancestral legends, early attempts to approach the mysteries that surround man's existence on earth. Several of the native myths, mainly in the Maya language and in Nahuatl, the tongue of the Toltecs and Aztecs, have been preserved. Some examples will be offered in this book. Other texts that we attribute to the anonymous endeavors of the groups of priests and sages who resided close to the temples or in the schools are conveyors of "The Ancient Word" (*Huehuetlatolli*), speeches and other forms of expression to communicate the group's wisdom about the gods, particularly the supreme Giver of Life, the norms of behavior, the principles of education, the beliefs concerning the afterlife, and so forth.

Besides this rather abundant corpus of compositions, other more personal expressions of the ideas and feelings of the sages living in ancient Mexico will be quoted. To better convey their thoughts, deep experiences, and intuition, the pre-Columbian sages frequently had recourse to distinct forms of poetry. There were on the one hand the sacred hymns addressed to this or that god, mainly at the feasts held at regular intervals according to the calendar. On the other hand, and that may be of particular interest for us, numerous compositions have survived that speak of the spiritual concerns of sages about whose names and lives information has reached us. In these compositions one probably can discover the best examples of the specific kind of spirituality attained by these ancient Americans.

Focusing now on the case of the Aztecs, in the midst of whom lived the sages I am talking about, it is important to remember that, far from being a monolithic culture, theirs was a world where opposed views often coexisted. According to the Aztec official beliefs, it was a national destiny to perform the duties of the chosen people of the Sun. This included, among other things, providing the supreme Sun God with the vital energy of blood, which was to be obtained from sacrificial victims. Only in this way could the Sun be fortified and a cosmic cataclysm be avoided.

Many among the Aztecs thus spent *their time* engaged in all sorts of war, mainly ceremonial warfare, the principal way of procuring victims for the sacrifices. In this form, fighting and conquering many other peoples became a fundamental activity in their social, political, religious, and national life. A people that had thus oriented its destiny came to develop what can be described as a mystic militarism.

This warlike mysticism may appear utterly repulsive to modern man, who nonetheless also commits himself to martial enterprises and, on account of them, brings about the sacrifice of his brethren by the millions. But this is obviously less significant than the existence of early native testimonies already expressing an open op-

INTRODUCTION

position to any sort of warfare. I refer to the officially proclaimed need and value of war. Two examples will suffice at this point:

Arrogant stand the warriors,
those who snatch whatever is
precious,
gold, splendorous feathers, turquoises . . .
Those intoxicated with the liquor of
death . . .

Let us spend our lives
in peace and pleasure . . .
Fury and wrath are not for man,
The earth is vast indeed![1]

Inebriation with death, war, and conquests is not a path to the Giver of Life. Thus the same sages added:

To invoke Him
with the strength
of the eagle and the jaguar,
with the force of the warriors,
will lead only to the speaking of false words on earth . . .[2]

Some sages, going further, also questioned other officially supported practices and beliefs. A craving for meaning was at the core of their concern. In their texts we find questions like these: "What is your heart seeking? What is perchance stable and lasting? Does man possess any roots? Do we really live on earth? Do we speak the truth here?"[3]

They accepted the evanescent quality of all that exists on earth. "Although it be jade," they said, "it will be broken, although it be gold, it will be crushed. Here nothing forever grows green. We only dream, everything is like a dream."[4]

---

1. *Collection of Mexican Songs.*, Preserved at the National Library of Mexico, fol. 16 r.
2. *Ibid.*, fol. 13 r.
3. Compositions in which these and other questions are expressed will be included in parts 5 and 6 of the present book.
4. *Collection of Mexican Songs*, fol. 17 r.

INTRODUCTION

Such recognition of the ephemeral destiny of whatever appears on earth confirmed in their eyes the uselessness of warlike endeavors as a means of preventing the death of the Sun.

Research has revealed the names of some of those who supported the militaristic ideology so closely related to Aztec official religion. And, also, we have been able to identify "the faces and hearts"—the personalities—of others who opposed it and sought different paths in their search for meaning. In the present book I will include compositions that were the personal creation of some of these sages whose names and lives are known to us.

Several of their extant poems, the best testimony I know of the ancient Mexicans' spirituality, permit us to say something about the search and approaches of these sages. They were certainly eager to find an entrance into the mysteries that surround man's existence on earth, and we are fortunate in being able to say that the surviving texts let us glimpse what they finally discovered or thought they had unveiled.

This assertion brings us close to the last of the questions we have raised: Whatever meaning we discern in these compositions, why are they presented here, side by side with the spiritual masters of Western civilization?

To answer this, let us consider first some of the possible levels of meaning inherent in the texts that convey ancient Mesoamerican spirituality. There is a most profound level we have to accept as unattainable to us. I refer to that kind of meaning which was fully understandable only to those who participated, from the inside, in the same cultural realm. Obviously we confront here an insurmountable epistemological problem. In this respect we have to recognize that these ancient Mesoamerican texts are extremely remote. They are further removed from Western culture than, let us say, an ancient Jewish composition, as they are not related to it either as an antecedent or as a creation in any possible way derived from it.

Are then these Mesoamerican productions completely unconnected with the cultural heritage of Western man?

A first kind of answer can be stated in terms of the humanism that at times has flourished in Western civilization. These ancient Mesoamerican compositions, as well as the great classics of India or China, are not unrelated to the cultural heritage of Western man because he has attained a level of interest that permits him to identify himself with the Latin sentence, *Homo sum, nihil humanum a me*

INTRODUCTION

alienum puto (Being a man, nothing human is strange to me). And it must be added that, while Western man is guilty of many forms of cultural aggression, imposition, ethnocentrism, he has also developed forms of comprehension that facilitate his understanding of culturally different peoples. This is the aim of disciplines like cultural anthropology, ethnology, philology, and world history, all of which have attained an extraordinary development in the context of Western civilization.

Nevertheless, no matter how far Western scholars, trained in these and other disciplines, penetrate into the meaning of texts such as these from ancient Mesoamerica, the fact remains that they inevitably must approach them from the outside. Is there perhaps another way to reach a fuller understanding of our Mesoamerican compositions? Let us briefly discuss a possibility that may eventually allow us to enter a deeper level of meaning.

To most Americans of European descent it seems that their civilization and culture are vigorous outgrowths, in many ways tremendously enriched, of the so-called Western world. In this sense the New World appears in their eyes as an originally empty though fertile realm where it became feasible to transplant that culture whose main ingredients are the Egyptian, Mesopotamian, Jewish, Greek, Roman and Christian legacies. It is said that the most distinguished bearers of Western culture in the modern age—when people began to discover and settle the Americas—were those of Anglo-Saxon, or more generically of Germanic, origin who brought with them beliefs, ideas, and forms of action derived from their own conception of Christianity. Now, to most of those who for years have thus thought of themselves and of the America in which they live, it will naturally sound absurd to hear about an "Indian" ingredient in their culture, particularly in its spiritual aspect.

My point is not to discuss whether it is incongruous or not to think of an aboriginal cultural influence in the case of white Anglo Saxon Christian Americans. My intention is to contrast the aforementioned attitude with that which prevails among other people who also live in the Americas and for whom native culture and history are in fact a part of their legacy. This is the case of the majority of the Mexicans, the Central Americans, the inhabitants of the Andean nations, and also of a large number of persons living in the United States Southwest.

As a consequence of various centuries of uninterrupted ethnic and cultural mixture in these areas, a bridge exists that communicates what is Western with what is native American. And if this communication has brought many times, from the part of the dominant society, attempts and achievements of cultural absorption, it is also undeniable that this bridge exists as truly as the faces of many millions of Mestizo people.

In the particular case of Mexico it can be stated that many languages and many of the cultural traits of the native Americans are still alive. Elements pertaining to the ancient indigenous peoples have also been incorporated into the forms of life of the Mestizo majority. Mention can be made not only of items as obvious as those present in the diet, arts, dress and so on—there are also the traditions and beliefs, and the extremely polite manners and sensibility of indigenous origin.

Now, individuals endowed with the knowledge of the native languages, and above all with that sense of participation from the inside in their approach to the expressions of native American spirituality, will probably have a deeper penetration into the meaning of texts whose rediscovery enriches a people sharing at the same time the institutions of Western civilization and something of the ancient indigenous culture. That a level of meaning linked somehow with the original connotations of the native texts can thus in some way be attainable implies an important consequence. These native American classics of spirituality—when properly dealt with—are no longer to be regarded as alien in the sense that there cannot exist a consubstantial bridge between them and the spiritual masters of the West. The contemporary researcher, properly equipped, can take advantage of this bridge's existence. A realm of unsuspected wisdom will then begin to manifest itself. By virtue of this cultural *mestizaje* or amalgamation we have been talking about, it will not sound aberrant to place side by side with the spiritual works of the West those so close to us of the indigenous man of the Americas.

The answers I have given to the questions raised explain why I accepted the idea and the invitation of the Paulist Press to prepare a "Mesoamerican book" for their series.

A Frame of Reference

To assist the reader, including the one totally unfamiliar with the civilization of Mesoamerica, in his approach to these indigenous classics of spirituality, it is of prime importance to provide him with

INTRODUCTION

a frame of reference. A concise analysis of the geographical and cultural meanings conveyed by the term Mesoamerica will be our first step in that direction.

Mesos is the Greek equivalent to the English *middle*, so the term *Meso america* appears as coined to point out that area situated between North America proper and the southern part of the New World. But the fact that such appellation has been introduced with intrinsically correlated geographical and cultural contents, adds to it a dynamic accent in function of which its most obvious meaning, the referred to territory, has to be understood as an entity subject to variations.

Mesoamerica implies no doubt an area in the above pointed out middle portion of this continent—that territory, very small at first, where a high culture was born, and then much larger where great cultural transformations continued to appear with ups and downs, resulting in further geographical expansions or contractions.

Around 1400 B.C., in just a small part of what later became the Mesoamerican area of high culture, some villages of agriculturalists and pottery makers grew into larger human settlements. More complex forms of social, economic, and political organization developed there. Division of labor; great artistic creations; an omnipresent religion, rooted in the ancient beliefs but enriched with new doctrines, rites, and ceremonies; a calendar and hieroglyphic writing, stand out among the most significant elements that came to integrate that constellation of achievements implied by a high culture. Afterwards, urban life and the formation of large chiefdoms, even empires of a sort, gave rise to new forms of existence. The style of life of a civilization commenced to consolidate and to influence other communities, reaching at given moments, through commerce or conquests, peoples separated by considerable distances.

In the span of life of autonomous development of the Mesoamerican civilization, during almost three thousand years before the Spanish arrival, moments of territorial expansion, followed by others of contraction, were not a rarity. Thus the geographical and the ethnic and linguistic components of Mesoamerica were not the same during the various periods of its long history. If the beginnings of Mesoamerican high culture are perhaps to be ascribed to one indigenous group, many other peoples participated later in the series of creations on account of which this great civilization of the New World can be defined.

INTRODUCTION

It will be enough for the moment to give the extension of Mesoamerica on the eve of the Spanish conquest. Its northern frontiers were at that time the Sinaloa River to the northwest (some six hundred kilometers to the south of the Arizona border) and the Panuco River to the northeast, (about 300 kilometers below the point where the Rio Grande has its mouth), while in the central part it did not extend beyond the basin of the Lerma River. Its southern limits were the Motagua, which empties into the Gulf of Honduras, in the Caribbean; the southern shores of Nicaragua Lake, and the Nicoya Peninsula in Costa Rica.[5]

Mesoamerica as an area where man succeeded in creating a high culture, its evolution, with particular emphasis on its spiritual achievements—religious beliefs, art, writing, and calendar—through the so-called Classic and Postclassic periods until the days of the Spanish Conquest, will be now the subject of our attention. With this background, I hope, the approach to our Mesoamerican classics will be meaningful.

---

5. Some German scholars, in particular Eduard Seler (1849–1922), introduced more than seventy years ago, the expression *Mittel Amerika* to connote the area where indigenous high culture flourished in Central and Southern Mexico and the adjacent territory of the northern Central American nations. Many years later, in 1943, Paul Kirchhoff published in Mexico a paper focusing his attention upon the geographic limits of the area he described as "Mesoamérica: sus límites geográficos, composición étnica y caracteres culturales", *Acta Anthropologica*, 1 (Escuela Nacional de Antropología, México, 1943), 92–107. Today *Mesoamerica* and *Middle America* are used as having an identical connotation.

2. The Cultural Evolution of Mesoamerica

Antecedents

Around 5,000 B.C. some groups living in what is now Central Mexico and in the Sierra of Tamaulipas (not very far from the Texas border) entered into a process of changes that ended up in the practice of agriculture. Discoveries made in caves such as the one of Cozcatlan, Puebla, show how, little by little, the former gatherers began the domestication of squash, chile, beans and corn. The production of pottery started considerably later, around 2300 B.C.

In various parts of central and southern Mexico and in Central America, villages of farmers and pottery makers began to proliferate. Some of these villages, probably those established in better environments—such as those on the banks of a stream or close to the sea—experienced an early growth in population. The inhabitants of the villages scattered over such a vast territory often differed ethnically and linguistically.

From among these different peoples, some were soon to stand out as initiators of new forms of life and creativity. Archaeological evidence shows that a series of extraordinary changes began to appear, commencing around 1300 B.C., in an area close to the Gulf of Mexico, in southern Veracruz and the neighboring state of Tabasco. That area has been known since the pre-Columbian days as "The Rubber Land," *Olman*, the land of the Olmecs.

Excavations made in Olmec centers such as Tres Zapotes, La Venta, San Lorenzo and others have revealed great cultural transformations. La Venta, the largest center, was built on a small island a few meters above sea level, in a swampy area near the Tonala River, sixteen Km. before it empties into the gulf of Mexico. Although available stone is more than seventy Km. distant, a number of colossal stone sculptures and other monuments have been unearthed there.

In La Venta, as in some other Olmec sites, a sort of proto-urbanism began to develop. The agriculturalist villagers who settled in the vicinity of La Venta had probably experienced, together with a population growth, various kinds of urges that stirred them from their old ways of subsistence. What they achieved presupposes, as well, changes in their socioeconomic, political and religious forms of organization.

INTRODUCTION

As far as known, the Olmecs rank first in time, in what was to be named Mesoamerica, as builders of large complexes of edifices mainly for religious purposes. Thus, the center of La Venta, skillfully planned, included mud-plastered pyramids, long and circular mounds, stone-carved altars, large stone boxes, rows of basalt columns, tombs, sarcophagi, stelae, colossal heads of basalt, and other smaller sculptures. The existence of large plazas seems to indicate that religious ceremonies were performed in the open air. Jaguar masks, formed with green mosaics, have been found in the floor of some of the open spaces in front of the religious buildings.

The existence of a division of labor can be asserted by inference. While many individuals continued to be concerned with agriculture and other subsistence activities, others specialized in different arts and crafts, in the task of providing the defense of the group, in commercial endeavors, in the cult of the gods and in the government, which probably was in the hands of the religious leaders.

Olmecs worshiped an omnipresent Jaguar God. Elements attached to the symbolism of what later became the Mesoamerican Rain God probably derived from the Jaguar God's mask. In the stelae and other monuments various representations of fantastic birds, often in association with jaguars, serpents, or human beings, are visible. The offerings found in burials give testimony to a cult of the dead with a belief in an afterlife. The earliest vestiges of the Mesoamerican calendar and writing are also linked to the series of achievements on account of which we can speak now about the birth of a high culture, that of the Olmecs.[6]

Some of the symbols and hieroglyphs used by the Olmecs survived through the various cultural stages of Mesoamerica. This, and the fact of the early diffusion of Olmec elements in different places, some far from the centers of origin, seems to confirm the character of a *mother high culture* that has been attributed to that developed by the Olmecs. Their influence—probably through commerce and perhaps also by a sort of "missionary" religious impulse—is manifest in many sites of the area close to the Gulf of Mexico, and also in the

---

6. For reliable general works about the origins, development and diffusion of Olmec culture see: Michael D. Coe, *America's First Civilization* (New York, 1968) and Ignacio Bernal, *The Olmec World*, (The University of California, Berkeley, 1969).

14

INTRODUCTION

Central Plateau, in Oaxaca, in the land of the Mayas and in Western Mexico (Guerrero and Michoacán).

Some few hundred years before the Christian era, when Olmec high culture had already declined, other centers in the above mentioned areas were about to flourish. They were the closest antecedent of the Classic period in Mesoamerica. Then an authentic civilization was born, which, as we will see, developed and diversified to different degrees as it became assimilated and enriched by a variety of peoples.

The Classic Period (c. A.D. 1 to 850)

Teotihuacan, the "metropolis of the gods," is the best example of what was the culmination of Classic civilization in the central plateau. There authentic urbanism came into being. Recent archaeological research has revealed that not only a large ceremonial center but whatever is implied by the idea of a city had developed there.

Teotihuacan did not grow at once. It took several centuries for generations of priests, architects, and sages to plan and realize, modify, enlarge, and enrich what perhaps was originally conceived as an entity to exist forever. Besides the two great pyramids and the Temple of Quetzalcoatl, the Plumed Serpent, other enclosures, palaces, schools, and different forms of buildings have been discovered. Large suburbs where the community had their homes surrounded the more compact religious and administrative center. Avenues and streets were paved and there also existed a well-planned drainage system. Pyramids, temples, palaces, and most of the houses of the rulers or members of the nobility were decorated with mural paintings. Gods, fantastic birds, serpents, jaguars, and various plants with flowers were represented in the paintings.

The metropolis of Teotihuacan, which at its zenith around the fifth century A.D. extended over a surface of around twenty square kilometers, probably had a population of some fifty thousand inhabitants.[7] Differences of status related to divisions of labor, an efficient army, extensive agriculture, and a well-organized commerce, with merchants going to distant places are some of the features that, by

---

7. René F. Millon, "The Study of Urbanism in Teotihuacan", *Mesoamerican Archaeology*. New Approaches, edited by Norman Hammond, (London, 1974), 313–334.

inference, can be recognized as appertaining to what probably was the socioeconomic structure of the Teotihuacan state. The many vestiges of its influence in various remote sites, in Oaxaca, Chiapas, and even in the Guatemalan highlands, seem to indicate that Teotihuacan was the center of a large kingdom or of a confederacy of different peoples.

Teotihuacans worshiped several gods that later were also to be invoked by other Nahua-speaking peoples. The names of these gods are Tlaloc and Chalchiuhtlicue, Lord and Lady of the Waters; Quetzalcoatl, the Feathered Serpent; Xiuhtecuhtli, Lord of Fire; and Xochipilli, Prince of the Flowers. As in the case of other institutions, the art that flourished in Teotihuacan was to influence, in various forms, other Mesoamerican peoples.

Parallel to the development of Teotihuacan—although in some cases a few centuries later—civilization developed also in other subareas of Mesoamerica. One early instance is offered by the site of Monte Alban in Central Oaxaca. There, in addition to the religious center built on a hilltop, numerous structures visible on the slopes give evidence of the existence of a rather large urban settlement. More complex forms of writing, with dates, place-names, and other hieroglyphs appearing in various inscriptions, are also a testimony of the high cultural level attained by the Zapotecs, who had built Monte Alban and ruled over many other groups in what is today Oaxaca.[8]

Thanks to archaeology we also know about more than fifty Maya centers of considerable importance that were built during the Classic period. Some of the most famous are Tikal, Uaxactun, and Piedras Negras in Guatemala; Copan and Quirigua in Honduras; Nakum in Belize; Yaxchilan, Palenque, and Bonampak in Chiapas; Dzibilchaltun, Coba, Labna, Kabah and the early phases of Uxmal and Chichen-Itza in the Yucatan peninsula.

Arguments have been offered to assert or to deny the urban nature of the Maya centers. Today it is generally recognized that such settlements built on the banks of rivers, as those close to the Usuma-

---

8. In relation with early forms of writing and the development of the calendar, see: Alfonso Caso, "Zapotec Writing and Calendar," *Handbook of Middle American Indians*, Austin, University of Texas Press, 1965, v. 3, p. 931–947; also: Hans J. Prem, "Calendrics and Writing, Observations on the Emergence of Civilization in Mesoamerica", *Contributions of the University of California, Archaeological Research Facility*, Berkeley, 1971, num. 11, p. 112–132.

cinta or, in general, within a dense tropical forest area, encompassed not only the sanctuaries for the gods and the palaces for the religious leaders but also residential quarters for the people. In some cases, as in Dzibilchaltun, archaeological research has been eloquent enough in that respect. In speaking about other various centers it is clear that the dwellings for the people, often thatchroofed, perishable pole structures, have left in most cases no detectable traces.

If our ignorance is great about the political and socioeconomic structures of the Classic Mayas, at least we can appreciate some of their extraordinary creations in the arts, hieroglyphic writing, calendrics, and astronomy. Mention has to be made here of their architecture, which included the corbeled vault, their sculpture, in particular the bas-reliefs, and their mural paintings, such as the famous ones of Bonampak in Chiapas. Thousands of hieroglyphic texts, inscribed on stone stelae, stairways, lintels, paintings, ceramics, and books or codices, force us to affirm that the Maya priests and sages were in possession of an extremely sophisticated high culture. Even if up to now we are unable to decipher most of the contents of the inscriptions, we can at least glimpse some of the concepts of which they were conveyers. Dates, commemorating events, calendrical and astronomical records and their corrections, prophecies, the names and deeds of some prominent warriors, chiefs, rulers, priests, and sages, emblems of places, hieroglyphic texts associated with various stone-carved scenes in which humans and or gods are represented, seem to be the most frequent themes of the inscriptions.[9]

Today we know that the Classic Mayas had various calendars of extreme precision. Thus their year-count was one ten-thousandth closer to the astronomical tropical year than is our own calendar after the Gregorian correction. On the other hand, the Mayas, inheriting this perhaps from the Olmecs, were also in possession of a concept and symbol for nought. Such a discovery, made several hundred years before the Hindu had developed the idea of zero, was a consequence of the fact that the Olmecs, Zapotecs and Mayas were already giving a positional value to the numbers in their vigesimal

9. A great contribution in this particular field is the one made by J. Eric S. Thompson, *Maya Hieroglyphic Writing: An Introduction (University of Oklahoma Press, Norman, 1960)* and *A Catalogue of Maya Hieroglyphs*, (University of Oklahoma Press, Norman, 1962).

system. Great surprises await those who will perhaps succeed in the complete deciphering of the Maya writing. A universe of ideas and symbols, the core of the Maya world view—what they thought about divinity, human destiny, and the earth on which they lived—will then be revealed.[10]

While it appears that Teotihuacan had a sudden end around A.D. 650, it is known that the Zapotec city built on Monte Alban prolonged its existence during a period of decadence until it was finally abandoned. In the case of the Maya centers, a moment arrived, in a sort of irreversible series, when the priests no longer raised stone-carved stelae with inscribed dates. Then, perhaps in a rather slow process, one by one or several at once, the old cities began to be deserted.

Beyond the conjectures to explain the whys of the collapse of the Classic period in Mesoamerica, the fact remains that between 650 and 90 A.D. a cultural downfall occurred. However such a decadence did not mean the death of high culture in this part of the New World. Other peoples in various ways inherited and developed many of the Classic attainments. Some of these achievements colored the following cultural evolution of Mesoamerica. Not a few of them survived the Spanish conquest and are even now ingredients in the culture of many native groups and at times of the Mestizo majority that inhabits this part of the continent.

Postclassic Period: The Toltecs (950–1150)

Many groups lived in the North beyond the territories subject to Teotihuacan, that is, beyond Mesoamerica. Mention has to be made here of those generically called Chichimecs, the barbarian seminomads, gatherers and hunters. Others already practiced agriculture to a limited degree. Archaeology has shown that the Teotihuacans had exerted, at least indirectly, some influence on some of these groups. This appears to be particularly true in the case of the Pueblo Indians, the most advanced in the vast territories north of Mexico. Evidence also exists of the presence of some groups, culturally and perhaps also politically related to Teotihua-

---

10. See: Miguel León-Portilla, *Time and Reality in the Thought of the Maya*, (Boston, 1972).

can, who had settled in the North as advanced outposts, to protect the frontier from incursions of the Chichimec barbarians.

Those who were later to be called Toltecs have to be included among the settlers in the advanced outposts. When the collapse of Teotihuacan became known to them, they apparently decided to "come back," as the native texts put it, to the land of their cultural origin, that is, Central Mexico. Various accounts speak about their wanderings before they reached small towns still inhabited by people of Teotihuacan origin. The Toltecs finally settled in Tula, a place about fifty miles to the north of present-day Mexico City. Tula or *Tollan* actually means metropolis. And that was precisely what the Toltecs were about to build, a town whose destiny was to follow the traces and glory of Teotihuacan.

Quetzalcoatl: The Priest and Sage

A central figure in Toltec history is the famous Quetzalcoatl, a sort of culture hero who derived his name from that of a god worshiped since the days of Teotihuacan. Numerous native books and texts in Nahuatl speak about his portentous birth, life, and deeds. It is said that while Quetzalcoatl was still young, he retired to Huapalcalco, a former settlement of the Teotihuacans, to devote himself to meditation. There he was taken by the Toltecs to act as their ruler and high priest.

Native books attribute to him whatever is good and great. He had induced his people to worship a benevolent supreme Dual God, *Ometeotl.* This same god was also invoked as the "Precious Feathered-Serpent" or "Precious-Feathered-Twins," as both meanings are actually implied by the term Quetzalcoatl, at once the name of the god and of his priest.

The golden age of the Toltecs encompassed all sorts of achievements.[11] Palaces and temples were built. Many towns and peoples accepted the rule of Quetzalcoatl. But some enemies, who were probably religious adversaries, attempted to destroy that age. Some texts, which we will include in this book as a part of the Mesoamerican classics of spirituality, speak about the appearance of the one

---

11. For a comprehensive study about Toltec culture, see: Claude Nigel Davies, *The Toltecs,* (University of Oklahoma Press, Norman, 1977).

INTRODUCTION

named *Tezcatlipoca,* "the Smoking Mirror," a god that came to Tula to force Quetzalcoatl to abandon his city and his followers. According to these accounts, the departure of the wise priest precipitated the ruin of Tula. Other texts speak about two different critical moments. The first was that of the flight of Quetzalcoatl. Although tragic indeed, it did not bring about the complete downfall of Tula. The second took place several decades later. Huemac was the king ruling at that time. His forced departure and death around 1150 marked the irreparable collapse of Tula.

The ruin of the Toltecs meant, on the other hand, a diffusion of their culture and their penetration among various distant peoples. The presence of the Toltecs is recorded in annals such as those of the Mixtecs of Oaxaca and the Mayas of Yucatan and Guatemala.

The Mixtecs and Mayas during the Postclassic Period

The Mixtecs succeeded the Zapotecs in Oaxaca after the cultural and political decline of the latter. To the Mixtecs has to be assigned the founding of new towns, such as those of Mitla, Tilantongo and Teozacualco, as well as the partial rebuilding of famous Zapotec cities and strongholds. They excelled also in the arts, particularly as goldsmiths. Metal work—gold, silver, copper and to some degree tin—was introduced in Mesoamerica around A.D. 950 as a consequence of a diffusion from its place of origin in the Andean zone. The Mixtecs are also well known for their books of historical content. A few of them have reached us with records that take us back to happenings as distant in time as A.D. 692.[12]

The Mayas, who then lived in the highlands of Chiapas and Guatemala and in the peninsula of Yucatan, had not recovered their former splendor. Nevertheless, some small kingdoms showed some signs of prosperity. This was the case of the Quiche and Cakchiquel regions in the highlands of Guatemala and the renewed centers of Uxmal and Chichen-Itza to which others, such as Mayapan and Tulum in the Yucatec peninsula, have to be added.

The arrival of groups of Toltec origin in Yucatan and Guatemala contributed to the alteration of the situation. Those who entered

---

12. In a posthumous publication of the Mexican scholar Alfonso Caso an analysis is offered of the contents of several Mixtec native books containing biographies of a good number of rulers and noblemen from 692 to 1515 A.D. *Reyes y Reinos de la Mixteca,* (Fondo de Cultura Económica, México, 1977).

Guatemala appeared as followers of Gucumatz, the Quiche and Cakchiquel translation of the name of Quetzalcoatl. In Yucatan the guide of the invaders was called Kukulcan, a word with an identical connotation. Many questions can be raised relative to this complex of Quetzalcoatl-Kukulcan-Gucumatz. Thus it has been said that numerous Toltecs and other peoples that left Central Mexico with them after the ruin of Tula marched to distant places following chieftains who posed as being endowed with the attributes of a Quetzalcoatl. The fact is that new Quetzalcoatls appeared, although at this time they were more militaristic minded than religiously inclined.

In Guatemala—as is told in the Sacred Book of the Quiches, the *Popol Vuh*—Gucumatz and his followers imposed themselves on the Mayas.[13] Thus a new mixture of peoples and cultures occurred. The Guatemalans to various degrees became "Toltequized." In Yucatan much the same thing took place. Toltec influence was so strong there that in Postclassic Chichen-Itza pyramids and other temples and palaces were built imitating those of the metropolis of Tula. However, neither the new blood nor the cultural elements that had arrived from the central plateau of Mexico brought about a renaissance in the Maya world. Its destiny was to survive with no splendor until the days of the Spanish conquest.

New Penetrations from the North:
The Arrival of the Aztecs (1200–1325)

The complete abandonment of Tula, as had been the case with the collapse of Teotihuacan, facilitated the entrance into the Valley of Mexico of groups that had lived beyond the northern frontier of Mesoamerica. This time barbarian Chichimecs were the first to burst into what used to be Toltec domains. Various native texts describe what happened then. The Chichimecs, in trying to take possession of the rich, abandoned territory, came to meet some families and groups of Toltecs who had remained in their homeland.

Although first contacts were far from friendly, little by little things changed for the better. Processes of acculturation, extremely interesting and fully documentable through various available

---

13. The *Popol Vuh* or "Book of Counsel" is one of the sources offering abundant examples of the myths and the lucubrations of the Mesoamerican sages.

sources, developed.[14] The food gatherers and hunters began to settle in the neighborhood of decadent towns where Toltec culture had flourished. The Chichimecs dominated from a political and military standpoint. However, those in possession of Toltec high culture were to influence the Chichimecs deeply. Reluctantly at first and willingly later, the latter accepted agriculture, urban life, Toltec religion, the calendar, and the art of writing.

Thus by the end of the thirteenth century, new states or chiefdoms existed in Central Mexico. Some were the result of a kind of renaissance in towns of Toltec or even Teotihuacan origin. Others were strictly new entities in which the cultures of Chichimecs and Toltecs had melded.

This was the situation in the Valley of Mexico and its surrounding areas when other groups from the North also entered it. This time those arriving did not speak a barbarian Chichimec tongue. Their language was Nahuatl, that which had been spoken by the Toltecs and by a good number of Teotihuacans. The various Nahuatlan groups—the so-called Seven Tribes—resembled, in some of their cultural traits, those Toltecs who had been living earlier in the northern outposts, on the frontier of Mesoamerica. In the texts left by some of them it is often repeated that "we are coming back from the north, we are returning to where we used to live. . . . "

Aztec penetration or, as it is often described, their "pilgrimage," had to overcome numerous obstacles. Many were the hardships, persecutions, attacks, and so on, that they had to face until they finally settled on the island of Tenochtitlan, in the lakes that covered a large part of the Valley of Mexico. This occurred, according to various sources, in 1325.

The Aztec Nation

When the Aztecs established themselves in the island of Mexico-Tenochtitlan their social and political organization was still that of a group basically linked by kinship. They were still governed by various aged priests.

In 1363, the year that the mountain Popocatepetl began to give forth smoke, the old chieftain Tenochtli died after having led the

---

14. See: Miguel León-Portilla, "La Aculturación de los Chichimecas de Xólotl", *Estudios de Cultura Náhuatl,* (Universidad Nacional de México, 1968) VII, 59–86.

INTRODUCTION

Aztecs for many years. The Aztecs considered then the possibility of being governed by a *tlatoani* or king, imitating other peoples who had that form of rule, such as the Culhuacans, a neighboring people of Toltec origin. The implicit thought was that Mexico-Tenochtitlan could not grow great unless it had its roots in the splendid past of the Toltecs. The Aztec elders remembered the king of Culhuacan. A group of them went then to ask from him, as a most great favor, that he should grant them one of his children to reign in Mexico-Tenochtitlan.

Thus the Aztecs had their first king, the one named Acamapichtli. From that moment on the available records about the Aztec past acquire a different tone. Myths and legendary accounts make way for a history in which political and social changes, as well as the deeds of well defined individuals, are carefully described. Thus we know, for instance, about some important achievements that took place during the reign of the first Aztec ruler.

The building of the city went forward, and little by little the face of the Aztecs became known, with features that began to recall those of the Toltecs. The Aztecs paid tribute to the Tepanecs of the kingdom of Azcapotzalco, owners of the island on which they had settled.

Acamapichtli died around 1390 and was succeeded by his son Huitzilihuitl. The new *tlatoani* was married to a daughter of Tezozomoc, lord of Azcapotzalco, and because of this he was able to obtain a mitigation of the heavy tributes the Aztecs had been paying. Huitzilihuitl used the period of friendship to give his full attention to the internal problems of his people. But the advances achieved by the Aztecs aroused suspicion and dislike among a number of the nobles of Azcapotzalco. Maxtlatzin, a son of the aged Tepanec ruler, began to plan the destruction of the Aztecs, for he believed they should not be permitted to maintain any form of independence.

The death of Huitzilihuitl in 1415 and the election of young Chimalpopoca as the third Aztec king seemed to offer a favorable opportunity for the realization of the designs of Maxtlatzin. The whole future of the Aztec people was then gravely threatened.

The Great Aztec Crisis and Its Consequences

When the king of Azcapotzalco died in 1426, his throne was taken over by Maxtlatzin. One of his first acts was to make patent his

23

hatred for the Aztecs. To learn about what he did, let us quote the native annals:

> In the year 12-Rabbit [1426], the Tepanecs of Azcapotzalco
> killed king Chimalpopoca, ruler of Tenochtitlan,
> son of Huitzilihuitl. . . .
> The Aztecs were filled with despair
> when they were told that Maxtlatzin and the Tepanecs
> were taking up arms against them,
> to surround and destroy them.[15]

Various native books and chronicles speak of the dilemma in which the Aztecs then found themselves. Now already under the guidance of a new king, Itzcoatl, they were forced to choose between accepting the will of Maxtlatzin, that is their total submission to Azcapotzalco, or revolting. At that moment a truly extraordinary figure took the floor for the first time. He was a young man named Tlacaelel, a member of the family of the former king Huitzilihuitl. He spoke boldly, rejecting the idea of any surrender to Maxtlatzin and convincing the Aztecs that they must fight the Tepanecs, even if it meant death.

To relate how the Aztecs defeated Azcapotzalco would be lengthy and out of place. It is sufficient to say that our sources attribute the victory to the leadership of Tlacaelel. For several decades he persevered as the wise counselor of various Aztec kings. And because of what he did, it can be stated about Tlacaelel that he contributed, as perhaps no one else, to the consolidation of Aztec greatness, the whole of the achievements that so deeply impressed the Spanish conquistadores not so many years later.[16]

Having gained the full independence of Mexico-Tenochtitlan, Tlacaelel with three acts laid the basis for a new structuring of the Aztec state. First, he created a military aristocracy by granting titles

---

15. Fernando Alvarado Tezozomoc, *Crónica Mexicayotl*, Text in the Nahuatl language translated into Spanish by Adrián Léon, (Universidad Nacional de México, 1949), 104.

16. About the person and deeds of Tlacaelel the already quoted work of the Aztec chronicler Alvarado Tezozomoc, *Crónica Mexicayotl*, is particularly rich in information. Tlacaelel's greatest achievement was to develop a mystic-militarism which later became part of the official dogma of the Aztecs. In this respect the thought of Tlacaelel deeply contrasts with the expressions of other Mesoamerican sages whose compositions will be included in the present book.

of nobility to warriors who had distinguished themselves in the fight against Azcapotzalco. Then he took land from the enemy in order to divide it among the Aztec ruler, the members of the group of noblemen, the newly formed military elite, and some of the *calpullis,* or corporate groups of kinsmen that were important units in the social organization of Mexico-Tenochtitlan. Finally, and perhaps most importantly, Tlacaelel set out to create for his people a new version of their history.

A brief text reports a meeting of Itzcoatl, Tlacaelel, and other Aztec leaders after the victory over Azcapotzalco. At that meeting they are supposed to have decided to burn their own books, as well as those of Azcapotzalco.

> A record of their history was kept. But then it was burned during the reign of Itzcoatl in Mexico. A resolution was taken; the Aztec chiefs said, it is not suitable that everyone should know the pictures of the books. The people, our subjects, would be ruined and the earth would move crookedly, because there is much falsehood therein, and many in such pictures are taken for gods.[17]

Clearly, the later Spanish book burners had their forerunners among the indigenous rulers of Aztec society. In the new version of history that was then promoted, the Aztecs claimed a direct relationship to Toltec nobility; and their divinities, especially their patron Huitzilopochtli, God of War, were raised to the same plane as the creator gods of old times. Above all, this new history exalted the military spirit of the "People of the Sun," the Aztecs themselves, as worshipers of the great heavenly body, already identified with their god Huitzilopochtli, whose mission was to subdue the other nations of the earth, which would provide the sacrificial blood to nourish the supreme Giver of Life.

This is not the place to describe the series of conquests and other achievements due to the various rulers who, in an uninterrupted succession, led the destinies of the Aztecs until the eve of the Spanish arrival. However, because their names are mentioned in some of

---

17. *Codex Matritensis,* preserved in the Library of the Spanish Royal Academy of History, folio 192.

INTRODUCTION

the texts included in this book, it will be pertinent to list them here: Montezuma I, Ilhuicamina (1440–1469), Axayacatl (1469–1481), Tizoc (1481–1486), Ahuitzotl (1486–1502), and Montezuma II, Xocoyotzin (1502–1520).

Visible consequences of the endeavors of these *tlatoque* or rulers of the Aztec nation were the extraordinary development of the metropolis of Mexico-Tenochtitlan, the rapid growth of its population as well as that of its confederate neighbors, and, of course, the fact that the Aztecs came to impose their rule on several million persons. The so-called Aztec empire stretched from the Pacific Ocean to the Gulf coast and from the Central Plateau of Mexico to territories of present-day Guatemala.

Hernando Cortes in his letters to Charles V, Bernal Diaz del Castillo in his *History,* and the other Spanish chroniclers of the Conquest described the beauty and magnificence of the Aztec metropolis, its palaces and temples, sculptures and mural paintings, great plaza and the seventy-eight ceremonial buildings, the market, the gardens and orchards, and the streets, canals, and causeways that linked the island with the mainland.

But it was not only the pyramids, sculptures, and paintings that astonished the conquerors. They saw the power and wealth of Montezuma, the shrewdness of the merchants, the endurance of the warriors and their captains, and the sagacity of the priests and leaders who not only presided over religious affairs but also advised the supreme ruler. The priests were in charge of educating the young people; they were custodians of esoteric knowledge, of the calendar, and of the art of writing in the painted books and inscriptions. Bernal Diaz del Castillo, the soldier and chronicler, described the houses and the schools and temples where priests and wise men guarded "the many books of paper folded like Castilian fabrics."[18]

In sharp contrast to all this, the conquistadores also contemplated things they regarded as the work of the Devil. They were particularly horrified by what seemed to them devilish visages of the idols, and perhaps even more by the sacrifices of men and the stains of blood everywhere, in the temples and in the faces of the gods and the priests.

---

18. Bernal Díaz del Castillo, *The Discovery and Conquest of Mexico,* (New York, 1958), 215–216.

3. The Contrasted World in Which the Mesoamerican Classics of Spirituality Were Preserved and Enriched

Aztec beliefs, rites, sacrifices, feasts, priesthood, and all aspects of worship, although already integrated as elements of a single religion, had, in many cases, diverse origins. Traditions of great antiquity persisted as a common inheritance of many peoples within Mesoamerica. Other forms of belief and worship appertained, for their part, to the specific heritage of the Aztecs, who had come at a much later date to settle in Central Mexico. Nevertheless, as a consequence of the work of the priests, what can be described as Aztec religion, far from being a mass of heterogeneous elements had rather a functional ordering.

Before we describe the origins and themes of the Mesoamerican classics that comprise this volume, it is necessary to see how, within the official religion of the Aztecs, beliefs and rituals had been reshaped in terms of their mystic-militaristic world view, in sharp contrast with which a truly spiritualistic wisdom had also developed.

According to the ancient Mesoamerican cosmogonic thought, the world had existed not in one, but in various consecutive times. The one called "first founding of the earth" had taken place thousands of years earlier, so much earlier that, altogether, there had already existed four suns and four earths prior to the present age. Through these eras or "suns" processes of evolution developed with the appearance form each time more perfected, of human beings, plants, and foodstuffs. Four primordial forces—earth, wind, water, and fire—in a curious similarity to classical thought, had ruled these ages until the arrival of the fifth or present epoch, that of the "Sun of Movement."[19]

---

19. The theme of the cosmic ages or suns is studied at length by Miguel León-Portilla, *Aztec Thought and Culture, A Study of the Ancient Nahuatl Mind*, Norman, University of Oklahoma Press, 1963 and various reprints. See particularly p. 25–61.

For a comparative analysis of the same doctrines about the cosmic origins, see: Roberto Moreno de los Arcos, "Los cinco soles cosmogónicos", *Estudios de Cultura Náhuatl*, v. 7, Instituto de Investigaciones Históricas, Universidad Nacional Autónoma de México, méxico, 1967, p. 183–210.

J. Eric S. Thompson, "Maya Creation Myths", *Estudios de Cultura Maya*, México, Universidad Nacional Autónoma de México, v. 5, 1965, p. 13–32.

INTRODUCTION

Perhaps evolving out of the sun and earth cults, the belief in an all-begetting Father and a universal Mother, as a supreme dual deity, came into being. Without losing his unity in that the ancient hymns always invoke him in the singular, this deity was known as *Ometeotl*, "The Dual god," He and She of our Flesh, *Tonacatecuhtli* and *Tonacacihuatl*, who in a mysterious cosmic coition originated all that exists.

The Dual God also is "Mother of the gods, Father of the gods." In a first unfolding of his own being his four sons were born, the *Tezcatlipocas*, "Smoking mirrors," white, black, red, and blue. These gods constituted the primordial forces that put in motion the sun and caused life to exist on the earth. In the beginning the four children of the Dual God all worked together. But once the first of the suns and ages existed, one of the Tezcatlipocas, in the hope of exalting himself, attempted to take absolute possession of it. Transforming himself into the sun, he formed with ashes the first human beings. Acorns were then the only available food. The other gods were angered at the daring of their brother and the wise god Quetzalcoatl intervened and destroyed that first sun and the earth. As a native text puts it, "everything disappeared, everything was carried off by water and the people became fish."

The other three suns that existed prior to the present era were also accompanied by an equal number of attempts by the children of the Dual God to surpass their brothers. Thus each time a great cosmic struggle developed. Each period of ascendancy in the evolutionary process represents a sun, an age; then destruction comes again. In the second age giants existed and their food consisted of "water-maize." During the third sun other humans were born formed with clay. What they ate was "something similar to maize." The earth in the fourth age was inhabited by men who were transformed into monkeys when the end of the sun arrived. Curiously no mention is made about their nourishment.

Because the universe had been destroyed four consecutive times in the struggles of the gods, they began to concern themselves with terminating such unfortunate occurrences. Thus they met in a mythical Teotihuacan to settle their jealousies and begin a new era, the fifth, in which the present human beings would be born. This fifth age was that of the "Sun of Movement." It had its beginning thanks to a voluntary sacrifice of all the gods, who with their blood caused it to exist and to be inhabited again.

28

INTRODUCTION

For this Sun of Movement to be born, a balance of power among the various gods—cosmic forces had been achieved. The sons of the Dual god had accepted an alternating distribution of supremacy, orientating their influences to the different directions of the world. Aztec priests believed that such influences were present not only in the physical universe but also in the life of each mortal. The auguries and destinies that were thus brought were revealed by the sages who consulted their astrological books, the *Tonalamatl*.

The final destiny of this fifth age was also to be a cataclysm, the rupture of the established harmony. But in spite of this pessimistic conclusion, the Aztecs did not lose their enthusiasm in life. On the contrary, this conclusion moved them forward in a remarkable way. If through the sacrifice of the gods the existence and motion of the sun was made possible, only through the sacrifice of men would the present age be preserved. The "People of the sun" undertook for themselves the mission of furnishing it with the vital energy found in the precious liquid that keeps man alive. Sacrifice, and ceremonial warfare to obtain victims for the sacrificial rites, were their central activities, the very core of their personal, social, military, and national life.[20]

Nonetheless, as has been pointed out, in sharp contrast with such a mystic-militaristic attitude, some sages who had turned away from it appear in the ancient testimonies, asking themselves basic questions about the meaning and destiny of what exists on the earth and the possibility of saying true words about what is above us—the beyond, or, as we would put it, the universe of ultimate realities. To these sages—the *tlamatinime*, "those who know something"—historical evidence permits us to attribute various forms of speculation, theological and philosophical meditations, and the texts that, escaping oblivion and destruction, bring to us an expression of their spiritual concerns.

Although it is quite true that we do not know the names and life stories of most of those sages, some of whose intellectual expressions have been preserved, nonetheless, a few cases do exist in which our Mesoamerican spiritual classics can be presented as the work of

---

20. Different interpretations have been expressed in relation with the human sacrifices practiced by the Aztecs. Although it is well known that many of their predecessors—peoples like the Toltecs and others—included in their ritual the sacrifice of men, it is generally accepted that the Aztecs considerably increased the number of human victims offered to their gods, in particular to the Sun God.

persons whose identity has been determined. In discussing the various works included here, I will describe their origins, forms of transmission, and distinct literary attributes, and also consider the question of their authorship.

Oral Tradition and Systems of Writing

The Mesoamericans, like many other peoples in other different contexts of culture, had spontaneously committed to memory what we now label as their cosmic myths, epic poems, legends and accounts about their past, sacred hymns, songs, poetry, and various forms of discourses. However, with the passing of time—in particular once urbanism and a division of labor became a reality—a specialization in the task of preserving that sort of knowledge developed. To some of the priests and other sages from among the nobles fell such a task.

In our sketchy presentation about the cultural evolution of Mesoamerica, while reference was made to various native compositions, inscriptions and even books or "codices" were also mentioned. In fact, both oral tradition and diverse forms of hieroglyphic writing coexisted as the means to preserve the memory of the ancient happenings and of distinct sorts of religious and literary productions. Our available sources describe the oral teaching and the systematic memorizing of the texts in the Mesoamerican schools as an indispensable complement to the contents of the inscriptions in the monuments or in the painted books.

Such a systematic learning by heart in the schools was obviously much more effective in terms of fidelity than any kind of spontaneous oral tradition. And probably in coincidence with the establishing of those first schools or religious centers of learning, the earliest forms of Mesoamerican writing began to be developed. As we have seen, the oldest Mesoamerican testimonies of hieroglyphic writing are to be ascribed to a period antedating the Christian era by several hundred years. I refer to the inscriptions carved on several stelae found in the archaelogical zone of Monte Alban, not far from the city of Oaxaca. The study of their glyphic repertory shows that while a considerable number of signs had a precise calendric meaning, others conveyed very different connotations, such as personal or place names and so on.

That early form of writing (c. 700 B.C.) is in itself an evidence of two extremely important cultural happenings. If a calendar was already employed, which discovery necessarily had been the result of prolonged astronomical observations, and if the carved hieroglyphs show a certain elegance and a clear standardization, it can be asserted that in Mesoamerica both calendar and writing had been the indispensable complement of oral tradition since at least the beginnings of the first millenium B.C.

We know that, with the passing of time, calendar and writing in the various subareas of Mesoamerica reached different forms of development. Outstanding achievements in this respect are to be acknowledged to the Mayas. Researchers have unveiled the precision of their calendar systems but until now they have succeeded only in a small part in the decipherment of this ancient and complex scripture.[21]

In Central Mexico, Nahuatl-speaking groups such as the Aztecs employed a simpler form of writing, almost certainly derived from the Mixtecs of Oaxaca. The latter, in their turn, had ultimately received the influence of those early inventors of the Mesoamerican hieroglyphs, the early inhabitants of Monte Alban, probably related to the Olmecs, to whom the origins of the Mesoamerican mother high culture have been ascribed.

Aztecs and other groups living in Central Mexico on the eve of the Spanish conquest employed a writing system in which three different forms of representation coexisted. On the one hand they had not abandoned the use of pictograms or schematic drawings of objects, an antecedent of writing conceived to exhibit the images of what is to be communicated. Several Aztec inscriptions and books show, for instance, stylized representations of *teomama* or priests carrying the patron gods on their shoulders, the *calli* (houses), the *teopan* (temples), *the tlachtli* (ball-game courts), the *tlatoque* (rulers) seated in their *icpalli* (chairs), the tributes which included bundles of corn, mantles, skins, cocoa and various fruits, weapons, plumage and so forth.

Ideograms, symbolic representations of ideas, constituted another very important form of script, developed in the early days of the Mesoamerican high culture and much later adapted to the needs

---

21. Several scholars in Mexico, the United States and in various European countries persevere in their research aimed at the complete decipherment of Mayan writing and of other forms of Mesoamerican scripture. Information about recent developments in this matter is offered by Elizabeth P. Benson (editor), *Mesoamerican Writing Systems*, Washington, D.C., Dumbarton Oaks, 1973.

INTRODUCTION

of the Aztec nation. It is true that Aztec ideographic script was a simplified version of other richer and more expressively precise forms of Mesoamerican ideography. Nonetheless, that which the Aztecs had inherited in this respect permitted them to represent the various periods of time in their calendric notations, all sorts of computes, and a large number of objects, as well as many abstract ideas. Examples of the latter were the hieroglyphs expressing *ollin* (movement), *yoliliztli* (life), *teotl* (a divine being), *yaoyotl* (war), *yohualli* (night), *tecuhyotl* (sovereignty), *yahualli* (circle), a new thing, *yancuic*, or an old one *zoltic*. Ideograms conveying the meaning of more concrete objects and actions were, for instance, those of *xihuitl* (turquoise), *chalchihuitl* (jade), *teocuitlatl* (precious metal), *tianquiztli* (marketplace), *tlalli* (earth), *tetl* (stone), *tepetl* (mountain, town), *panoa* (to cross), *coyahua* (to perforate), *atlacui* (to obtain water), *chihua* (to do, to produce), *choloa* (to flee, to escape).

In addition to pictographs and ideograms, the Aztecs made use of some forms of phonetic writing. Their hieroglyphs representing sounds were mainly syllabic. The phonetic elements adopted by the Aztec scribes enabled them to connote, among other things, the sounds of names of persons and places. For example, by painting a stylized "tooth" (*tlan-tli*), together with the ideogram of *yancuic* (something new), they meant to represent phonetically *yancuic-tlan*, "the new place, the new town," as the ending *-tlan* has the precise connotation of "locality."

A further step, probably a specific Aztec development, was to symbolize some single letter sounds: *a, e, o*, represented by stylized pictographs for *a-tl* (water), *e-tl* (beans) and *o-tli* (road).[22]

In the codices or painted books, made of animal skins or of the *amate*-tree bark, duly prepared so as to be transformed into a kind of thick paper, ancient wisdom, legends and history, the calendar and other forms of knowledge could be, at least in part, recorded. It is true that, in the particular case of Aztec script, the possibilities of expression were in many respects limited. The furthest that could thus be reached was a sort of schematical outline of the fundamentals of their knowledge and history. Thus, if the contents of the books and other inscriptions were of prime importance in the pro-

---

22. For more information about Aztec writing, see: Charles E. Dibble, "Writing in Central Mexico", *Handbook of Middle American Indians*, Austin, The University of Texas Press, 1971, v. 10, part 1, p. 322–332.

cesses of preserving, teaching, and learning, systematic memorizing of the commentaries on the books and of approved oral tradition were never abandoned as an essential part of education in the schools.[23]

The sages and teachers led their students and the people in general to memorize songs, poems, and discourses, closely related to what the hieroglyphs expressed in symbols. A poetical version of such procedure is conveyed by the following ancient Mesoamerican song:

> I sing the pictures of the book
> and see them propagating,
> I am a graceful bird
> for I can make the books speak
> within the house of the paintings.[24]

Oral tradition, the contents of books and other inscriptions in monuments or even in small objects, were the means Mesoamerican society created to preserve its own heritage of culture. As a result of the Spanish conquest many of these testimonies were lost forever. Nonetheless, what has remained permits us to reach a deeper understanding of the material vestiges unearthed by the archaeologists and also something of the thought of the sages, much more than a bit of the masterpieces of Mesoamerican spirituality.

The Rescuing of this Literature

We owe to the efforts of some groups of surviving native sages, and to the remarkable concern of several humanistic-minded friars, the rescue of a part of the great wealth of compositions conceived and expressed in various Mesoamerican languages. Fewer than twenty pre-Hispanic books escaped the furor of the Conquest or the action of time, adverse elements, ignorance, and neglect.

---

23. A comprehensive record of the many manuscripts which compose the extant treasure of the Mesoamerican literatures is offered by John B. Glass and Donald Robertson, "A Census of Native Middle American pictorial Manuscripts", *Handbook of Middle American Indians*, 1975, v. 14, p. 81–252, and Charles Gibson and John B. Glass, "A Census of Middle American Prose Manuscripts", *Handbook of Middle American Indians*, 1975, v. 15, p. 311–400.

24. *Collection of Mexican Songs* (in the Nahuatl language), fol. 14; v. The manuscript is found in the National Library of Mexico.

INTRODUCTION

As a compensation for this, there are more than a hundred books or codices of fundamental cultural interest that although painted and written after the Conquest, are either copies of the ancient manuscripts or appear to be deeply inspired by them. In addition to this, other extraordinary testimonies were also saved. They are closely related to the contents of the painted books. They are in fact transliterations, using the Spanish alphabet, to express with it, in the same native language, what was conveyed by the hieroglyphic script. In other cases they are a transcription of what the sages dictated from what was taught and learned by heart in the ancient schools.

I can not list here all the names of those who thus saved for us this heritage of culture.[25] I will mention at least the group of sages of Tlatelolco and also the Franciscan fray Bernardino de Sahagun whom modern social scientists have named "the father of anthropological research in the New World."

What they rescued in the sixteenth century was little known to most of their contemporaries. A fear of a revival of idolatry prevented its diffusion. It was not until late in the nineteenth century that the ancient manuscripts began to be rediscovered in the archives and libraries of Mexico, Guatemala, the United States, Spain, the Vatican, Italy, France, Great Britain, and other countries.

And it can be added that a truly humanistic study of many of these materials has taken place only in recent years.

---

25. Those interested in knowing more about the rescuing process of the various texts of Mesoamerican native origin, can consult Miguel León-Portilla, *Pre-Columbian Literatures of Mexico*, Norman, The University of Oklahoma Press, 1969 and several reprints.

4. The Texts Included in This Volume

In selecting, from among the literary wealth of Mesoamerica, the texts that better respond to the scope of the present book, I have kept in mind elements and traits enunciated in the preface, as intrinsically pertaining to a generic description of spirituality. In other words, I have attended to those compositions in which the native sages as well as the anonymous oral tradition, memorized in the ancient schools, appear most deeply concerned with that nonmaterial universe where other sources of meaning are believed to exist.

Some creation myths, religious doctrines—such as those related to the Supreme Being, Lord of the Near and Close (*Tloque Nahuaque*), the Giver of Life (*Ipalnemohuani*)[26]—or those dealing with the possible human destinies in the afterlife have thus been chosen. In addition, several hymns, other religious poems, and various examples of native forms of philosophic reflection that can be attributed to specific authors will also introduce us to the spiritual world of the creators of the indigenous civilization of Mesoamerica.

To simplify understanding of the selected texts, I have distributed them in six parts or sections. I will describe the contents of each one of them, including a reference about the origins and peculiarities of the corresponding compositions. As we will see, instead of taking the theme of the creation myths as a point of departure, our attention will focus upon various indigenous testimonies that disclose to our eyes how the Mesoamerican peoples managed to preserve, enrich, and transmit their culture. Therefore, texts related to education, the moral ideals, and wisdom, human and divine, will provide us with a key to some of the secrets of this different kind of spirituality.

Part 1: Examples of The Ancient Word
To the persevering of Fray Andrés de Olmos and Fray Bernardino de Sahagun we owe the two largest collections of *Huehetlatolli* [The ancient word], which have thus escaped oblivion. Olmos, who

---

26. These are some of the names with which the supreme Dual God was invoked. *Tloque Nahuaque* could perhaps be also translated as "Master of the Close Vicinity" or "He to whom Nearness and Vicinity belong". See: Miguel León-Portilla, *Aztec Thought and Culture, A Study of the Ancient Nahuatl Mind*, Norman, University of Oklahoma Press, 1963 and several reprints, p. 90–95.

arrived in Mexico in 1528, soon learned the Aztec or Nahuatl language. In 1531 he received from his superiors the order to investigate "the beliefs and superstitions of the Indians." An extremely important fruit of his research was the obtainment of a considerable number of native texts.

The compositions he collected, described in pre-Columbian Mesoamerica as The Ancient Word, are discourses and orations delivered in Nahuatl on particularly important occasions, such as the death of a ruler, the election of a new ruler, the birth of a child, or a marriage, when it was time for the fathers and mothers to let their children know about how life is on the earth. Other examples of this literary genre are offered also by the instructions on morals and ancient wisdom delivered by teachers and sages in the schools. These texts were written from the oral account given by some elders who had memorized them before the Spanish Conquest.[27]

Fray Bernardino de Sahagun, whose fundamental work of research has been mentioned already, rescued an even larger collection of *Huehuetlatolli*, testimonies of The Ancient Word.[28]

Other examples of this form of discourse have come to us thanks to the interest of some native sages and students, such as Antonio Valeriano, Martin Jacobita, Tezozomoc, and Chimalpahin.

To describe the contents of his collection of *Huehuetlatolli*, Sahagun wrote in the Spanish text of his *History of the Things of New Spain* that such texts dealt with:

> The rhetoric and moral philosophy and theology of the Mexican people, in which there are many niceties with respect to the elegance of their language, that is, their rhetorical language.[29]

---

27. For a detailed description of the research carried out by Fray Andres de Olmos, see: Angel Ma. Garibay K., *Historia de la Literatura Náhuatl*, 2. v., México, Editorial Porrúa, 1953–1954, t.II p. 28–36.

28. Scholarly research during the last four decades has resulted in a large number of contributions about the life and the work of Bernardino de Sahagun. The most recent and authoritative series of studies on this subject, due to ten specialists, historians and anthropologists, has been published by Munro S. Edmonson (editor), *Sixteenth Century Mexico, The Work of Sahagún*, Santa Fe, N. Mexico, School of American Research, 1974.

29. Fray Bernardino de Sahagun, *Florentine Codex, History of the Things of New Spain*, edited and translated into English by Charles E. Dibble and J. O. Arthur Anderson, II v., Santa Fe, N. Mexico, School of American Research and The University of Utah, 1950–1969, t. VI, p. XII.

INTRODUCTION

Other prominent sixteenth century personages who became acquainted with at least a Spanish translation of the collection assembled by Fray Andres de Olmos praised also the spirituality and
didactic value of such examples of The Ancient Word. Among others, the famous Fray Bartolome de las Casas left the following appreciation in his *Apologetic History:*

> Are there any better conceived, or more spontaneous dis-
> courses, and more pertinent, to transform human life into
> virtuous action? Could perhaps Plato, Socrates or Pythago-
> ras, or after them Aristotle, think of something more ade-
> quate than these discourses with which so constantly these
> peoples instructed their sons? What else is taught by the
> Christian law, with the exception of what pertains to the
> faith . . .?[30]

To such a degree was The Ancient Word accepted in sixteenth-
century Mexico as an extraordinary testimony of the indigenous
wisdom that the collection of Olmos became the subject of a special
treatment that no other indigenous text received. Such a collection,
with minor alterations, was published in Mexico City in 1600 in the
Aztec language with an abridged version in Spanish.[31]

It is important to recall here that the Spanish royal authorities,
including the Holy Office of the Inquisition, far from being inclined
to preserve testimonies of the ancient culture, had ordered in many
instances the confiscation and destruction of all sorts of "idolatrous
objects," in particular idols and native books. Fray Bernardino de
Sahagun himself had to face in 1577 the consequences of a Royal Cedula of Philip II, which stated:

> From letters written in those provinces we have learned
> that Fray Bernardino de Sahagun . . . has composed a Uni-
> versal History of the most noteworthy things of New

---

30. Bartolomé de Las Casas, *Apologética Historia Sumaria*, edited and with an Introduction by Edmundo O' Gorman, 2v., Mexico, National University of Mexico Press,
1967, t. II, p. 448.

31. Fray Juan Bautista, *Huehuetlatolli Pláticas que antiguamente usaban los indios desta
Nueva España*, Mexico 1600 (?) Only two copies are known of this book and in both
the front-page is missing. I have consulted a photographic reproduction of the one
found in The John Carter Brown Library, Providence, R. I.

INTRODUCTION

Spain. . . . It is an abundant collection of all the rites . . . in the native language.

. . . it seems that it is not proper that this book be published or disseminated in those places, for several reasons. We thus command that, upon receiving this Cedula, you obtain these books with great care and diligence; that you make sure that no original or copy of them is left there; and that you have them sent in good hands at the first opportunity to our Council of Indies in order that they may be examined there. And you are warned absolutely not to allow any person to write concerning the superstitions and ways of life of these Indians in any language, for this is not proper to God's service and to ours.[32]

Only in this context will the publishing of the *Huehuetlatolli* or speeches of the elders, those collected by Fray Andres de Olmos, be properly appreciated. And it can be added that no other indigenous text was ever published until the nineteenth century.

On the one hand the presentation here of some of the speeches that are a part of The Ancient Word will introduce us to some aspects of everyday life of the Aztecs, with a particular emphasis on their moral ideals and practices.[33] On the other hand it is important to underline that the ideals and wisdom mirrored in these texts were mainly a prerogative of the nobles, those who attended the *calmecacs* or centers of higher learning. The following discourses make up Part 1 of our book:

1. The words with which the father admonishes his daughter when she has already reached the age of discretion

---

32. The complete text of this Royal Order can be found in *Codice Franciscano*, Joaquín García Icazbalceta (editor), *Nueva Colección de Documentos para la Historia de México*, 5 v., México, 1886–1892, First reprint, S. Chavez Hayhoe, 1941, p. 240–250.

33. Various collections of *Huehuetlatolli* have come down to us. I will mention here the following: the one compiled by father Olmos, published only in part. 16th century copies of this collection or of parts of it are found in the National Library of Spain (Madrid), The National Library of France (Paris), The Bancroft Library (Berkeley, Cal.), The National Library of Mexico and The Library of Congress, (Washington, D.C.). The *Huehuetlatolli* rescued by Sahagun are included in Book 6 of the *Florentine Codex* and appear distributed there in forty-three chapters in both Nahuatl and Spanish. Mention can also be made of other *Huehuetlatolli*, of uncertain provenance, preserved now in various repositories of Mexico, the United States and Europe.

INTRODUCTION

2. The answer of the noble mother telling her daughter tender words, that she will always remember the discourse of her father

3. The discourse of the father with which he admonishes his son that he should look to the knowledge of one self in order to be pleasing to the gods and to men

4. The manner in which the father exhorts his son to provoke him to chastity

As a complement to these compositions, other texts will be included here, all of them related to education as it was imparted in the pre-Columbian schools:

1. A discourse in which it is told how the parents promised their new born sons to the *calmecac* (schools of higher learning) or *telpuchcalli* (young people's houses) so that in due time they could enter them

2. The words that were exchanged when the parents actually left their sons in any of these schools

3. A discourse about the usages of those instructed in the young peoples' houses

4. An account of the punishments that were imposed in the above mentioned schools

5. The rules observed in the *calmecac*

6. An account about how the high priests were chosen from among those who had followed the precepts of the *calmecac.*

Many of the stylistic procedures, distinctive of the literature expressed in the Nahuatl language, will be apparent to the reader of these texts, as an effort has been made to adhere to them while translating them into English. Among other things, one will thus perceive the frequent use of parallel sentences expressing the same idea in different ways, a kind of rhythm in the phrases and the employment of metaphors and idiomatic expressions characteristic of the Mesoamerican compositions. The plumage of the quetzal bird will connote the idea of beauty; necklaces of precious stones will mean lineage and descent; jade stands for life; flower and song, for poetry; eagles and ocelots signify brave warriors. . . . But, what is more important, the reading of The Ancient Word will be perhaps the best way to come near to the wisdom of Mesoamerica. In fact, evidence exists that some of these texts, or at least the ideals they convey, were part of the legacy the Aztecs had received from predecessors as renowned as the Toltecs.

INTRODUCTION

Part 2: Creation Myths

Teotlatolli and *Teocuicatl*, "divine words" and "divine songs," were the designations the Nahuatl-speaking Mesoamericans gave to those compositions we describe now as their myths. I will transcribe here in faithful English versions some Quiche Maya and Nahuatl accounts in which the different births and collapses of the world, the successive formations of various kinds of human beings, the discovery of maize and the legend of the culture hero Quetzalcoatl, are recalled.

As has been already mentioned in this Introduction, a basic Mesoamerican belief was that other ages or cosmogonic suns had succeeded each other before our present era. Those ages or "suns" were named in function of the force or divine element which violently put an end to each one of them: earth, wind, water, and fire. Human beings who existed in them were also different. While some Nahuatl accounts speak of four previous ages, the Maya versions recall only three before the present one described as that of "the Sun of Movement."[34]

The extant indigenous books and other native texts transcribed after the Conquest speak of the supreme Dual God, Our Mother–Our Father, the origin of whatever exists on the earth, and above and below it. This can be seen in pre-Columbian books such as those known with the following names (often derived from some of their possessors or from the places where they are kept): *Codex Vindobonensis* and *Codex Selden* (of Mixtec origin); *Borgia*, *Vaticanus*, *Cospi*, *Laud* and *Fejérvary-Mayer* (of Central Mexico), *Dresden*, *Tro-Cortesiano* and *Parisinus* (of Maya provenance).[35]

Here texts will be offered representative of some of these var-

---

34. The theme of the cosmic ages or suns is studied at length by Miguel León-Portilla, *Aztec Thought and Culture, A Study of the Ancient Nahuatl Mind*, Norman, University of Oklahoma Press, 1973 and various reprints. See particularly p. 25–61.
For a comparative analysis of the same doctrines about the cosmic origins, see: Roberto Moreno de los Arcos, "Los cinco soles cosmogónicos", *Estudios de Cultura Náhuatl*, v. 7, Instituto de Investigaciones Históricas, Universidad Nacional Autónoma de México, México, 1967, p. 183–210 and J. Eric S. Thompson, "Maya Creation Myths", *Estudios de Cultura Maya*, México, Universidad Nacional Autónoma de México, v. 5, 1965, p. 13–32.
35. The names of these pre-Columbian Mesoamerican books or codices are derived either from that of the place where they are kept or from that of one of their better known possessors. For a description of the physical features and contents of these and other native books, see: John B. Glass, "A Survey of Native Middle American Pictorial Manuscripts", *Handbook of Middle American Indians*, 1975, v. 14, p. 3–80.

INTRODUCTION

ious Mesoamerican subareas. The account of the successive "creations" of the world, according to the Quiche-Maya version of the *Popol Vuh* [The Book of Counsel], will mark the beginning of the present approach to the realm of Mesoamerican myths. The *Popol Vuh* is probably one of the most widely known native American compositions. While written in the Colonial days of Guatemala and containing manifest interpolations of Christian origin, it conveys pre-Columbian tradition and history. To Fray Francisco Ximenez, parish priest of the small town of Chichicastenango, we owe the discovery, early in the eighteenth century, of the old manuscript.

Apparently the original text in the Quiche-Maya language was a compilation made "by one or more descendants of the Quiche race, according to the tradition of their forefathers." Munro S. Edmonson, the scholar to whom the most accurate English rendition of the *Popol Vuh* is due, believes the subject of this native book, though multiple, has a complete coherence:

> [Its theme] is the greatness of the Quiche, the people, the place and the religious mysteries which were all called by that name [The Book of Counsel]. It is a tragic theme, but its treatment is not tragic; it is Mayan. The rise and fall of Quiche glory is placed in the cosmic cycling of all creation, and when it is ended like the cycles of Mayan time, it stops.[36]

"The root of the former word," as it is stated at the beginning of the *Popol Vuh*, gives life to what is known about the Quiche-Maya people and their predecessors who existed in previous ages. Thanks to this root of the former word we can know about the various unsuccessful divine essays to make and shape some beings capable of understanding and of worshiping the gods. And also thanks to this book we will hear about the final creation, that of our own cosmic age when the gods, after discovering the intelligence with which their creatures were endowed, decided to throw a vapor on the eyes of man so that he could see only what was near, what was close to him.

---

36. Munro S. Edmonson (editor), *The Book of Counsel: The Popol Vuh of the Quiche Maya of Guatemala*, New Orleans, Middle American Research Institute, Tulane University, Publication 33, 1971, p. XIV

INTRODUCTION

The Nahuatl and Mixtec parallel accounts about the various ages or cosmic suns, which will be appended here to the Quiche-Maya narrative, while showing some variants, basically coincide with it, which in fact confirms the existence of a Mesoamerican universal participation in the same cultural traditions.[37]

Other myths in the Nahuatl language, describing the visit of Quetzalcoatl, the wise god whose emblem is the Feathered Serpent, to the *Mictlan*, the Place of the Dead, and his later intervention to rescue or to steal for us the precious seeds of maize, will complement this series related to the cosmic and human origins.

Part 3: The Story of the High Priest Quetzalcoatl, Lord of the Toltecs

As has been mentioned, around A.D. 950 a famous priest and sage, a culture hero, reigned in the metropolis of Tula. He had derived his name from that of the benevolent god whose cult he preached.

The saga, rich in symbolism about this high priest Quetzalcoatl, will also be included in this Mesoamerican volume, in accordance with the Nahuatl compilation transcribed by Fray Bernardino de Sahagun and his native disciples. Quetzalcoatl, as we have seen in our panoramic study of the historical evolution of Mesoamerica, appears as the religious leader of the Toltecs during the second half of the tenth century A.D. He lived in palaces of different colors that he had built in Tula, the Toltec metropolis, oriented toward the four cosmic points. There, in fasting and chastity, he devoted his life to meditation and to enriching in every form the culture of the Toltecs. Thus his reign is depicted as an epoch of abundance with all sorts of achievements.

But one day three wizards appeared in Tula. They insisted that they had to speak with the wise priest and ruler. Apparently they wanted to introduce into Tula the rites of human sacrifice. Quetzalcoatl accepted at last to receive them. The three wizards gave him a mirror in which he saw himself as very old, weighed down by the years. The wizards had in mind to confuse Quetzalcoatl's heart and thus to bring about his ruin. They urged him to taste a remedy they had brought with them to give him back the force of youth. At this

---

37. In the present Introduction—when dealing with "The Documentary Sources and the present Translation"—specific reference will be made to the codices and other documents in which these texts are found.

point they offered him a drink. Quetzalcoatl, at first resisting, tasted the drink, finally drank of it, then all of it, and became inebriated.

Then the wizards brought about several portents by which many Toltecs perished and by which they ruined Tula. When Quetzalcoatl realized what had happened, he was very much troubled and decided to abandon his city, to go away to the Region of Light, the east, the Land of Wisdom, of the Red and the Black. When he arrived at the edge of the divine waters, he then disappeared. According to some testimonies, he embarked on a raft of serpents; according to another, he cast himself into a great fire. From it emerged his heart as the morning star.

The story of Quetzalcoatl, the culture hero who is also mentioned by the Yucatec-Maya and the Quiche-Maya with the names of Kukulkan and Gucumatz (designations that convey the same meaning), can be taken as perhaps the most beautiful and rich in symbolism of the Mesoamerican stories.[38]

Part 4: The Official Dogma and the Doubts of the Sages about Afterlife

The Mesoamerican peoples, and to a considerable degree also their modern descendants, among them the millions of contemporary *Mestizo* Mexicans, have been and continue to be fascinated by the many mysteries surrounding death. Man in this part of the Americas has most often placed a rather limited value on life on the earth. Nahuatl poets remind us that:

> It is not true, it is not true
> that we came to live here.
> We came only to sleep, only to dream.[39]

Or, as it is proclaimed even more directly, in another composition:

> Truly, earth is not the place of reality,
> indeed one must go elsewhere.... [40]

---

38. An early attempt to offer the English-speaking readers the story of Quetzalcoatl is due to John H. Cornyn who, in a limited edition, published in 1930 his somehow sophisticated version of it in English: *The Song of Quetzalcoatl*, Yellow Springs, Ohio, 1930.

39. *Collection of Mexican Songs*, fol. 17, r.

40. *Ibid.*, fol. 1, v.

INTRODUCTION

The native books and other texts transcribed after the Conquest are eloquent indeed in this respect. Through them we can learn about the Mesoamerican beliefs, thoughts and doubts related to death. It is of particular interest to note that there existed great differences between what can be described as the official dogma in this matter and the speculations of several sages.

In the religious beliefs, especially in those prevalent during the time of the Aztec splendor, death in battle, death of the sacrificed victims, death of women in childbirth, are always exalted. It was believed that all those who died in one of these forms would have a glorious destiny, as they would go to the house of the Sun god to reside with him in the heavens.

In the texts there are also descriptions of other places or destinations in the beyond. One is the *Mictlan*, "The Place of the Dead," which existed in the underworld and was also known as "The-Place-of-the-fleshless", *Ximoayan,* and "Our-common-place-where-we-lose-ourselves," *Tocenpopolihuiyan.* Persons who had a natural death went there, but to reach it they had to overcome on the road a number of obstacles. Mention is also made in several religious testimonies of the Tlalocan, a sort of paradise of Tlaloc, the Rain God, to which some chosen people were destined.[41]

In contrast to these beliefs about death, derived from the ancient dogma, more personal compositions stand out where different concepts, doubts, and assertions are expressed regarding the afterlife. A conviction that the mystery will never be completely unveiled by man on earth appears and reappears in these compositions. The beauty of the poems carries at times the voice of hope but also the clamor of pessimism. A deep spiritual concern is at the core of the question: whether or not it is possible to say true words about the beyond and the survival of one self.

The presentation here of the two forms of expression, dogma and personal anguished inquiries, will help to disclose another aspect of the spiritual world of the ancient Mesoamericans.

Part 5: Anonymous Religious Poetry and Other Related Texts
Sacred hymns from the Maya and Nahuatl cultural subareas, as well as other religious songs and poems, some of them denoting a

---

41. More about this can be found in M. León-Portilla, *Aztec Thought and Culture,* p. 124–128.

44

INTRODUCTION

considerable antiquity, comprise another rich corpus within the Mesoamerican classics of spirituality. In approaching these compositions it is important to underline that all or the great part of them are to be attributed to the schools or congregations of native priests and sages. Specific reference to this is made in some texts that speak about a regulation according to which, if someone composed a religious song or poem, he had to submit it to the examination and eventual approval of a priest whose duty it was to preserve the purity of the dogma:

> The tonsured priest of "The Mother of Pearl Serpent" was concerned with the songs. If someone composed a song, he consulted with him, so that he could provide, he could dispatch the singers to his house. When someone composed a song, he had to pass judgment upon it.[42]

The obtention of the approval meant, among other things, that the submitted composition could be intoned in public, as nothing in it was found against the prevalent dogma. Evidence exists that not only the sacred or "official" hymns, which were chanted in the religious ceremonies throughout the year, but also many of the poems were conceived to be sung in one way or another. Thus for the native Mesoamericans, as has been the case in other ancient cultures, the universe of poetry existed closely related to music and also to dancing, the participants often dressed in a variety of costumes, in a sort of performance, anticipating the appearance of drama. Some of the extant poetical texts in Nahuatl are in fact accompanied by musical notations and imply besides the active participation of various persons. Their singing takes at times the form of a dialogue through which human and divine beings communicate. According to Fray Diego Duran, a sixteenth century Dominican missionary,

> ... there were long rehearsals of songs and dances ... and with each new song they brought out different costumes, with mantles and feathers and false hair and masks, according to the songs they had composed and what they were about.[43]

---

42. *Codex Matritensis* of the Royal Palace, Madrid, fol. 260 r.
43. Diego Durán, *Historia de las Indias de Nueva España*, t.II, p. 231.

INTRODUCTION

The analysis of a considerable number of the thus chanted and enacted compositions permits us to say something about their more relevant stylistic traits. Here also, as is the case with the discourses that appertain to The Ancient Word, parallel expressions, almost repetitive verses, are a frequent procedure. Some examples are in order.

The first is taken from an old composition in which the portentous fight between the Aztec god of war, Huitzilopochtli, and the Four Hundred warriors of the South is recalled.

> He pursued the Four Hundred gods of the South,
> he chased them,
> drove them off the top of the Mountain of the Snake ...
>
> In vain they tried to rally against him,
> in vain they turned to attack him ...
>
> Nothing could they do,
> nothing could they gain,
> with nothing could they defend themselves ...[44]

In a different vein, when the sage asks about the meaning of life, we hear:

> What have you been seeking?
> Where has your heart been wandering?[45]

Parallel expression is also a device in these lines taken from a song in which the departure of the culture hero Quetzalcoatl is evoked:

> My lord is gone, he of the fine feathers,
> he has left me fatherless ...
> How will your courtyards remain forsaken?
> How will your palaces remain forsaken?[46]

---

44. *Codex Matritensis* of the Spanish Royal Academy of History, fol.
45. *Collection of Mexican Songs*, fol. 2, v.
46. *Ibid.*, fol. 26, v.

INTRODUCTION

Metaphors and clusters of metaphors, carrying specific indigenous connotations, have to be reckoned among the most frequent stylistic devices in Mesoamerican poetry. In reading it, one enters a flowery garden where a magnificent variety of gems, plants, birds, and colors give new meanings to whatever is born and exists on the earth. Metaphor here seems to be a fundamental part of expression.

"Recurrent phrases," appearing here and there, strategically placed along the sequence of a poem, impress a main concept or a feeling in those who are listening. "Beginning and ending words" are another form of repetition introduced to evoke the same metaphor and mainly to cause the persuasion that an idea or a feeling has attained completeness.

The metrics of this poetry have been studied only in part. Beyond any doubt there were various forms of rhythm and measure in it. Our translations into English imply at least an effort to preserve the feeling of this, inherent in the original text.

Part 5 of this Mesoamerican book includes the following series of anonymous hymns, poems, or songs: The sacred hymns intoned by the Aztecs in their religious feasts throughout the year, which were rescued by Father Sahagun and his native students. To compensate for the many obscurities that will be found in these ancient and esoteric compositions, a number of notes will be added to clarify them.

Other religious songs, also in Nahuatl, that have come down to us from various places and times will form another part of this selection. Their themes are: the attributes of the gods or more generally of the divinity; what is good or bad on the earth; the meaning of friendship, and the evanescent quality of whatever exists.

Yucatec-Maya excerpts from *The Book of Songs of Dzitbalche* and from *The Chilam Balam Book of Chumayel* will exemplify various aspects of the spirituality whose expression is the poetry of the ancient inhabitants of that part of Mesoamerica.

Part 6: The Poetry of Nezahualcoyotl (1402–1472) and of Other Priests and Sages Known to Us

I have been able to study the lives and works of twenty of the Mesoamerican poets and sages.[47] It has been of enormous interest to

---

47. In a book I have published only in Spanish the lives and compositions of thirteen Nahuatl poets are studied at some length. See M. León-Portilla, *Trece Poetas del*

find in the sources a rather large number of compositions which are attributed to authors whose identity has been determined. And the registered names of those who are presented as authors of one or several poems are actually more than twenty.

However, to firmly establish a relation between a composition and a given Mesoamerican author, various steps have to be taken. A fundamental one is to look for reliable information about the referred-to person. If it is possible to gain some knowledge about his life and deeds, one has to search also for other sources of evidence about his reputation as a composer of poems or songs.

In some instances the native chronicles can give an answer: Such a person is mentioned as distinguished in this or that and besides, or perhaps particularly, because of his literary productions. At other times his colleagues, that is, other sages and poets, prize him on account of his works. The desired and necessary relation can thus be established.

But this is not always the case. Names mentioned as those of the authors of specific songs, can unfortunately remain for us a sort of mystery as no indication about them is found in other testimonies. And the opposite also happens: We know that a given Mesoamerican was a famous poet in pre-Conquest times, but not a single composition attributable to him has come down to us.

From among the twenty sages and poets about whose persons and works we know something thus far, Nezahualcoyotl, the ruler of the chiefdom of Texcoco, is probably the one enjoying the greatest well-deserved renown. He was born in the town bearing the same name as his chiefdom in the year 1-Rabbit, which corresponded to 1402. Although he had to endure many persecutions and sufferings from his childhood (his father was murdered by political adversaries), he received a careful education thanks to which he could assimilate the ancient wisdom inherited from the Toltecs. Several years later, assisted by the rulers of Mexico and other smaller chiefdoms, Nezahualcoyotl defeated the adversaries of his father and was elected the supreme governor of Texcoco.

He reigned for more than forty years, during which time his

mundo Azteca, Mexico, National University of Mexico Press, 1967 and several reprints. Also I have dealt in particular with the figure and poetic work of Aquiauhtzin, in: "The Chalca Cihuacuicatl of Aquiauhtzin, Erotic Poetry of the Nahuas", *New Scholar,* San Diego, University of California, v. 5, num. 2, p. 235–262.

vassals enjoyed a golden age. Besides, he was constantly consulted by the monarchs of Mexico and other neighboring nations. He gave them advice on a great variety of matters, which included political, social, and economic issues, and the construction of new roads and of the ditch or embankment to separate the fresh from the salt waters in the lakes that then covered a large part of the Valley of Mexico. But, above all, Nezahualcoyotl had a great reputation as a sage in the divine things and as a master of the word, a poet.

The compositions we can attribute to him are more than thirty. Some of them became so famous that they are reproduced in more than one of the ancient manuscripts. The main themes recurring in the poetry of Nezahualcoyotl oblige us to describe him as a Mesoamerican philosopher. He reflects on the fugacity of all that exists on the earth, the mysteries surrounding death, the possibility of uttering true words here, the purpose and value of human action, and the inscrutability and at once all-embracing attraction of the supreme Giver of Life.

There is reason to believe that only a small part of the poetry of Nezahualcoyotl has reached us. Nonetheless, on the basis of what we have and know of it, we can affirm that it offers one of the best testimonies of the spirituality that flourished in Mesoamerica.[48] I have prepared for this book an English translation with the idea of being as faithful as possible to the original texts in Nahuatl.

The extant work of some others, from among the twenty identified poets, will also be included here. I will list the names (with a micro-biography) of those whose compositions will be offered.

Tlaltecatzin, born around 1350, in Cuauhchinanco, within what is the present Mexican state of Puebla, deserves particular consideration. A number of other well known native poets praise his songs. To him can be attributed a composition probably strange to us, in which his invocation of the Giver of Life, his acceptance of death—provided it will arrive without violence—intermingle with his craving for pleasure, intensely portrayed in an imaginary dialogue with an *ahuiani*, which literally means "she who makes others glad," the

---

48. Several biographies and studies of the poetry of Nezahualcoyotl have been published. See: Frances Gillmor, *Flute of the Smoking Mirror, a portrait of Nezahualcoyotl, poet-king of the Aztecs*, Albuquerque, University of New Mexico Press, 1949; Miguel León-Portilla, *Nezahualcoyotl, su poesía y pensamiento*, Texcoco, Enciclopedia del Estado de México, 1972; Jose Luis Martínez, *Nezahualcoyotl, vida y obra*, México, Fondo de Cultura Económica, 1973.

INTRODUCTION

woman who is sought for the sake of mere pleasure. This poem of Tlaltecatzin will be reproduced in our book as an unsuspected instance of Mesoamerican spirituality transmitted with the language of sensuous attraction.[49]

Tochihuitzin Coyolxiuhqui, who was active as a poet during the second half of the fifteenth century, was born in the Aztec metropolis, one of the many sons of Itzcoatl, sovereign of the Aztecs from 1426 to 1440. From the days of his youth he frequented the wise Nezahualcoyotl, by whose teachings he was probably influenced. Tochihuitzin is mentioned on two occasions together with other celebrated poets from Central Mexico. The sources that give us his name also include two of his compositions. In them he appears deeply concerned with discovering the meaning of life. One poem is the Aztec expression of the universal inclination to conceive human existence as a dream. The other proclaims that only the sages can live the song and somehow disclose the mystery of the flower.

Another wise man, a contemporary of Tochihuitzin, was the one described as "The White Eagle of Tecamachalco," the famous poet Ayocuan. His hometown, Tecamachalco, is situated in the modern state of Puebla. The information we have about him is rather abundant. In summary form I will recall that Ayocuan was the son of Cuetzpaltzin, who governed the towns of Cohuayocan and Cuauhtepec and later became the ruler of Tecamachalco. Thanks to his father's care, Ayocuan was sent to Quimixtlan to receive his education. In that village, whose name means "the place shrouded in clouds," he was introduced to the ancient wisdom and beliefs.

Once an adult, Ayocuan passed most of his time conversing with other sages and poets, acting also as mediator in various circumstances and reciting his own productions in places such as Tlaxcala and Huexotzinco. Numerous mentions about this and his great prestige as a poet are found in the ancient manuscripts. The remaining examples of Ayocuan's poetry speak clearly of his deep religious insights. Concerned with the transitoriness of all that exists, he believed in art and symbolism. But, as he proclaimed in one of his poems, "in this region of the fleeting moment. . ., our yearning itself deforms our flowers and songs. . . . "

---

49. More information about Tlaltecatzin and the other poets whose compositions will be included in this book is offered in: M. León-Portilla, *Trece poetas del mundo Azteca*, Mexico, National University of Mexico Press, 1967 and several reprints.

INTRODUCTION

A beautiful example of the tenderness of the Mesoamerican women and their talent for poetry is offered by Macuilxochitzin in the testimony of her expression that has come down to us. Born around 1435 and a native of Mexico-Tenochtitlan, Macuilxochitzin was a daughter of the renowned counselor of several Aztec rulers, Tlacaelel. Undoubtly she was carefully educated and she must have heard from the lips of her father the advice of The Ancient Word, spoken to her, "the little girl, who is like a jade and a precious quetzal feather.... "

Macuilxochitzin lived during the years of the greatest Aztec splendor. In the single poem we have from her, she revives an Aztec campaign planned by her father and carried out by the Supreme ruler Axayacatzin. As she describes it, the expedition was conceived to conquer the Matlatzincas of the Valley of Toluca.

But her intention in composing this poem is not only to exalt the triumph achieved by the Aztecs. She wants to praise the Giver of Life with her song and also to save from oblivion the decisive intervention of a group of women, related by blood to those who had been defeated. Showing her feminine tenderness, she depicts in a compassionate way how those women saved the life of the vanquished Otomi warrior who had wounded the Aztec ruler Axayacatzin in battle.

Tecayehuatzin from Huexotzinco, who lived during the second half of the fifteenth century and the early years of the following century, stands out among the most celebrated Nahuatl sages and poets. Nevertheless, the study of the native sources convinces us that Tecayehuatzin actually had to live two different forms of existence. If as a poet he concentrated on the meaning of symbolism and ultimate realities, as a statesman, ruling the chiefdom of Huexotzinco, he felt forced to practice intrigue and deceit.

To him we owe some personal compositions and, what is of greater interest, a long dialogue in which he discusses with other sages the possible meanings of "flower and song," that is, poetry itself, symbolism, and art.

Tecayehuatzin, as the text expresses it, conceived the idea of inviting poets and sages from various places to participate in such a dialogue. The actual encounter was probably held around 1490 in a garden near Tecayehuatzin's palace. Acting as a friendly host, before expressing what is his intention in the meeting, he treats his colleagues with a foaming chocolate drink and a generous distribution of tobacco. In due time he opens the discussion he has in mind to provoke, with a eulogy of the symbolism of flower and song. He also proclaims that, at least for a brief time, he has borrowed the presence of his friends, poets and sages who are to him "precious stones, quetzal feathers," the most marvelous reality on earth. And in parallel form, once he has invoked the Giver of Life, he asks himself if flower and song—poetry, symbolism, art—are the only truth man is able to reach on the earth.

One by one the participants try to answer the question Tecayehuatzin has proposed. Ayocuan, the poet about whose life and works something has already been said, appears inclined to answer with new questions. He would like to know the ultimate origin of flowers and songs. Are they perhaps a gift of the gods? Can it be said, in consequence, that they constitute the best language for speaking with the Giver of Life? Or are they only a memento of man's days on earth?

Another poet, some of whose creations are also included in the native manuscripts, Aquiauhtzin of Ayapanco, insists that flower and song can convey the best invocation to the Giver of Life. To him, the supreme god reveals his presence through the inspiration of poetry and art.

Cuautencoztli, another poet of the previously mentioned town of Huexotzinco, doubting about the *truth* that man himself can possess on earth, appears hesitant about the value of the songs he can compose. If we do not know anything about the ultimate reality and destiny of man, how can we dare to affirm that our poetry conveys any truth?

Prince Motenehuatzin counteracts then what he considers the pessimistic attitude of Cuauhtencoztli. He is convinced that flower and song, though so often uneven, are perhaps the best thing man has to drive away sorrow.

Tecayehuatzin speaks again in a kind of interlude. He begs the assembled poets to be cheerful. His friend Monencauhtzin echoes his words, insisting that flowers and songs are the wealth and joy of the princes and sages.

Now the dialogue takes a different direction. A new participant, Xayacamach of Tlaxcala, declares that flower and song, like the hallucinogenic mushrooms, are good means to intoxicate one's own heart to free it from sadness and suffering. When in the sacred ceremonies the mushrooms are consumed, one sees marvelous visions, evanescent forms of multiple colors, all even more real than reality itself. But this world of color vanishes later as if it were a dream; afterwards, man finds himself weary, forced to face again the somber problems of life. This is for Xayacamach the meaning of flower and song.

Other opinions are expressed on the same theme of poetry, art, and the symbols. One says he collects flowers to bedeck his own little hut, thus to be close to the abode of the Giver of Life. Finally, the dialogue draws to a close. Tecayehuatzin speaks again. His heart has remained open to doubt. He appears still anxious to know whether flower and song are the only way to pronounce true words on earth. The answers so far have been diverse. Nevertheless, he trusts that he will say something on which all will agree: at least flower and song make possible friendship on earth.

The reading of the dialogue of flower and song, which in its entirety is included in this book, will probably be the most eloquent confirmation of the value inherent in these classics of Mesoamerican spirituality. The pre-Columbian sages accepted that it was perhaps impossible for man to arrive at absolute answers, but at the same time they admitted that, through metaphors and symbols, all things could be questioned while at once they could become an inexhaustible source of meaning.[50]

I believe the moment has arrived to end this Introduction, devised to facilitate the reading, analysis, and study of the message left by our Mesoamerican sages. Now we know that, although they spoke various languages and developed regional differences, they all participated in their own ways in the same complex processes that caused the flourishing of high culture and civilization in this part of the New World. Mesoamerica was a universe of culture where, independently, man also discovered the means to preserve the memory of his life and thought.

Mesoamerican development was mortally threatened when, in the sixteenth century, the Spanish arrival brought in many radical and traumatic transformations.

It was fortunate that, at least in part, the Ancient Word of the sages did not fall into oblivion. An even greater reality is the contemporary presence of several millions of descendants of those an-

---

50. Complementary information about the various connotations of "flower and song" can be found in León-Portilla, *Aztec Thought and Culture*, p. 73–81.

INTRODUCTION

cient Mesoamericans. Thanks to them, who in many forms and so deeply have influenced the life of the *Mestizo* country that is Mexico, we have the above mentioned consubstantial bridge to cross the gaps of time and cultural differences that separate modern man from his native ancestors. Taking advantage of this bridge, we benefit from that wisdom, the best of the Mesoamerican legacy to the peoples of the four quadrants of the world.

5. The Documentary Sources and the Present Translation

Although several mentions have been made already of the documents and codices that contain the native texts I will include in this book, it seems appropriate to add some more specific information about them. To do this, I will make systematic reference to the various consulted sources, indicating at once which are the texts that proceed from them.

The Codices Matritenses and Florentine comprise the texts compiled by Fray Bernardino de Sahagun in Nahuatl. He began his work of research in 1547 in Tepepulco (in the state of Hidalgo, in Central Mexico) and continued it in other towns during more than thirty years. Consulting ancient native books and transcribing the narrative of several native elders who repeated what they had learned by memory in the pre-Columbian schools, he succeeded in assembling an immense treasure of compositions and other data related to The Ancient Word, the myths, other religious testimonies, and, in general, to many other aspects of Aztec culture.

The texts that compromise the whole of parts 1 and 3 and various sections of parts 2 and 4 of this book derive from such primary sources. *Codices Matritenses* are preserved, a first part in the Library of the Royal Palace, Madrid, and a second in the Library of the Royal Spanish Academy of History, also in the capital of Spain. *Codex Florentinus* forms part of the rich collection of manuscripts of the Laurentian Library in Florence.[51]

In our book we follow the translation into English of the materials derived from the latter manuscript, prepared by the distinguished scholars Charles E. Dibble and Arthur J. O. Anderson of

---

51. An excellent facsimile edition of the *Codices Matritenses* was published in 3 volumes by the Mexican Scholar Francisco del Paso y Troncoso, Madrid, 1905–1907. Researchers in Mexico (National University) and in Germany (Iberoamerikanische Bibliothek, Berlin) have translated and published several parts of the contents of these *Codices*. Their works are registered in our Bibliography.

There is an English edition of the *Florentine Codex* (Bernardino de Sahagun's, *General History of the Things of New Spain*), edited and translated by J. O. Anderson and Charles E. Dibble, 11 v., Santa Fe, N. Nexico, School of American Research and the University of Utah, 1950–1969.

Of the Nahuatl text which corresponds to Books 1, 3 and 10 of the *Codex* a revised version has been published by the same scholars, (1973–1978).

the School of American Research, Santa Fe, New Mexico, and the University of Utah. I ought to say that I have introduced minor modifications to said translation having in mind to offer a text as easy to understand and faithful to the original Nahuatl as possible. In particular I have tried to preserve the abundance of metaphors so characteristic of the indigenous expression. I want to repeat here the testimony of my gratitude to my colleagues Dibble and Anderson for their generous permission to take advantage of their first translation into English of the *Codex Florentinus*.

In the case of the texts from the *Codices Matritenses*—as, for instance, the twenty sacred hymns to the gods—the English translation is the result of my own effort to offer the reader a new version of these compositions so rich in archaisms which denote their old age.

The *Popol Vuh*, or "Book of the Counsel," is the source, in the Quiche-Maya language, from which the account about the cosmic ages and successive creations of human beings is taken as it appears in our part 2. Several copies are known, preserved now in various libraries of the United States and Guatemala. I have been granted the privilege of transcribing here the text of the excellent and first direct translation into English prepared by my friend professor Munro S. Edmonson, from Tulane University.[52]

The Mixtec parallel myth about the cosmic and human origins, included in part 2 of this book, comes from a transcription preserved in the Monastery of Cuilapa, state of Oaxaca, Mexico, and later copied again by Fray Gregorio Garcia, vicar in that place. This narrative corresponds also to the contents of the first pages of the Mixtec pre-Columbian manuscript known as *Codex Vindobonensis*, now in the National Library in Vienna. I have translated this text into English, trying to convey the nuances of its original version.[53]

---

52. Several editions of the *Popol Vuh* have been published with translations into Spanish, French, English, German and Japanese. The available translations into English are: *Popol Vuh: The Sacred Book of the Ancient Quiche Maya*. English version by D. Goetz and S. Morley from the translation into Spanish of Adrian Recinos, Norman, University of Oklahoma Press, 1950; *The Book of Counsel: The Popol Vuh of the Quiche Maya of Guatemala*, edited and translated by Munro S. Edmonson, New Orleans, Middle American Research Institute, Tulane University, 1971. By far this new and direct translation prepared by professor Edmonson is the best ever published and an example of philological and ethnolinguistic scholarship.

53. *Codex Vindobonensis*, as its designation indicates, is preserved at the National Library in Vienna. Together with *Codices Becker 1 and 2, Codex Bodleianus, Columbinus, Nuttal* and *Selden*, this manuscript integrates the rich *corpus* of Mixtec pre-Columbian

INTRODUCTION

Two Collections of Mexican songs and poems, inestimable possessions of the National Library of Mexico and of the Latin American Section of the Library of the University of Texas (Austin), are the sources of the texts that form parts 5 and 6 of our book. The one in Mexico, known as *Colección de Cantares Mexicanos*, is a manuscript of eighty-five sheets, written on both sides. Several hundred compositions are inscribed in it with the Latin alphabet. Such transcription, prepared during the second half of the sixteenth century, is due to some anonymous native sages who could consult the ancient testimonies, oral traditions, and codices.[54]

More specific information can be given about the manuscript existing in Texas. Composed of forty-two sheets, also written on both sides, it is almost surely a result of the research carried out by the sixteen-century Mestizo chronicler Juan Bautista Pomar. According to his own testimony, he could collect this corpus of native poetry

> consulting with old natives, intelligent in their antiquities
> ... and locating very old songs, from which [sources] [he]
> took what has been written . . .[55]

For the most part, the compositions included in both manuscripts appear as anonymous. Nevertheless, in some cases, as has been already indicated, precise reference is made to verified authors. It is also important to note that in several instances the same poem or song is included in the two manuscripts. This is above all rele-

---

documents. The text from the Monastery of Cuilapa, Oaxaca was originally published by Fray Gregorio García, *Origen de los Indios del Nuevo Mundo e Islas Occidentales*, Madrid, 1729, p. 137–138.

54. The late scholar Angel M. Garibay translated into Spanish and published numerous compositions included in this *Collection of Mexican Songs*, found in the National Library of Mexico. See in particular: *Poesía Nahuatl* II and III, paleography, translation into Spanish and introduction by A.M. Garibay, Mexico, National University Press, 1965–1968. At present several researchers in Mexico, The United States, France and Germany continue deeply interested in the study and complete publication of this rich literary source in the Nahuatl language.

55. Juan Bautista Pomar, "Relación de Texcoco", included in: A.M. Garibay, *Poesía Nahuatl I*, Mexico, National University Press, 1963. In this first volume of the *Nahuatl Poetry Series*, Garibay included the paleography, Spanish version and an Introduction relative to the manuscript kept in The Latin American Collection of The Library of the University of Texas (Austin). The original and curious title appearing in this manuscript is "Romances de los Señores de la Nueva España", ("Ballads of the Lords of New Spain").

INTRODUCTION

vant from a critical point of view. If, as is the case, we have here two compilations, prepared and transcribed by different persons at different times, the coincidences reveal not only the authenticity of the composition but also its ample diffusion among the native Mesoamericans. In preparing all the direct translations into English of the poems and songs derived from these sources, I have done my best to maintain, as far as possible, the flavor and nuances of the original compositions. Particular attention has thus been given to those traits and elements I have already described as distinctive of the poetry in Nahuatl.

The Book of Songs of Dzitbalche, which contains fifteen poems in the Mayan language of Yucatan, permits us an appreciation of lyric compositions conceived by the ancient Mayan priests and sages. Rescued by Professor Alfredo Barrera Vasquez of the Yucatec Institute of Anthropology in Merida, Yucatan, this manuscript is of prime importance to an approach of Mayan spirituality. The poems included in part 5 of our book have been translated into English following the Spanish version due to Barrera Vasquez.[56]

The Book of Chilam Balam of Chumayel, one of the most significant creations from among what is known of the Yucatec-Mayan literature, is the last of the sources I have taken into account in preparing this book.[57] The Chilams were high-ranking priests who most often served as teachers and prophets. *Balam,* a word that means jaguar, is "the name of the most famous of the chilams who lived a little before the arrival of the white men."[58] Eighteen *Chilam Balam* books remain but only four of them have been studied in part. These contain mythical and historical passages, sacred hymns, and prophecies of the days, years, and other periods of time. Some late Christian interpolations are evident in the *Chilam Balam* manuscripts that have come down to us. In part 2 of the present book examples are offered of the mythical narrative characteristic of this

---

56. An edition and translation into Spanish of all the poems included in this manuscript is due to Professor Alfredo Barrera Vasquez, *El libro de los cantares de Dzitbalché,* Mexico, National Institute of Anthropology and History, 1965.

57. The translations of this book, into Spanish and English, prepared respectively by Alfredo Barrera Vasquez and Ralph L. Roys, deserve special mention: *El libro de los libros de Chilam Balam,* Mexico, Fondo de Cultura Económica, 1948 and *The Book of Chilam Balam of Chumayel,* Washington, Publication 438, Carnegie Institution of Washington, 1933 (A reprint has been issued by the University of Oklahoma Press, 1967).

58. Barrera Vasquez, *op. cit.,* p. 14.

INTRODUCTION

Chilam series, an authentic expression of the religious thought of the Mayas.

One final comment: The footnotes to the texts comprise much more than the mere references to the documentary sources and other bibliographical precisions. Conceived to facilitate the comprehension of divers points needing clarification, they will often bring in information derived from other sources describing the correspondent cultural background and will be, therefore, relatively abundant. I want to repeat that my main concern here has been to take advantage of whatever leads to consolidate that "bridge" which will permit the approach and sympathetic understanding of our Mesoamerican classics of spirituality at once so distant from and so close to us.

Part One
THE ANCIENT WORD

Here it is related how the rulers admonished their daughters when they had already reached the age of discretion.

Here you are, my little girl, my necklace of precious stones, my plumage, my human creation, born of me. You are my blood, my color, my image.[1]

Now listen, understand. You are alive, you have been born; Our Lord, the Lord of the Near and the Close, the maker of people, the inventor of men, has sent you to earth.[2]

Now that you begin to look around you, be aware. Here it is like this: There is no happiness, no pleasure. There is heartache, worry, fatigue. Here spring up and grow suffering and distress.

Here on earth is the place of much wailing, the place where our strength is worn out, where we are well acquainted with bitterness and discouragement. A wind blows; sharp as obsidian it slides over us.

They say truly that we are burned by the force of the sun and the wind. This is the place where one almost perishes of thirst and hunger. This is the way it is here on earth.

Listen well, my child, my little girl. There is no place of well-being on the earth, there is no happiness, no pleasure. They say that the earth is the place of painful pleasure, of grievous happiness.

The elders have always said: "So that we should not go round always moaning, that we should not be filled with sadness, the Lord has given us laughter, sleep, food, our strength and fortitude, and finally the act by which men propagate."

All this sweetens life on earth so that we are not always moaning. But even though it be like this, even though it be true that there is only suffering and this is the way things are on eaath, even so, should we always be afraid? Should we always be fearful? Must we live weeping?

But see, there is life on the earth, there are the lords; there is au-

---

1. Expressions like these, addressed to the beloved ones, rich in metaphors, are frequent in the extant examples of the *Huehuetlatolli*, The Ancient Word.

2. Several of the titles of the supreme Dual God are given here: *Tloque Nahuaque*, "Lord of the Near and the Close," is an expression derived from two adverbs to both of which a suffix of possession is attached. *Tloc* means "close to" and *Nahuac* means "near." The suffix *-e* connotes the idea of "to whom belongs something": in this case, "to be close and near." I have also translated this expression as "Lord of the Close Vicinity" or "Lord of the Everywhere." *Techihuani*, "The maker of people," and *Teyocoyani*, "The inventor of men," constitute an example of the parallelism so frequent in the literature of the Nahuas.

63

thority, there is nobility, there are eagles and tigers [knights]. And who is always saying that so it is on earth? Who goes about trying to put an end to his life? There is ambition, there is struggle, work. One looks for a wife, one looks for a husband.

But now, my little one, listen well, look carefully: Here is your mother, our lady, from whose bosom, from whose womb you appeared, you came forth. As the leaf opens, so you grew, you flowered, as if you had been sleeping and awakened.

Listen, look, understand, for thus it is on earth. Do not be idle, do not walk aimlessly, do not wander without a destination. How should you live? How should you go on for a short time? They say it is very difficult to live on the earth, a place of terrific struggle, my little lady, my little bird, my little one.

Be careful, because you come from a renowned family, you descend from them, you are born from illustrious people. You are the thorn, the offshoot of our lords. The lords have left us, those who governed; they are standing in line there, those who came to take command in the world; they gave renown and fame to the nobility.[3]

Listen. Much do I want you to understand that you are noble. See that you are very precious, even while you are still only a little lady. You are a precious stone, you are a turquoise. You have been formed, shaped; you have the blood, the color; you are the offshoot and the stem; you are a descendant of noble lineage.

And now I am going to tell you this. Perhaps you do not understand very well? Are you still playing with earth and potsherds? Perhaps you are still sitting on the ground? Truly, you must listen a little for you already understand these things; by yourself you are gaining experience.

See that you do not dishonor yourself and our lords, the princes, the governors who preceded us. Do not act like the common people of the village, do not become an ordinary person. As long as you live on the earth, near and close to the people, be always a true little lady.

Look now at your work, that which you have to do: During night and day, devote yourself to the things of God; think often how

3. These and other similar statements in this text confirm what has been said in the Introduction: that most of the *Huehuetlatolli* were discourses transmitted and delivered by members of the Pre-Columbian nobility.

He is like the night and the wind.[4] Pray to Him, invoke Him, call to Him, beg Him earnestly when you are in the place where you sleep. This way your sleep will be pleasant.

Waken, get up in the middle of the night, prostrate yourself on your knees and your elbows, raise your neck and your shoulders. Invoke Him, call the Lord, our Lord, He who is as the night and the wind. He will be merciful, He will hear you in the night, He will look upon you with compassion; then He will grant you your destiny, what is set aside for you.[5]

And if the destiny should be bad, the portion which they gave you when it was still night, what came with you at birth, when you came into life, with this supplication it will be made good, rectified; the Lord will change it, our Lord of the Near and the Close.

Watch for the dawn, get up quickly, extend your hands, extend your arms, raise your face, wash your hands, cleanse your mouth, take up the broom quickly, begin to sweep. Do not be idle, do not stay there close to the fire; wash the mouths of your little brothers; burn copal incense, do not forget it, for thus you will have the mercy of Our Lord.

And this being done, when you will be prepared, what will you do? How will you fulfill your womanly duties? Will you not prepare the food, the drink? Will you not spin and weave? Look well how are the food and drink, how they are made, that they should be good; know how good food and good drink are prepared.

These things that are sometimes called "things appropriate for persons of distinction," they are the duty of the wives of those who govern; for this they are called things that belong to the nobles, the food proper for one who governs, his drink. Be skillful in preparing the drink, in preparing the food. Pay attention, dedicate yourself, apply yourself to see how this is done; thus life will pass, thus you will be at peace. Thus you will be highly esteemed. Let it be not in vain if Our Lord some time may send you misfortune. Sometimes

---

4. "He is like the night and the wind": *Yohualli, Ehecatl*, the one invisible as the night and intangible as the wind.

5. The destiny (the *tonalli*) is "what is set aside for everyone." This text makes reference to the deeply rooted Mesoamerican belief about the destiny that the supreme God granted to every individual when he was conceived in the womb of his mother. As the text goes on to say, if the destiny were bad, supplications to the Lord of the Near and the Close could eventually change it, rectify it.

there is poverty among the nobles. Face it; then take hold of it, for this is the duty of a woman: spinning and weaving.

Open well your eyes to see what is the Toltec art, what is the art of feathers;[6] how to embroider in colors and how to interweave the threads; how women dye them, those who are like you, our wives, the noble women. How they place the threads on the loom, how to make the woof of the cloth, how to hold it fast. Pay attention, apply yourself, be not idle, do not stand idly by, be strict with yourself.

Now is the right time, there is still plenty of time, because there is still jade in your heart, turquoise.[7] It is still fresh, it has not been spoiled, it has not been altered, nothing has twisted it. We are still here, we your parents, who have brought you here to suffer; because in this way the world continues. Thus it is said, thus the word was given, thus Our Lord arranged it, so that there should be always, there should be offspring on the earth.

We are still here, it is still our time, not yet has come the stick and the stone of Our Lord. We are not yet dead, we have not perished. Of what are you thinking, child, little bird, little one? When Our Lord will have hidden us, you will be cared for by another, for it is not your destiny, it was not meant for you to sell vegetables, wood, handfuls of chili, pots of salt, *tesquesquite* stone,[8] standing at the doorways of the houses, because you are noble. Learn to spin, to weave, to prepare food and drink.

May no one's heart ever become disdainful of you, say anything about you, point a finger at you, talk about you. If things come out badly, how will you react to misfortune? Because of this will we be blamed? When Our Lord will have taken us to Himself, will we be reprimanded in the Region of the Dead? But as for you, do not put

---

6. Mention has been made in the Introduction about the esteem in which Toltec art, and in general Toltec culture, were held by the various peoples who flourished later in Mesoamerica. In part 5 of this book texts will be offered that speak about the various Toltec arts.

7. Jades and turquoises were symbols of life and precious things. When a person died a jade, or in the case of the poor people a cheap green stone, was introduced into his mouth, conveying the meaning of the life that such person was believed to enjoy in the beyond.

8. *Tequesquite stone* means saltpeter. Here a description is made of the occupations of the common people to contrast them with what was thought to be the destiny of a young lady belonging to the nobility.

into motion the stick and the stone against yourself. Do not cause them to come against you.

But even if you are attentive, cannot censure fall upon you? And if you are praised too much by others, let not your countenance become proud, do not act as if you had the rank of eagle or tiger, as if you held Huitzilopochtli's shield in your hand, as if it were due to you that our heads are raised, that our countenances are magnified.[9] But if you do nothing, then will you not be like a block of stone? They will not speak of you, you will have little praise. Be and act according to what Our Lord wishes for you.

Look now at something else that I want to impress on you, communicate to you, my human creation, my little daughter. Do not permit the lords from whom you are born to be mocked. Do not throw dust or rubbish on them; do not cast any uncleanness on their history, on their black and red ink, on their fame.[10]

Do not insult them in any way, such as wanting things of this earth, such as seeking to enjoy them out of season, those which are called sexual things. And if you do not withdraw from them, can you ever come near the gods? Better that you should perish immediately.

So now calmly, very calmly, pay attention; if thus Our Lord sees it, if someone should speak of you, if they should say something about you, do not scorn it, do not kick with your foot what may be an inspiration of Our Lord; take it up; do not withdraw so that it would have to come back to you two or three times. Even though you be our very daughter, because you are born of us, do not become proud, forgetting Our Lord in your heart. For thus you will fall into the dust and rubbish, which is the life of public women.[11] And then Our Lord will scoff at you, will do with you as He chooses.

---

9. "As if you held Huitzilopochtli's shield in your hand," that is, if you had the power and the dignity of what is reserved to the god of war, the tutelar god of the Aztecs, Huitzilopochtli.

10. Black and red inks, *Tlilli, Tlapalli*, symbolize in the mythology and religious thought of the Nahuas the knowledge about things difficult to understand and about the beyond. "Black and red inks" imply also the painted books where history was preserved and, in general, such expression appears as a metaphor to denote writing and wisdom.

11. Public women were not a rarity in the context of Mesoamerican society. In the Nahuatl language they were called *ahuianime*, "gladdeners," "those who gladden men."

Do not seek him who will be your companion as if in a market place; do not call to him as if you were aflame in the springtime, do not go about desiring him. But also, take care not to disdain the one who may be your companion, the one chosen by the Lord. For if you look down on him, it might be that Our Lord would scoff at you, and finally you might become as a public woman.

But prepare yourself; watch who is your enemy so that no one should make light of you. Do not give yourself to a wastrel, to one who seeks you for his own pleasure, a depraved boy. Nor should two or three faces you may have seen know you. Whoever may be your companion, you two must go to the end of life together. Do not leave him, hold to him, cling to him even though he be a poor man, even though he be only a small eagle, a small tiger,[12] an unhappy soldier, a poor noble, sometimes tired, lacking goods; not for that do you neglect him.

May Our Lord look upon you, may He strengthen you, He who knows man, the Investor of people, the Maker of human beings.

With these words from my mouth do I give all this to you. Thus before Our Lord, I fulfill my duty. And if perchance you cast this away, still you know it. I have fulfilled my duty, my little woman, my little daughter. May you be happy, may Our Lord bring you success.[13]

*   *   *

Here it is told how, when the father had spoken, the mother then replies. She tells her daughter tender words that she will always keep, will always place in her interior, the discourse of her father.

Dove, little dove, little child, little daughter, my little girl: You have received your father's words, the discourse of your lord and father.[14]

---

12. An eagle, a tiger, or more properly an ocelot: a metaphorical expression to mean the warriors.

13. *Florentine Codex*, book 6, chapter 18. Translated by Miguel Leon-Portilla.

14. Whether this Ancient Word was a composition to be attributed to a priestess or to a male sage is difficult to state. It is known at least that some women stood out for their poetical creations. In this book we will quote a poem attributed to the poetess Macuilxochitzin. In any form this *Huehuetlatolli* confirms the active participation of women in fields of such an importance as education.

What you have received is nothing common, is not given to the ordinary people: It was treasured and well guarded in your father's heart.

And he has not merely loaned it to you, for you are of his blood and his color, he has made himself known in you. Although you are a young girl, you are his image.

But what can I say further, what remains to tell you? I would gladly give you advice, but he spoke fully on all matters, made you aware of everything, there is nothing left to tell you.

Yet I must give you something, in order to fulfill my duty. You must never reject anywhere the words of your lord and father, because they are excellent and precious things, because only good things come from the word of our lord, since his language is truly that of a great person.

His words are as valuable as precious stones, as fine turquoises, rounded and grooved. Treasure them, keep them as a treasure in your heart, let them be as a painting in your heart.[15] If you live, you will educate your sons with them, will make them men; all this you will give them, will say to them.

There is a second word that I give you, I tell you, my child, you, little one. Look, I am your mother. In my bosom, for several months, I carried you. And then, when you were born, often I lulled you to sleep. I often laid you in your cradle. I placed you on my thigh. And in truth, with my milk I nourished you . . .

This is the way you must follow, the way of those who educated you, the way of the ladies, the noble women, the aged, white-haired women that preceded us. Do not think they left us all their wisdom in their discourses. They gave us only a few words, they told us little. Here is all they said:

Listen well, for now is the time to learn here on the earth, and this is the word. Heed it and learn how your life should be lived, how you should shape it.

We travel through a difficult region here, we wander about on the earth, with an abyss on one side, a ravine on the other. If you do

---

15. The words of wisdom of the father are here compared to a precious stone and to the contents of the painted books where knowledge about things human and divine was preserved.

not walk between them you will fall on one side or the other. One can live only in the middle, walk safely only in the middle.[16]

Little daughter, little dove, little child, place this counsel in your heart and treasure it there. Do not forget it, but let it be your torch, your light, during all the time you live here on the earth.

There remains only one other matter, with which I will end my words. If you live for a time, if you go on living on this earth for a time, do not deliver up your body foolishly, my little daughter, my child, my little dove, my little girl. Do not give yourself to this one or that one, for if you surrender yourself so carelessly, you are lost, and will never be under the protection of one who truly loves you.

You will never be able to forget it, you will always be burdened with misery and anguish. You will not be able to live in calmness and in peace. Your husband will always be suspicious of you.

My little daughter, my little dove, if you live here on the earth, do not allow two men to know you. And heed this warning always, keep it in mind all your life.[17]

And when you are a married woman, do not think secret thoughts, but govern yourself, and do not allow your heart to stray foolishly to other men. Do not run risks with your husband. Do not foolishly deceive him, that is, do not be an adultress.

Because, my little daughter, my little girl, if this occurs there is no remedy, there is no return. If you are seen, if it becomes known, you will be cast out into the streets, you will be dragged about, they will crush your skull with stones, they will utterly destroy you.

You will cause fright. You will give a bad name to our forebears, to those of the lineage that gave you birth. You will scatter dust and dung on the books of paintings in which their history is preserved.[18] You will make them figures of fun. It will end forever,

---

16. "To wander about on the earth, with an abyss on one side, a ravine on the other" appears as the Nahuatl version of that universal statement about the "virtue being in the middle," "*in medio est virtus.*"

17. Permanent concern with sexual morality in these Mesoamerican texts must have impressed the Christian missionaries very favorably. This probably explains why several of these *Huehuetlatolli* were rescued and even published, as in the particular case I have mentioned of the collection assembled by Father Andres de Olmos.

18. As in the previously transcribed *Huehuetlatolli*, here also the same idea is expressed: Immoral behavior means to scatter dust and dung on the books of paintings in which the history of the forebears is preserved. Thus it was believed that there was a sort of communication between those living at present on the earth and those who had passed away.

the book of paintings in which your memory was to have been preserved.

You will no longer be called exemplary. They will talk about you, gossip about you, call you "She that is sunk in the dust." And even if no one should see you, even if your husband should not see you, bear in mind that the Lord of the Near and Close will see you. He will be angered, He will provoke the anger of the people, He will avenge it. He will send you that which He will determine, perhaps paralysis, blindness, or putrescence. And you, then, you will deserve to be in tatters, in rags.[19] This will happen on earth, because you despised your man. Or perhaps He will trample your feet, will make you disappear, will send you to Our-Common-House, The Place of the Dead.

The Master, Our lord is merciful.[20] But if you do such a thing, if you behave improperly, if you betray your companion, even if the Lord of the Near and Close does not make it known, you will not be in peace, will not live in peace. Our Lord will inflame your man; he will become infuriated, he will be enraged.

Therefore, my little child, my little daughter, my little dear, live in calmness and peace during the time given you to live. Do not misbehave, do not bring infamy on those from whom you came to this life. As for ourselves, may you bring us renown, may you cause us to be glorified. And as for yourself, may you be happy, my child, my little daughter, my little dear. Enter With Our Lord, the Lord of the Near and Close.[21]

*   *   *

Here is told the manner of the discourse of the father, ruler or nobleman, with which he admonished his son that he should look to the humble life, to the bowing, to the knowledge of oneself in order to be pleasing to the gods and to men. Many are the marvelous dis-

---

19. Some scholars have affirmed about the supreme Lord of the Near and Close that he was to the Mesoamericans a sort of "idle king," a divine entity extremely far from human affairs. Here these Huehuetlatolli appear to indicate the contrary as it is the Lord of the Near and Close who will be angered because of the inconvenient behavior and will avenge it by punishing the transgressor.

20. The Lord of the Near and Close is also merciful. The final words of these *Huehuetlatolli* insist upon this: "Enter with Our Lord, the Lord of the Near and Close."

21. *Florentine Codex*, book VI, chapter 19. Translated by Miguel Leon-Portilla.

courses, and the figures of speech, and the different words of the discourse.[22]

O my son, O my youth, O boy, O servitor, listen, for Our Lord has placed you here. And now, to you who are my son, who are my child, who are my precious necklace, who are my precious feather, who are my oldest [my second, my youngest son][23], I speak, I call out a word or two. Verily, now I form, I say, I reflect on the word or two that I shall give you of my motherhood, of my fatherhood. I shall perform my obligation, lest tomorrow, the next day, Our Lord, the Lord of the Near and Close, will have hidden us. Certainly no one enjoys the hard, the heavy. Certainly our living on earth is not assured.

And grasp this, hear this: May you follow Our Lord for a little while. May you live on earth. May you linger long. Give utmost attention. Be deliberate. Take much care. Certainly it is a dangerous place, a revolting place, a boundless place, a place of no repose, a frightful place, and a painful and afflicting place. And it is very true, as our mothers, our fathers,[24] the old men go saying, that no one escapes our ultimate home, the place of the winds, of the shattering winds, where reside the wind people, the flower people.[25] There is mocking of others on earth. There is rejoicing over the misfortunes of others, there is laughing at others, there is ridicule on earth. And what they say, what they praise, what they tell one is not true; there is only ridicule.

Here is what you are to do, what you are to realize: It is that which is guarded, that which is bound; the secret knowledge that

22. This and the following texts included in this part 1 of our book have been translated into English by J. O. Arthur Anderson and Charles E. Dibble. As I have stated in the Introduction, their translation has been revised, with the permission of Professors Anderson and Dibble, preserving its fidelity to the original Nahuatl text, but introducing in it some minor changes to facilitate understanding by nonspecialists.

23. The words in brackets indicate that this discourse, learned from oral tradition, could be addressed by the father to his various sons.

24. After describing some of the attributes of the earth, the place where humans have to exist, the father makes reference to "Our mothers, our fathers, the old men," that is, to his sources of knowledge. Thanks to them, he can also say something about "our ultimate home."

25. "The wind people" (*Hecamecatl*), "the flower people" (*Xochimecatl*), mentioned here are those who inhabit some of the levels of the underworld, in the *Mictlan*, the Place of the Dead. See part 4 of the present book, which deals with "The Official Dogma about the Afterlife."

the old men, the old women, those who go white-haired, those who go white-headed, those who go emaciated with age, our forefathers, left as they departed.[26] For they came to live on earth; for they came to live with others. And they came to occupy position and authority among the people.

They practiced the bowing of the head, the lowering of the head, the bending of the neck, the weeping, the tears, the sighs. Our forefathers came to know only their misery when they went leaving us. They came living on earth in sadness, in affliction; they came not as fools, they came not panting as they walked, out of breath as they walked. Although they went doing such as that, they were revered. They came exercising military command; in their hands rested the eagle tube, the eagle vessel; they led the eagle warriors; they provided drink for the sun, for Tlaltecutli, the Lord of the Earth.[27]

And although Our Lord showed them mercy when, for a while, for a brief time, they came to occupy the realm, those who came ordering things well for Our Lord of the Near and Close, who came bathing the vassals, who came suppressing their tears, who came determining sentences of death, this made no difference to them. Not for this reason did they lose humility; not for this reason did they become drunk; not for this reason did they become perverted. And this although they enjoyed that which was the property of Our Lord. The prosperous enjoyed the flowers, the tubes of tobacco, the breech clouts, the capes, the large cotton capes, the clothing. And they came enjoying the land, the houses. And the prosperous enjoyed all manner of drink, of food. And they came honoring one with shields, devices, lip pendants, head bands, ear plugs, lip plugs. And before them there was trembling.[28]

Perchance—since such as this happened to them—perchance did they become brazen? Did those mentioned perhaps act superior? Did they perhaps become presumptuous? Did they perhaps, for this reason, come belittling one? Did they perhaps, for this reason, come

26. Once more it is affirmed that what will be communicated is the knowledge left by the ancestors.

27. *Tlaltecutli*, the deity of the earth, had actually male-female countenances, in other words he-she was a manifestation of the supreme Dual God, as related specifically to the earth. On the other hand, *Tlaltlecutli* appears also in this text as a counterpart of the Sun God.

28. For more information about all that was the property of the members of the nobility see *Florentine Codex*, book 8.

regarding no one with consideration? And did they perhaps, also for this reason, come forgetting? Did they lose their judgment? Not at all did they end their humility. Most certainly they came humbling themselves, came becoming meek. Most certainly they came becoming contrite. Most certainly they came depreciating themselves, came belittling themselves. The more they were honored, the more they wept, suffered affliction, sighed; they became most humble, most meek, most contrite.

In such a manner lived on earth those who were the old men, those who go leaving us, your great-grandfathers, your forefathers. You are their offspring; from them you are descended. Regard them; look them in the face. And their memory, their torch, their mirror that, departing, they left: take, place, set the mirror before you. See therein how you are; compare your way of life, your being. Seeing exactly how you are, then you are to discover where are your blotches, your blemishes.

Behold, here is yet a word. Heed it; you are my eagle, you are my ocelot, you are my son! And know, remember, that it is a time of pain, a time of affliction in which you have gained your desert, in which you have gained your merit, in which Our Lord has sent you; that I, your mother, I your father am poor, miserable. Although they went as great men who went leaving us, did they perhaps bequeath us their skills? For already poverty, misery, the misery of old men, the misery of old women dominate.

O my son, look in your ashes, in your heart. All is permeated by pain, by affliction; misery, inhumanity dominate; pain, affliction are known; starvation dominates. We are in want as to that which hangs from our hips, from our necks. In truth we turn it around: From whence comes the wind, there we place it. And look at us! By the grace of our Lord of the Near and Close, we go dying of hunger and thirst; we go like skeletons.

And look at your male cousins, female cousins. Do they perhaps reside, do they perhaps exist, do they enjoy abundance by the grace of the Lord of the Near and Close? Do they perhaps remain possessors of property? Do they perhaps remain glorified? Can you not see how they live? For it spread on earth; for there is drudgery; all are fatigued. With that, how can you be proud, arrogant? That would be but virtual drunkenness, extreme foolishness. This is how you came forth; this is how you were born. And this is how it is in your house, and so are these of your household, your residents. If you would in some manner suffer. And will you not so bow your head, will you not so hang your head? For in such a time as this were you born. And still behold, I place all before you, I cause you to see all. The third oldest brother, your responsibility, your younger brother,[29] do you not look to him, take example from him, learn from him, depend upon him whom Our Lord has humbled? Already he commanded the city; he has procured his realm; already in his hands rest the blue water, the yellow water; already he washed, he bathed the vassals; already in his hands, in his mouth is castigation; Our Lord has placed him in authority, him whom Our Lord has humbled. Already he is called *Tecutlato, Tlacatecutli;*[30] so the city has called him.

The prudent one to serve the city existed, lived not. The noblemen, the precious noblemen, the sons of rulers exist not, live not. But there are none at all. However, if there had been any, the Lord of the Near and Close would have selected them, and the city would have taken one of them. Can he be the tender youth? I am weeping for him. Perhaps he will sink there, perhaps Our Lord searched for another. Is Our Lord perchance wanting in friends?

And how did he live? How did you see him? Did he perhaps go panting? Did he perhaps go like a fool? Did he perhaps go brazenly? Did he perhaps perform impetuously? Was he perhaps disdainful? For certainly he went bowed. Certainly he acted in humility. Certainly he went crying out in sadness unto Our Lord, the Lord of the Near and Close. At night he held vigil; in truth, he went crawling on elbows and knees at midnight; at the parting of the night he went sighing. So was he by nature. And he arose promptly, he seized the broom, he became diligent in the sweeping, the cleaning, the fanning.[31]

And in truth, how does he now live? How does he perchance behave? Does he perhaps act superior? Is he perhaps proud? Does he perhaps say, "Already I am this"? Rather, he goes bowed; rather, he is humble, he weeps, sighs, calls out, calls to Our Lord in sadness, in tears. You do not now see that he perhaps says, "I am this," and "Al-

---

29. To understand these references to the various brothers, see note 23.

30. *Tecutlato:* the one holding the rank and the attributes of a judge. *Tlacatecutli:* an assisting dignatary to the supreme ruler. His duties were related to military affairs.

31. Several mentions are made in this and other similar texts of the practice of arising promptly to do the sweeping, the cleaning. This was actually a ritual practice that is described at length in *Codex Matritense,* fol. 255 v.

ready I am like this." For he holds vigil at night, quickly takes the sweeping, and is diligent with the incense ladle, the incense, the offering of incense. Blessed is he, for you are the older brother and he is your younger brother, O my son.

Behold, here is yet a word like a thorn, like a spine, like a biting wind, which will urge you on, which will press you, bear you to the ground that you may humble yourself, that you may become meek. Hear it and know it. Know that it is a time of misery, a time of poverty in which you have come forth, in which you were born, into which Our Lord, the Lord of the Near and Close, has sent you.

Look at us. In what condition are we who are your mothers, who are your fathers? And how do we live? For what is our glory, what is our renown? Although our forefathers went as great people, departed, leaving us, did they perhaps leave their skills? Did they bequeath them as they left? And look at your relatives, neighbors: In nothing can Our Lord be served, for they bring need.

And who are you? You are of noble lineage; you are one's hair, you are one's fingernail;[32] you are a ruler's son, you are a palace nobleman, you are a precious one, you are nobleman; you are to go holding this, raising it, before your gaze. Note that the humbling, the bowing, the inclining, the weeping, the tears, the sighing, the meekness, these are nobility, the estimable, the valued; these are honor. Note that no brazen one, no vain one, no dissolute or, as is said, shameless one has become ruler. And no inconsiderate one, no impetuous one, no hasty one, no one untrustworthy with secrets, no rash one has become ruler, has been in the rulership.

And if, at times, a dignitary was seen who spoke in jest, who ridiculed, who was fitful, they gave him the displeasing name of *teccuecuechtli;*[33] and the rulership they entrusted to no one who was wicked but to a brave warrior, one furious in battle. The wicked but brave warriors, those furious in battle, those who only came paying the tribute of death, were called *quaquachictin, Otomi tlaotonxinti.*[34] Those who came to occupy the rulership, those who came to oversee the vassals, those who came to direct the eagle warriors, the ocelot

---

32. "One's hair, one's fingernail" (one's offspring), another example of the frequent use in the Nahuatl language of paired metaphors.
33. *Teccuecuechtli,* a rascal, a coaxer.
34. High ranks in the Aztec army.

warriors, were the weepers, the sighers, those who humbled themselves, those who inclined themselves, the bowers, those who became meek, those called the secure, the peaceful, the calm, the gentle.

You know, you remember that there is only one ruler, the heart of the city, and that there are two assisting dignitaries, one from the military, one from the nobility. The one from the military is the *Tlacatecutli;* the one from the nobility is the *Tlacochtecutli.*[35] And of the commanders also, one is from the military, the *Tlacateccatl;* one also is from the nobility, the *Tlacochcalcatl.*[36] And in this way does Our Lord govern, if it is to continue. And the military one, the *Tlacateutli,* the *Tlacochtecutli,* the *Tlacateccatl,* or the *Tlacochcalcatl,* did he then come to life in this position? Was he born in it? Did perhaps his mother, his father bequeath it to him? No. For one is just elected on earth, one is commissioned, endowed by Him by Whom we live.

O my son, O my son, take it to heart. In what manner do you behave? Perhaps it is to no purpose that you will be able to do something? Perhaps He by Whom we live will yet designate you for something. And if possibly you will be assigned to a position on earth, in what manner do you do in your heart? Do not praise yourself, do not take it lightly, do not claim it to yourself; be not vain, be not proud, be not presumptuous. Vanity, presumption, pride, truly provoke the annoyance, the anger of the Lord of the Near and Close. Perhaps something is your merit. Perhaps in something you will honor Our Lord. Perhaps you will be something, perhaps you will be nothing. Just conduct yourself; especially be your head bowed, your arms folded, your head lowered. Be there your weeping, your sadness, your sighing, your humility, your meekness.

And yet hear: You are to render, to declare your very heart unto Our Lord. Your humility is not to appear only on the surface, for it will be said of you that you are a charlatan, a deceiver. And verily, Our Lord is looking to you; he knows, he sees the interior of stones, of wood. He knows one's heart, he hears, he sees within us, what we merit. Do not harden your heart in your humility. As a

---

35. *Tlacatecutli:* See note 30. *Tlacochtecutli:* "lord of the spears," also a high degree in the army. It was a charge to be served by a member of the nobility.

36. The *Tlacochcalcatl,* "lord of the house of the spears," and the *Tlacateccatl,* "commander of men," mentioned a few lines later, were the supreme chiefs of the Aztec armies.

precious green stone, as a well-formed precious turquoise, offer your humility to Our Lord. Be not a hypocrite.[37]

*   *   *

Here is told the discourse, the manner in which the father, ruler or nobleman, exhorted his son in order to provoke him to chastity. Here he said that the gods befriend, love much those who can be abstinent. Many similes and examples are given expression. Very good are the discourses and the many other things that furnish pleasure.

You who are my son, you who are my youth, hear the words; place, inscribe in the chambers of your heart the word or two that our forefathers left departing; the old men, the old women, the regarded ones, the admired ones, and the advised ones on earth. Here is that which they gave us, entrusted to us as they left, the words of the old men, that which is bound, the well-guarded words.[38] They went saying that the pure life is considered as a well-smoked, precious turquoise; as a round, reedlike, well-formed, precious green stone.[39] There is no blotch, no blemish. Those perfect in their hearts, in their manner of life, those of pure life, are like the precious green stone, the precious turquoise, which is glistening, shining before the Lord of the Near and Close. Like them are the precious feathers, the dark green ones, broad, well-formed, which arch over the earth. They are those of pure life, those called good-hearted.

Heed what the old men went saying: that the children, the youths, the maidens, are the real friends, the really beloved of the Lord of the Near and Close. They live with him; they rejoice with him; he makes friends of them.

Because of this, for this reason, the old men, those especially devout in the penance, in the fasting, in the offering of incense, go especially confident in those who are children, youths, maidens. The

---

37. *Florentine Codex*, book 6, chapter 20.

38. Insistently it is repeated that "the words of the old men," that is, tradition, are "the well-guarded words."

39. The metaphors of the turquoise and of the precious green stone convey here not merely the idea of life and existence but in particular that of the purity of life, the existence without blotch or blemish.

students of the old men, their sons, they awaken while it is yet dark and while they want the pleasure of sleeping; they strip them; they sprinkle them with water. These sweep; they offer incense; the women wash the mouths. It is said that the Lord of the Near and Close yet hears, receives their weeping, their sorrow, their sighs, their prayers, because, it is said, they are good of heart, undefiled, still clean, untouched, pure, still true precious green stones, still true precious turquoises. So, it is said, through them the earth yet endures. They are our intercessors.

And then there are the priests, the penitents, for they are those who live in chastity; clean, good, fine, precious, washed, white are their hearts. Their way of life is undefiled, without ordure, without dust, without filth. For this reason they approach, they stand before the Lord of the Near and Close; they offer him incense, they pray to him, they pray to him on behalf of the city. And the ruler names them the priests of his gods because of their goodness, their clean life.

And the old people, the wise ones, the keepers of the books,[40] go saying that the pure in heart are very precious; those who nowhere find and who rejoice not in vice, in filth, those who know it not, are so precious that the gods require them, seek them, call out to them. He who goes pure, who dies in war, they say, the Sun summons; he calls out to him.[41] He lives hard by, nigh unto the Sun, the valiant warrior. He goes gladdening him, giving cries to him, causing him to rejoice. Always forever, he lives in pleasure, he rejoices; ever glad, without pain, he sucks the different flowers, the savory ones, the fragrant ones. For verily he lives in the House of the Sun, which is a place of wealth, a place of joy.

And such as these who die in war are well honored; they are considered very precious on earth, and they are also very much desired. Also they are much envied, so that all people desire, seek, long for this death, for such are much praised.

---

40. The sages are described here as those in possession of the books. See in this respect a text from the *Codex Matritensis*, included in part 5 of this book, about the ideal image of the sage.

41. Here the destiny of the valiant warriors is described. In part 4 of this book a text is included that confirms and amplifies what is the happiness awaiting those destined to the House of the Sun, those who died in the battle.

Thus is it said of one who died in war, a small youth who came to die in war in Mexico. He was an inhabitant of Uexotzinco, named Mixcoatl. His song is intoned; it is told:[42]

You, Mixcoatl, merit the song.
You will live on earth;
You will live among Uexotzinco's drums,
Will gladden the nobles.
Your friends will behold you.

Here is the reply to this song to give much praise to Mixcoatzin, the small youth who died in war. It says:

Like fine burnished turquoise you give your heart.
It comes to the sun.
You will yet germinate—
Will once again blossom
On earth.
You will live among Uexotzinco's drums,
Will gladden the nobles.
Your friends will behold you.

And then those who have been drowned, those struck by lightning: the old men went saying that they who are good of heart are struck by lightning because the Tlaloque desire them; they long for them.[43] They take them there to their home, Tlalocan. They live by the master, Xoxouhqui, he who is provided with rubber, with incense, Tlamacazqui, Lord of Tlalocan. For verily in Tlalocan those who enter, those taken, those struck are submerged there. They live in eternal spring; never is there withering; forever there is sprouting, there is verdure; it is eternally green.

And then here are the words that tell of those who die prematurely, the tender youths, the tender maidens, the inexperienced,

---

42. Poems such as this about the warrior *Mixcoatl* are sometimes offered in discourses like the present one and also in various chronicles and stories.

43. The discourse attends now to the destiny in the afterlife of those who are chosen by Tlaloc, the "Lord of Rain," or by his servants, the Tlaloque. The God of Rain is here described as the Master *Xoxouqui*, "the blue-greenish one," and as *Tlamacazqui*, "the offering priest." See part 4 of this book for a more detailed description of the *Tlalocan* or paradise of the God of Rain.

the uninstructed on earth. To him who went not experiencing, not approaching vice, filth, it is said, Our Lord showed bounteous mercy. The tender youth, the tender maiden are like precious bracelets, like precious green stones.

And still here is a word to be guarded, to be taken, to be heard, for it is said that the children who die become as precious green stones, as precious turquoises, as precious bracelets. When they die they go not there where it is fearful, the place of sharp winds, the region of the dead.[44] They go there to the home of Tonacatecutli;[45] they live in the garden of Tonacatecutli, suck the flowers of Tonacatecutli, live by the tree of Tonacatecutli; by it they suck the flowers.

It is not in vain, O my son, that children, babies are buried in front of the maize bin, for this means that they go to a good place, a fine place, because they are still as precious green stones, still as precious bracelets; still pure, they become as precious turquoises.

And here is still a little: The babies, the children are very precious; they are beloved, desired, because they are the clean, the yet-pure ones. They become as precious green stones, as precious bracelets, as precious turquoises: precious.

Behold also the good, the fine, the good of heart, those worthy of confidence. They are respected, honored. They do nothing reprehensible, they are nowhere reprehensible. And they live in happiness and peace. Nowhere do they spread fear; they live in contentment.

And now, O my beloved son, O my youth, take heed if you are to continue with Our Lord awhile. Listen to the way in which you are to live. You are not to lust for vice, for filth; you are not to take pleasure in that which defiles one, which corrupts one, that which, it is said, drives one to excess, which harms, destroys one: that which is deadly.[46] So the old men went saying: In childhood, in the yet tender years, then is when Our Lord shows compassion for one. Then is when he distributes, gives as one's desert, the rulership, the governed, valiant warriorhood. And then, then in the time of childhood, in the tender years, at that time the Lord of the Near and

---

44. An allusion is made here to the third region existing in the beyond, the *Mictlan*, "Place of the Dead." See also part 4.

45. *Tonacatecutli*, a title given here to the God of Rain but also used as an invocation of the supreme Dual God. It literally means "Lord of Our Flesh."

46. As in the previously presented examples of the Ancient Word, it is important to note here the emphasis given to the idea of moderation.

Close gives one, gives one as merit, joy and prosperity. And in the time of childhood, still in the time of purity, the good death is merited.

Take heed, O my son: also such is the condition in the peopling, the replenishing of the world. For the Lord of the Near and Close has said, you are ordained one woman for one man. However, you are not to ruin yourself impetuously; you are not to devour, to gulp down the carnal life as if you were a dog.

Especially are you to become courageous, are you yet to become strong, are you yet to reach maturity. Even as the maguey, you are to form a stalk, you are to ripen. Then, thereby, you will become strong in the union, in the marriage your children will be rugged, agile, and they will be polished, beautiful, clean. And well will you enter into your carnal life: In your carnal life you will be rugged, strong, swift; diligent will you be.

And if you ruin yourself impetuously, if too soon you seduce, you discover women on earth, verily the old men went saying, you will interrupt your development, you will be stunted, your tongue will be white, your mouth will become swollen, puffed; you will go tasting your nasal mucus, you will be pale, you will go pale on earth, nasal mucus will go dripping, you will go coughing, you will be enfeebled, weakened, emaciated; you will become a tuft of hair. Possibly already you will linger a short time on earth, very soon to be old, old and wrinkled.

And you are as the bored maguey,[47] you are as the maguey: Soon you will cease to give forth liquid. Perhaps it is so with you, a man, when already you consume yourself, when you can no longer say anything, no longer do anything, to your spouse. Soon she hates you, soon she detests you, for verily you starve her. Perhaps presently there arises her desire; she longs for the carnal relations that you owe your spouse. Already you are finished, you have completed all. Perhaps you are incapable. She will ignore you, she will betray you. Verily, you have ruined impetuously, you have consumed yourself.

Heed yet. May you in good time reach manhood. You are not to ruin yourself impetuously. Although she is your spouse, your body,

---

47. The *maguey* plant, an American agave, was cultivated among other reasons for its sap, which when fermented became *pulque* or *octli*, a spirituous native beverage. It actually took several years before one could bore the maguey to obtain its sap. Once the maguey was bored, it gave forth liquid for a rather limited span of time.

when you will know her, it is as with food that you are not to eat hastily; that is to say, you are not to live lustfully; do not give yourself excessively to it. Moderately, temperately are you to perform the act. Perhaps otherwise to no avail comes to pass that you think to find pleasure when you give yourself excessively to pleasure, for already you kill yourself, you endanger yourself.

The old men said, as they left, as they went leaving their commandments: You are only a maguey that they have sucked excessively. Be not so. The cape wetted, washed, when tightly wrung, quickly dries; also you are the same when you have given yourself excessively to the carnal act. Not only are you useless, but soon your nasal mucus goes hanging; you will go toothless, you will go on hand and knees, you will go pale.

Behold, it came to pass that a man was seized, was imprisoned— a decrepit old man, white-headed—because he knew another's woman; he had committed adultery. And he was asked if it were possible that he still required the carnal act. He said that presently was aroused his desire for the carnal act, because in the time of his childhood, in the time of his youth, he looked not upon a woman, nor did he ever anywhere know carnality. In the period of his virility, already in the time of his old age, then he went seeking the carnal act.

Behold, here is yet a word or two. Let it inspire you, that all may be your measuring stick, your model. You are to take all as an example, as to how to live in purity on earth.

In the time of the lord Nezahualcoyotzin, two old women were seized.[48] They were white-headed; their heads were like snow; it was as if they were wearing shredded maguey fiber. They were imprisoned because they had committed adultery, had betrayed their spouses, their old men. It was young priests, youths, who had violated them.

The ruler Nezahualocyotzin inquired of them; he said to them: "O our grandmothers, listen! What is it? Do you perhaps still require the carnal act? Are you not satiated, being as old as you are? And how did you live while still in your girlhood? Just say it, just tell me, since you are here for this reason."

They said to him: "Master, ruler, Our Lord, receive it, hear it.

---

48. Special mention has been made in the Introduction of the famous Lord and sage Nezahualcoyotzin (1402–1472). His poetical work is presented in part 6 of this book.

You men, you are sluggish, you are depleted, you have ruined yourselves impetuously. It is all gone. There is no more. There is nothing to be desired. But of this, we who are women, we are not the
sluggish ones. In us is a cave, a gorge, whose only function is to
await that which is given, whose only function is to receive. And of
this, if you have become impotent, if you no longer arouse anything,
what other purpose will you serve?"

And this, O my son: Be very careful on earth. Live very calmly,
very peacefully. Live not in filth. Do not live in filth on earth.[49]

*   *   *

*Here it is related how the common folk left their sons there in the
young men's house, and how they observed the customs there in the
young men's house; how they were trained, reared.*

When a boy was born, then they placed him in the *calmecac*
[center of higher religious preparation] or in the *telpuchcalli* [young
men's house]. That is to say, the parents promised him, gave him as
a gift, made an offering of him in the temple, in the *calmecac* in order
that the boy would become a priest or a young warrior.[50]

If they put him in the young men's house, they promised him to
it, they prepared drink, food. They summoned, they assembled, they
entreated the rulers of the youths. The parent entreated them; they
said:[51]

"Here Our Lord, the Lord of the Near and Close, has placed
you. Here you grasp, you are notified, that Our Lord has given a
jewel, a precious feather; a child has arrived. And behold, in truth
now he wishes to be hardened. Already he is a jewel. Shall we perchance lay in his hand a spindle? A weaving stick? He is your property, he is your child, he is your son.

---

49. *Florentine Codex*, book 6, chapter 21.

50. The *Calmecacs* were centers of high learning, in which nobles and future priests
were educated. The *Telpuchcalli*, "houses for the young people," were attended by the
children of the commoners. From the *Telpuchcalli* they emerged as warriors and also
well trained in agricultural techniques. For an introduction to the Aztec systems of
education see M. Leon-Portilla, *Aztec Thought and Culture*, pp. 137–150.

51. This ceremony of promising the recently born sons either to the *calmecac* or to
the *telpuchcalli* was obviously a ritual practice. The most significant part of this text is
precisely the discourse of the parent who promised his son. Such discourse is another
example of the Ancient Word.

"In your laps, in the cradle of your arms we place him. For there are your sons; you instruct them, you educate them, you make eagle warriors, you make ocelot warriors. You instruct them for Our Mother, Our Father, Tlaltecutli, the Lord of the Earth, Tonatiuh, the Sun.[52]

"And now we dedicate the boy to Him Who is the Night, the Wind, the Lord, the Youth, Yaotzin, the Warrior, Titlacauan, Tezcatlipoca.[53] Perchance Our Lord will sustain him a little.

"We leave him. He will become a young warrior. He will live there in the house of penances, the house of weeping, the house of tears, the young men's house, where live, where are born the eagle warriors, the ocelot warriors, there where secrets are taken from the lap, the bosom of Our Lord.

"And there He instructs them, there He gives them gifts, there He shows them compassion. He gives the eagle mat, the ocelot mat to him who weeps, to him who sorrows. From there Our Lord drew them forth. The known ones of Our Lord protect, guard the reed mat, the reed seat of authority.

"And should we perchance be wont to weep, should we be wont to sorrow? Will something be our desert, our merit?[54] Will he perchance mature? Will he be instructed? Perhaps not. It has come to pass that we are unfortunate, we poor old men, we poor old women.

"Receive him, take him. Let him follow, let him know those

---

52. The priests in whose arms the baby is now placed will in due time educate him, transform him into an eagle, an ocelot. In doing this they will serve the Lord of the Earth, who is here explicitly described as "Our Mother, Our Father," that is, as a manifestation of the supreme Dual God. See in this context note 27.

53. God *Tezcatlipoca*, the "Smoking Mirror," is here invoked with the title of "He who is the Night and the Wind," which, as we have seen, were also attributes of the supreme Dual God. According to the ancient text of the *Historia de los mexicanos por sus pinturas* [History of the ancient Mexicans through their paintings], there were four *Tezcatlipocas*, the children of the Dual God, conceived as the primary forces that activate the universe. The symbolism of their colors—red, black, white, and blue—permits us to trace their identifications with the natural elements, the directions of space, and the spans of time under their respective influences. Appearing at times as a single individual, *Tezcatlipoca* was worshiped in the figure of a young warrior (*Yaotzin*). On the other hand, several other titles were also given to him, such as *Titlacauan*, which means "He whose servants we are." *Tezcatlipoca* appears here as the patron god of the *Telpuchcalli* (the young men's houses).

54. "Our desert, our merit (*tolhuil, tomacehual*), is another example of the paired metaphors so frequently seen in Nahuatl. The expression literally means "what is our day, what is our merit," that is, "our destiny."

who are instructed, who are educated, the sons of others, and the poor sons of the poor eagle warrior, of poor ocelot warriors."

And here is how the others returned the word, how they answered.[55] They said:

"Incline your hearts. Here we have listened on behalf of Our Lord, the Master, the Youth, He Who is the Night, the Wind, Yaotzin. To Him you pray, you call; to Him you give your jewel, your precious feather, your offspring. We merely take, we accept what you give Our Lord; we have only listened for Him.

"What is Our Lord requiring of, what is He requiring for your jewel, your precious feather? Indeed, we do our best, we common folk. We speak of the time of darkness.[56] In what manner is Our Lord, the Lord of the Near and Close, disposing for the child? In what manner was he adorned? How was it ordained in the time of darkness? In what was he arrayed? What did he bring with him when he was born? And what is his destiny? And further, on what day sign was he bathed?[57] What is the child's merit? What are his deserts?

"Verily, we common folk imagine it in vain. Will one perchance later be adorned on earth? Certainly we bring it with us. Certainly in the place of darkness it came forth as our property.

"But let him put his efforts to the sweeping, the gathering up of rubbish, the arranging of things at one side or the other, and the laying of fires.[58] May he remove secrets from the bosom, the lap of Our Lord, the Night, the Wind.

"May there be placed here above in the light whatever are his gifts with which he came bedecked, whatever was given with which he was ornamented in the time of darkness. Perchance in truth now Our Lord will take him there; perchance He will destroy him utterly. Perchance it is our desert, perchance it is our merit. Perchance

---

55. Those who answer to the speech of the father of the recently born baby are the priests of the *Telpuchcalli*.

56. "We speak of the time of darkness," that is, of the time when the supreme Dual God had determined the destiny of the baby.

57. Reference is made here to the ritual bath in which the baby received his name. It was necessary to consult the soothsayer to select the most adequate date for such a ceremony. Other Ancient Words are of particular interest in this context. See *Florentine Codex*, book 6, chapters 36–38.

58. The meaning of this paragraph is that, through sacrifice and the purifying ritual practices, the destiny and the gifts with which the baby was born could be somehow improved.

he will live to be a small child. Or perchance he will mature. Or perchance he will become an old man.

"But now how will we speak? Shall we perchance console you? Shall we perchance say: 'So it will be; this will be; this will he do; this will Our Lord change; so will he be; he will be something; he will attain honor; he will live on earth'?

"But perhaps it is our desert, our merit that he will live plunged in vice and filth on earth. Perchance he will take things from others' pots, others' vessels; perhaps he will take someone else's woman; he will have a gay time. And perchance he will experience misery, misfortune.

"Let us instruct children; let us educate children. Let the word, the statement, motherhood, fatherhood come forth.[59] Shall we perchance enclose it within him? Shall we be reassured? And likewise you who have the jewel, you who have the precious feather?

"And now may you bring about entreaties, weeping, tears. Do not abandon sorrow; yet live calling out for compassion to the Lord of the Near and Close, as to what He requires of you, what He says."[60]

*   *   *

Here it is told how the rulers, the noblemen left their children there at the calmecac, *and what manner of customs were observed at the place called* calmecac.

Rulers, noblemen, and still others, well mothered, well sired, these same entered their children, promised them, there in the *calmecac;* and still others did so who wished it.[61]

All became priests, the noblemen, because the place of instruction, the *calmecac,* was a place where one was admonished, where one was instructed, a place where one lived chastely, a place where fleetness of foot was tested, a place of prudence, a place of wisdom, a

---

59. "The word, the statement, motherhood, fatherhood," mean here the wisdom of the elders and sages.

60 *Florentine Codex,* book 3, chapter 4.

61. The actual entering into the *Calmecac,* the centers of high learning, of those promised to them by their parents is described in this text. Although it is expressly stated that those entering into the *Calmecac* were the children of noblemen, it is also affirmed that others (that is commoners) could take their children there, probably if they had showed a relevant intellectual capacity.

place of making good, of making righteous. In no way was there filth, vice; there was nothing reprehensible in the priests' lives, in the education of the *calmecac*.

The ruler, nobleman, lord, or anyone who was rich,[62] when he vowed that he would put his son in the *calmecac*, prepared drink, food. He summoned, he assembled the priests, and he summoned the head-taking priest, and he assembled the well-mothered, the well-sired ones, the old men. The old persons made an entreaty; they besought the priests; they said to them:

"O our lords, O priests, you have come to come here; you have used your feet; perhaps straws, grass you have somewhere touched with your feet; perhaps somewhere you have injured your feet; you have stumbled against something.

"Our Lord has placed you here. You grasp, you hear now that, in truth, Our Lord, the Lord of the Near and Close, has given a jewel, a precious feather.

"We dream; we see in our dreams. In truth, now, what will the small boy, the small child be? Shall we perchance give him a spindle, a batten? He is your property, your possession. Now we speak to the Master, Topiltzin Quetzalcoatl, Tlilpotonqui,[63] that He may enter the *calmecac*, the house of weeping, the house of tears, the house of sorrows, where there is instructing, there is educating of the sons of our lords.

"And there is the importuning of the Lord of the Near and Close, in that place there is the taking of secrets from the lap, the bosom of Our Lord; there, there is the ardent desiring with weeping, with tears, with sighs. And there He gives one gifts, there He selects one, for there we speak in His house. There are forged, are perforated our lords, the children of lords, there where Our Lord will bring about the sweeping, the gathering of rubbish at one side or the other, the arranging of things.

"In your laps, on your backs, in the cradle of your arms we place him. May your hearts to inclined, for we give you our child. May your hearts be inclined: Grant him gifts. May he follow, may he struggle when he is instructed, when he is educated, when he does penances all night, all day on elbow, on knee, so that he hastens

---

62. This sentence has to be understood in relation to the gifts offered when children were promised to the *Calmecac*.

63. The god *Quetzalcoatl*, also invoked as *Topilzin*, "Our son," *Tlilpotonqui*, "the one adorned with feathers," was the patron deity of the *Calmecac*.

while he calls to, while he cries out to Our Lord; while he weeps, sorrows, sighs.

"Enough. You have grasped it, you have heard it, O priests."

Here is how the priests answered, how they returned the word:

"Here we grasp, we take your breath, your words. Let us not admire ourselves; let us not falsely claim our deserts, let us not falsely claim our merits. Here your breath, your words come forth telling how because of, for the sake of your jewel, your precious feather, you are in torment. We hear only on behalf of Our Lord To-piltzin Quetzalcoatl Tlilpotonqui. So what will He require of your jewel, your precious feather? And so what will He require of you? So what will the jewel, the precious feather, be?

"Shall we indeed say: 'Let it be thus; let this be the case?' Let us put our trust in the Lord of the Near and Close. What does He require of us? Let us yet have faith."

Then they bore the child into the temple. The parents carried paper, incense. Rulers or noblemen took breech clouts, capes, neck bands, precious feathers, green stones, which they gave as gifts. The poor man took only paltry papers, incense, herbs, which became their gifts.[64]

When they had taken the children there, then they anointed them with black, they blackened their faces well with soot. Then they gave them only neck bands of the *tlacopatli* plant.[65] Poor people gave their children only neck bands of loose cotton. Then they cut his ears; they cast the child's blood on the image of the god. If he was still a small child, the parents still took him with them. If he was a ruler's child, they left his neck band there in the temple; the priests took it.

Then the priests taught him all of the life, the ordering, as it was lived in the *calmecac.*[66]

$$* \qquad * \qquad *$$

Here it is told about the usages of those instructed, educated, in the young men's house by which they lived: the things they did, the services they rendered.

64. This last sentence confirms that besides the noblemen, the rulers and rich people, the poor could also take their children to be educated in the *Calmecac.*

65. The *Tlacopatli* plant was used against poisonous bites of different animals. Apparently it corresponds to the *Aristolochya subdusa Wats.*

66. *Florentine Codex*, book 6, chapter 7.

And when he entered the young men's house, there indeed they charged him with the sweeping, the laying of fires.[67] And then began the penances. At that time there was singing, which was called song with dance. There he lived with the others, with the others he danced, with the others it was said that there was song with dance.

And when he was already an untried youth, then they took him to the forest. They had him bear upon his back logs of wood, perchance yet only one, or then, there, two. Thus they tested him, whether perchance he would do well in war, when already indeed an untried youth they took him to war. Yet it was only a shield that he went carrying on his back.

And when he was already indeed a youth, if he was instructed, if he was prudent, if he was reliable of speech, and especially if he was of benign heart, then he was made a master of youths; he was named *Tiachcauh*.[68] And if he was a well-accomplished man, if yet especially well instructed, then he was named a *Telpochtlato*, ruler of youths.[69] He governed them all; he represented all the youths. If one harmed anything, he judged him, he sentenced him, he corrected him. He dealt justice.

And if he became a brave man, if in the battle he was a captor of four captives, from there issued the commanding general, the general, the leader. And also from there issued the one they called *achcauhtli* [constable], who today is the equal, the equivalent, of the staff-bearer, for also in times past there were there staves, and it was just these who arrested one, who confined one.[70]

These were all the honors, the preferments, of the youths.

And in this way of life, only few showed understanding, educated themselves in it. Innumerable were those called youths, because in no way was the life of youths harsh. When yet small boys, there they slept together in what they called the young men's house. There they lived all together.

---

67. Once more, in describing the ways of life followed in the *Telpuchcalli*, the young men's houses, mention at first is made of the sweeping and the laying of fires. The sweeping, as has been explained, was a ritual act conveying the idea of cleaning the surrounding space as a preliminary step to the self-purification.

68. *Tiachcauh* literally means "the first, he who leads the others." His duty was to train the younger students in the use of the various weapons.

69. *Telpochtlato*, as is explained in the following sentence, besides governing the younger students of the *Telpuchcalli* acted as a judge to settle their differences.

70. This commentary, expressed also in the Nahuatl text, obviously denotes that it

And he who was absent, who slept not in the young men's house, him they punished. And they ate in their homes. And they all went in a group where they did something, perhaps they undertook the preparation of mud for adobes, walls, agricultural land, canals. They went in a bunch or they divided into groups. And they went to the forest. They took, they carried on their backs what they called torches for the singing.

And when only a little sun was left in the afternoon, they quit whatever they did. They then bedecked themselves, ornamented themselves. First they bathed themselves; then they rubbed black on themselves, not also, they say, on their faces. Then they put on their neck bands.

The valiant men, the chief warriors put on neck bands of large white gastropod shells or of gold. Long shells were applied; leather was applied. Then they painted their faces with stripes. It was said that they applied black sweat to themselves; they pasted on iron pyrites. As one's adornment ear plugs were worn, turquoise ear plugs were worn, heron feathers were worn, netted capes were worn. This netted cape was of twisted maguey fiber, knotted, like a net set with small, white gastropod shells. The rulers had golden gastropod shells in their netted capes. Of the netted capes of the shorn ones it was said: "They are provided with fruit." For this reason was it said: "They are provided with fruit," that very large fiber balls hung from them.

When the sun had already set, then they laid a fire at the place which they called *Cuicacalco*, the song house. On the hearth the youths laid the fire. When it was dark, then was begun the singing. Everyone danced until the half division of the night passed, until midnight passed.

And in those times no one covered himself with anything. All thus danced, wrapped only in netted capes, not a little as if indeed they went naked.[71]

*   *   *

Here the punishments, the imposed penances with which they were punished when some youth became a little drunk, are related.

was transmitted by a person inclined to make comparisons with the uses that were prevalent in the colonial days of the New Spain, that is Mexico.

71. *Florentine Codex*, book 3, chapter 4.

When there was instructing in the young men's house, great was the care that was taken of the sweeping. No one at all drank *octli*, the intoxicating beverage.

But when they were indeed already men, when already they had grown up, he who drank octli hid himself well. Not at all did he drink in public. Most secretly, likewise not often, did he drink.

And if it was seen that some youth became a little drunk, if it was seen that he had come upon *octli*—perchance he lay fallen, or sang—or if it was seen that somewhere with others he had become a little drunk, then because of this there was a gathering up, because of this there was a rounding up.

And because of this fear descended. If he was only a commoner, or someone of no importance, he was beaten before the others. He fell under wooden staves; he died under wooden staves. Or he was made to suffer the rope.

But if he was a nobleman's son, they strangled him secretly.[72]

And these youths had their paramours by twos, by threes.[73] Perchance one was in her own house, perchance several lay scattered.[74] And when, they said, youth was laid down, he paid his debt. In order to leave, the youth left large cotton capes, perhaps ten, perhaps twenty if he was rich.

When the masters of the youths had consented, when they had given their leave, then it was said he married. Only one woman did he take; he kept her at his home.

And when a youth was educated, not merely of his own will did

---

72. The severe prohibition against drinking *octli* and the vigor with which the violators were punished are confirmed by various other sources. The sixteenth-century chronicler Diego Duran gives the following testimony:

No one used to dare drink pulque [*octli*] or become drunk unless he was an old man, for warmth and comfort in his old age, and this applied as much to the ruling class as to the rest of the people. So I have heard it affirmed that if a noble was caught in a drunk state..., he was deprived of his position and could even be executed if he went too far." (Diego Durán, *Historia de las Indias de la Nueva España, Book of the Gods and Rites, and the Ancient Calendar,* translated into English and edited by Fernando Horcasitas and Doris Heiden, Foreward by Miguel Leon-Portilla [Norman: University Oklahoma Press, 1973], p. 289).

73. That is, two or three young students shared the same paramour.

74. Pre-Colombian Mesoamericans were rather liberal in permitting the young people to have a paramour. Several ancient testimonies confirm this. I refer the reader to part 6 of the present book where a poem is included in which the sage Tlaltecatzin appears intoning a chant to a prostitute.

he leave the estate of youth. He grew very old there where the youths were. But if he willed, the ruler gave him leave to go.

But not very often from the youths' place came, perchance, lords: only commanding generals, generals, chief warriors were taken thence. Lords of men, lords of the arsenal did not come from there, because the manner of life of the youths was not very good; because they were given to women, to vicious life;[75] because they took up mocking, vain talk; they talked coarsely, grossly, uncouthly.[76]

*   *   *

Here it is told about the way of life that was observed in the calmecac, *where lived or were educated those who were to become the fire priests and the offering priests.*

First: All slept there in the *calmecac.*[77]

Second: It was brought about that everyone swept when it was yet dark.

Third: When it was already daytime, those already a little strong then went to seek maguey thorns. As they said, they broke off the maguey thorns.[78]

Fourth: When they were already indeed novice priests of whatever kind, they went forth when it was still dark, or at midnight. They started to go to the forest; they took the wood; they carried on their backs what they called logs, which they burned at the *calmecac* all night as the priests kept watch. And if somewhere preparation of mud for adobes, a wall, agricultural land, a canal, were to be undertaken, there was going forth when it was still quite dark; there was going, leaving those who were to guard and then those who went to serve the food. They went in a group. None were absent. In good order they passed the whole day.[79]

---

75. I feel inclined to think that this last comment probably reflects the Christian morals either of the Indian informant or of Fray Bernardino de Sahagun, who ordered the transcription of these texts. The reason to make this supposition has to do with the already mentioned liberal attitude of the natives that permitted the young people to have their paramours.

76. *Florentine Codex*, book 3, chapter 6.

77. Clearly, the ways of life in the *Calmecac*, the centers of high learning, were more rigid than those prevalent in the *Telpuchcalli*.

78. The maguey thorns were used for the various kinds of self-sacrifice.

79. The distribution of time in the *Calmecac* included various forms of manual

Fifth: Soon after they ceased working they went to see to their godly obligations, the obligations to the *calmecac*, the doing of penances. When there was still a little sun, or when night had already fallen, it was said they cut maguey spines. When it was quite dark, when it was already deep night, then the priests began, as was said, the placing of the maguey spines. No more than one at a time they went. First they bathed; then they took the shell trumpets and the incense ladles, the bag that went full of incense, and they took up pine torches. Thereupon began the placing of the maguey spines. They went naked. Those who performed great penances went perhaps two leagues; maguey spines were placed perhaps in the forest, perhaps in the desert, perhaps by the water. The younger ones or he who wished went perhaps half a league for the placing of the maguey spines. They had their shell trumpets. They went blowing them. Wherever they placed the maguey spines, when they went arriving, there they went blowing trumpets.

Sixth: When the priests slept, no two lay together. All lay by themselves. None were covered together.

Seventh: The food they ate they prepared together only for themselves, for what they ate was their own. And if anyone gave one his food, not by himself did he eat it.

Eighth: At midnight, when, as was said, night divided in half, everyone arose; they prayed. If one failed to do so because he slept, if one did not awake, then, for this, there was a gathering together. They drew blood from his ears, his breast, his thighs, the calves of his legs. Verily, because of this, fear descended.

Ninth: No one at all became proud; no one at all became vain. Well ordered was living. If at times it appeared that one perhaps drank *octli*, perhaps was given to women or committed a great fault, then they went to apprehend him. No mercy was shown.[80] He was burned, or strangled, or burned alive, or shot with arrows. If he sinned only lightly, they drew blood from his ears, his flanks, his thighs, with maguey spines or with a sharpened bone.

Tenth: The small boys were so educated that if they did noth-

work, as a sort of preliminary step to the practices of self-control, the worshiping of the gods, and the learning of the ancient wisdom.

80. The rigid character of the rules prevalent in the *Calmecac* appears here. While in the *Telpuchcalli* the students were permitted to have their paramours, it was considered a great fault if those studying in a *Calmecac* were given to women.

ing of great evil, they then drew blood from their ears or switched them with nettles.

Eleventh: At midnight the principal priest went down to the water. They bathed themselves in the water.[81]

Twelfth: When it was a time of fasting, indeed all observed it. Verily when midday arrived, all the small boys ate. But when it was the time of fasting they called *Atamalqualo*,[82] they tasted nothing at all. Some ate at midnight; they went to eat the next midnight. Some ate at noon; the next time, next day at noon they went to eat. No chili, no salt did they eat. Not, in order to sleep, did they even drink water. They said the fast was broken if they ate, if they drank, a little bit.

Thirteenth: Most especially was there teaching of good discourse.[83] He who spoke not well, who greeted others not well, they then drew blood from him with maguey spines.

Fourteenth: Especially was there teaching of songs they called the divine songs inscribed in books.[84] And especially was there teaching of the count of days, the book of dreams, and the book of years.

Fifteenth: A strict vow of the priests was that of chastity, a pure life, that nowhere would they look upon a woman. A strict vow of theirs was a life of moderation. No one whatever lied. The priests were very devout. They were very god-fearing.

---

81. This eleventh rule, as well as the second of this same text, is also eloquent testimony about the emphasis given by the Mesoamericans to practices of purification. According to the second rule, everyone swept the patio of the school and the adjacent temple when it was yet dark. Now in the eleventh rule special mention is made of the ritual baths.

82. *Atamalqualo* or *Atamalqualiztli*, the feast when one eats only "water-Tamales," that is the Indian maize cakes, but prepared then without chili, with neither salt nor lime. It was a special food eaten in that feast of penance, which was observed every eight years and also included a seven-day fast. The feast of *Atamalqualiztli* is probably mentioned here as a mere example of the various periods of fasting in accordance with the ritual calendar.

83. "Good discourse" (*in qualli tlatolli*), the way of speaking that corresponds to the educated people. Several other texts mention this preoccupation with the elegant and adequate form of expression. The good discourse was at times described as *tecpillatolli*, "the discourse of the nobles."

84. In this fourteenth rule, as in the previous one, we have a brief though precise description of the intellectual education offered to the students in the *Calmecac*. Basically it included the following points: teaching the good discourse; the songs, those called the divine songs, according to their books; the calendar or count of the days; the books of the dreams; and the books of years or annals.

Enough of this. Here is told what the way of life of the priests was. Yet much is left unsaid that is required to be said. It will be told in another place.[85]

* * *

Here it is told how the high priests, the Quetzalcoatl priests, were established, were chosen. The first was named Totec Tlamacazqui, Our Lord offering priest, the second Tlaloc Tlamacazqui, the offering priest of the God of Rain. Always they set up those who were especially wise, prudent.[86]

And one who had distinguished his way of life and otherwise had followed the precepts, the way of life of the priests, this one was taken, this one was chosen. He became a keeper of the god. The ruler and the great judges and all the other rulers elected him. They gave him the name of Quetzalcoatl. There were two Quetzalcoatl priests: One was named Totec Tlamacazqui, one was named Tlaloc Tlamacazqui.[87]

The Quetzalcoatl priest called Totec Tlamacazqui was dedicated to Uitzilopochtli;[88] the Tlaloc was dedicated to the lord of Tlalocan, the God of Rain. These were exactly equal in rank.

And though he were poor, though he were in need, though his father, his mother were the poorest of the poor, if he well carried out the way of life, the precepts of the priests, this one was taken, this one was given the name of Quetzalcoatl. He was named either Totec Tlamacazqui or Tlaloc.

Not lineage was considered, only a good life.[89] This indeed was considered. Indeed this one was sought out, one of good life, one of

---

85. *Florentine Codex*, book 3, chapter 8.

86. The enunciation of this text shows that already in the Aztec days there were two high priests who had adopted the title or name of the famous religious leader of the Toltecs, *Quetzalcoatl*. These two priests had to be extremely virtuous persons who had followed the wisdom of *Quetzalcoatl*.

87. *Totec Tlamacazqui*, "Our lord, the offering priest," and *Tlaloc Tlamacazqui*, "the offering priest of Tlaloc."

88. The *Totec Tlamacazqui* Quetzalcoatl, "Our lord the offering priest, Quetzalcoatl," was in charge of the cult of Huitzilopochtili, the patron deity of the Aztecs.

89. After describing the qualities on account of which a priest was chosen to receive the title of *Quetzalcoatl*, it is expressly stated that in such a selection lineage did not matter. This is particularly important as it implied a sort of social mobility within the religious sphere. To reach the highest rank of *Quetzalcoatl*, only good life and purity of heart were considered.

righteous life, of pure heart, of good heart, of compassionate heart; one who was resigned, one who was firm, one who was tranquil, one who was not vindictive, one who was strong of heart, one who was of constant heart, one who was of pungent heart, one who made much of others, one who embraced others, one who esteemed others, one who was compassionate of others, one who wept for others, who had awe in his heart, one said to be godly of heart, who was devout, who was god-fearing, one who wept, one who sorrowed, one who sighed.

And when one started out, he was still called a novice priest, then an offering priest, then a fire priest already respected was this one. Then from there was taken the one named the Quetzalcoatl priest.[90]

And this priesthood lived moderately circumstanced, moderately well as they followed a specialized way of life; because rather severe was the way of life of the priests.

Just there was the manner of educating of the priesthood distinct from that of the young warriors.[91]

---

90. In this paragraph, as in a synthesis, the various ranks within the priesthood are mentioned, beginning with the so-called novice priests and ending up with the one who receives the title of *Quetzalcoatl*.

91. *Florentine Codex*, book 3, chapter 9.

Part Two
CREATION MYTHS

The *Popol Vuh:*
The Book of Counsel[1]

The First Creations[2]

This is the root of the former word.
Here is Quiche by name.[3]
Here we shall write then,
we shall start out then, the former words,
the beginnings and the taproots
of everything done in the Quiche town,
the tribe of the Quiche people.
So this is what we shall collect then,
the decipherment, the clarification, and the explanation
of the mysteries and the illumination
by Former, and Shaper;[4]
Bearer and Engenderer are their names,[5]
Hunter Possum and Hunter Coyote,[6]
Great White Pig and Coati,[7]

---

1. According to Munro S. Edmonson, to whom we owe this translation into English, the expression *Popol Vuh* "may be literally rendered 'the book of the man of the mat.'" To which it can be added that the man of the mat can be as well the ruler or the sage.

2. Under this title of "The First Creations" I include the early attempts of the gods to create a being capable of understanding and intelligent enough to worship those who had formed and shaped him.

3. The Quiche Indians speak a language that belongs to the Maya family. At present the descendants of the Pre-Columbian Quiche live in scattered communities in central and western Guatemala.

4. The Former (*Tzakol*) is a name that, according to Munro S. Edmonson, means "Maker," as referred to such things as cooking and building. Shaper (*Bitol*) means also "Maker," but as applied "to such things as pottery manufacture."

5. Bearer (*Alom*) and Engenderer (*Q'aholom*) mean, according to Edmonson, "*Alom*, a woman who has been caused to bear children; *Q'aholom*, a man who has been caused to engender sons." This series of paired designations obviously connotes the dual character of the supreme deity.

6. Hunter Possum, according to Edmonson, probably connotes the idea of the "blowgun hunter [which] is the name of the twentieth day of the calendar." On the other hand, possum, probably *Didelphis yucatanensis*, "presides over the hours before dawn." In other words this name, applied to one aspect of the supreme Dual God, has a double calendrical connotation. Hunter-coyote (*canis latrans*) is probably another magical name of the divine Engenderer.

7. Great White Pig and the Coati are other animals magically impersonating the divine creating forces of the Former and Shaper.

Majesty and Quetzal Serpent,[8]
The Heart of the Lake[9]
and the Heart of the Sea,
Green Plate Spirit
and Blue Bowl Spirit, as it is said,[10]
Who are likewise called,
Who are likewise spoken of
as the Woman with Grandchildren
and Man with Grandchildren,
Xpiacoc and Xmucane by name,[11]
Shelterer and Protector,
Great-Grandmother
and Great-Grandfather,
as it is said in Quiche words.
Then they said everything
and did it furthermore,
in the bright existence and bright words.
This we shall write already within the word of God,
already in Christianity we shall save it,[12]
because there is no longer
a sight of the Book of Counsel,
a sight of the bright things come
from beside the sea,
the description of our shadows,[13]

---

8. Edmonson translates the word *tepeu*, which is a loan from Nahuatl, as "Majesty." I incline toward understanding it as "Conqueror." Quetzal Serpent is the translation of Gucumatz, the Quiche version of the name of Quetzalcoatl. If we remember at this point that Quetzalcoatl appears in some Quiche texts as the Lord of the Orient, from whom all the tribes received the insignia and the power to govern, it will be easier to understand why the word *tepeu*, "conqueror, ruler," is here attached to the Quiche version of the name of the high priest of the Toltecs, Gucumatz-Quetzalcoatl.

9. Lake Atitlan was familiar to the Quiche-Mayas. The Pacific Ocean, although distant, was not unknown to them. The text describes in parallel form the supreme creator as the lord of both lake and sea.

10. According to Edmonson, "the plate and bowl may refer to earth and heaven and also to ceremonial vessels used in the ritual count of the months."

11. According to Adrian Recinos, the modern translator of this text into Spanish, these two names complement the idea of the dual nature of the supreme god. He translates them as "the old man, the old woman."

12. The native sage who transcribed the testimony of the *Popol Vub* shows himself conscious of the importance of his effort to save the ancient words, "living already in Christianity."

13. The word *shadows* probably means here "in the past," before the appearance of the Christians in the Quiche land.

a sight of the bright like, as it is called.
There was once the manuscript of it,
and it was written long ago,
only hiding his face is the reader of it,
the meditator of it.[14]
Great was its account and its description
of when there was finished
the birth of all of heaven and earth:
The four creations,
the four humiliations,
the knowledge of the four punishments,
the rope of tying together,[15]
the line of tying together,
the womb of heaven,
the womb of earth.
Four creations, four humiliations, it was told
by the Former and Shaper,
the Mother and Father
of Life and Mankind,
The Inspirer and Heartener,
Bearer and Heartener of
Light and the Race,
Children of the Mother of Light,
Sons of the Father of Light,
The Meditator, The Thinker
of everything, whatever exists:
heaven, earth,
lake, and sea.

Here is the description
of these things:
truly it was yet quiet,
truly it was yet stilled.
It was quiet.
Truly it was calm.

---

14. The probable meaning of these lines is that those interested in knowing and meditating about the contents of the ancient book have now, "already in Christianity," to hide their faces, to conceal their interest.

15. As Edmonson points it out, "the reference here is probably to the tying of the years, at the end of the 52-year cycle."

Truly it was solitary
And it was also still empty,
the womb of heaven.

These are truly then the first words,
the first utterances.
There was not one person yet,
one animal,
deer, bird, fish, crab,
tree, rock, hole,
canyon,
meadow or forest.
All by itself the sky existed.
The face of the earth was not yet visible.
All by itself the sea lay dammed,
and the womb of heaven,
everything.
There was nothing whatever
silenced or at rest.
Each thing was made silent,
each thing was made calm,
was made invisible,
was made to rest in heaven.
There was not, then, anything in fact
that was standing there.
Only the pooled water,
only the flat sea.[16]
All by itself it lay dammed.
There was not, then, anything in fact
that might have existed.
It was just still, it was quiet
in the darkness, in the night.
All alone the Former and Shaper,
Majesty, and Quetzal Serpent,
The Mothers and Fathers
were in the water.

---

16. It is interesting to note that, after the insistent description of the fact that there was nothing standing or visible, an exception is made to affirm that the sea lay dammed, that there was "the pooled water, only the flat sea."

Brilliant they were then,
and wrapped in quetzal
and dove feathers.
Thence came the name
of Quetzal Serpent.[17]
Great sages they were
and great thinkers in their essence,
for indeed there is heaven
and there is also the Heart of Heaven.
That is the name
of the deity, it is said.

So then came His word here.[18]
It reached to Majesty
and Quetzal Serpent,
there in the obscurity, in the nighttime.
It spoke to Majesty
and Quetzal Serpent, and they spoke.
Then they thought;
then they pondered.
Then they found themselves.
They assembled their words, their thoughts.
Then they gave birth,
then they heartened themselves.
Then they caused to be created
and they bore men.[19]
Then they thought about the birth,
the creation
of trees and shrubs,
and the birth of life and humanity
in the obscurity, in the nighttime
through him who is the Heart of Heaven,
One Leg by name.[20]

---

17. This is a poetical explanation of the name of Quetzalcoatl: the brilliant reality of the divinity who appeared as wrapped in the feathers of the quetzal bird, floating on the waters of the sea.

18. Notwithstanding the use of the plural in the former lines that give the names of the Dual God, now it is stated in the singular that "then came His word here."

19. The supreme Dual God is described as in a dialogue, and the text says, in the plural, that "they thought, they pondered, they assembled their words. . . . "

20. As Edmonson notes, "One Leg is certainly a calendar name but not in Quiche.

One Leg Lightning is the first,
and the second is Dwarf Lightning.
Third then is Green Lightning,
so that the three of them are the Heart of Heaven.[21]
Then they came to Majesty
and Quetzal Serpent,
and then was the invention
of light and life.
"What if it were planted?
Then something would brighten
a supporter, a nourisher.[22]
So be it.
You must decide on it.
There is the water to get rid of,
to be emptied out,
to create this, the earth,
and have it surfaced and leveled
when it is planted,
when it is brightened,
heaven and earth.
But there can be no adoration or glorification
of what we have formed,
what we have shaped,
until we have created a human form,
a human shape," so they said.
So then this, the earth, was created by them,
only their word was the creation of it.
To create the earth, "Earth," they said.
Immediately it was created.
It was just like a cloud,
like a mist then,
the creation then, the whirlwind.
Then the mountain was asked to come from the water.

Yucatec has a day 'leg' (*oc*), corresponding to the Quiche God (*tz'i*) . . . the *Popol Vuh* suggests that the 16th century Quiche were familiar with the count of days in Quiche, Nahuatl, Mam, and perhaps Yucatec."

21. Once more our text accumulates here numerous titles or names attributed to the creator, the Heart of Heaven.

22. Human beings, the creatures expected to worship their gods, are of course the "supporter, nourisher."

Straightaway there were great mountains.
Just their power, just their magic
caused the making of then, the invention
of mountains and valleys.
At a stroke there were also created
cedar groves on them
and pine forests on them.
So Quetzal Serpent then rejoiced,
"It is good that you have come,
O Heart of Heaven,
O One Leg
and you, Dwarf Lightning
and Green Lightning.
Our forming is successful,
and our shaping," they said.
And once they had created
the earth, the mountains and valleys,
the paths of the waters were unraveled
and they proceeded to twist along among the hills.
So the rivers then became more divided
as the great mountains were appearing.
And thus was the creation of the earth
when it was created by Him
Who is the Heart of Heaven,
The Heart of Earth,
as they are called.
And they were the first to think of it.
The sky was rounded out there
and the earth was rounded out in the water.
And thus it was invented as they thought,
as they reflected on its perfection,
its being made by them.

Then they thought further
of the wild animals,
guardians of the forest,
and all the population of the wild:
deer, birds, panthers, jaguars,
serpents, rattlers, yellowmouths,

guardians of plants.
The Mother said this, and the Father:
"Should it only be still,
or should it not be silent
under the trees and shrubs?
Indeed, it would be good if there were
guardians for them" they said,
And when they thought and talked,
at a stroke there came to be
and were created
deer and birds.
Then they awarded homes also
to the deer and birds.
You, deer, on the rivers
and in the canyons
will you sleep then.
There will you be then,
in the grass, in the fruits,
in the wilderness will you multiply yourselves then.
On all fours your walk,
your gait will be."
They were told,
and then they designated
the homes of the little birds
and the big birds.
"You, O birds, in the trees, in the bushes,
make your homes then,
make your houses then.
Multiply there then, increase then
on the branches of trees,
on the branches of shrubs,"
the deer were told and the birds.
When they had done their creating,
they gave them everything:
their nests and lairs.
And so the homes of the animals were the earth.
They gave it, the Mother and Father.
There was completed the assignment
of all the deer and birds.

Then also they were told,
the deer and birds
by Former and Shaper,
the Mother and Father,
"Talk, then, call, then.
Don't warble; don't cry.
Make yourselves understood to each other
in each species, in each grouping,"
the deer were told and the birds,
panthers, jaguars, serpents, and snakes.
"Now then pronounce our names,
worship us, your Mother and your Father.
Now then, say this:
One Leg,
Dwarf Lightning, Green Lightning,
The Heart of Heaven,
The Heart of Earth,
Former, Shaper,
Mother and Father.
Talk then and call to us.
Worship us,"
they were told.[23]
But they did not succeed in talking like men.
They just pretended to.
They just rattled;
and they just croaked.
The form of their speech did not emerge.
Differently they made cries, each one apart.
When Former heard it and Shaper,
"It is not yet arranged
so they can talk."
They repeated to each other,
"They do not succeed in pronouncing
our names,

---

23. In an almost childish way the gods, so deeply concerned with having creatures capable of worshiping them, ask the various animals they had created to manifest their capacities. As the animals were not able to talk, even if they pretended to, they were reprimanded by the gods.

109

Although we are their Former
and we are their Shaper."
"It isn't good," they repeated to each other,
they, the Mother and Father.
And they were told,
"Just change yourselves,
Because it is not yet successful
since you do not speak.
We shall therefore change our word,
your food, your nourishment,
your sleeping places, your lairs,
what has been yours
has now become
the canyons and the wilderness,
because our worship has not been achieved;
you do not yet call upon us.
Indeed there is, or there should be,
a worshiper, a praiser whom we shall yet make
who will just take your places,
and your flesh will just be eaten.
So be it then,
and there may you serve,"
they were told.[24]
So they were commanded,
the little animals
and big animals who are upon the earth.
And then it was necessary for them
to try their luck again.
It was necessary for them
to make another attempt,
and it was necessary for them
to arrange again for worship.
For they could not catch
their speech among themselves.
For it could not be understood,
as it was not made that way.
And so their flesh was humbled; they served.

---

24. This statement of the gods justified, in the eyes of the Quiche, the eating of the
flesh of the animals.

They were eaten; they were killed,
the animals that were here on the face of the earth.
And so there was another effort
To form man, to shape man
by the Former and Shaper,
The Mother and Father.
"Let us just try again.
Already it has approached
the planting, the brightening.
Let us make a supporter for us,
a nourisher for us.
How then can we be called upon
and be remembered upon the earth?
We have already tried with the first of our formings,
our shapings.[25]
We did not attain our being worshiped
and being glorified by them.
And so let us try now to make
a praiser, a worshiper,
a supporter, a nourisher," they said.
For then there was the forming
and the working
of earth and mud.
Its body they made,
but it did not look good to them.
It just kept coming apart.
It was just absorbent.
It was just soggy.
It was just damp.
It was just crumbling
and it was just dissolving.
Its head was not rounded.
Its face was just one-sided.
Its eyes were just veiled
and could not be looked into.
As soon as it spoke

---

25. Man thus appears to the eyes of the Quiche-Maya as the creature most needed by the gods. The divine mother and father are able to make mistakes and that is why they have to try several times their forming and shaping.

it made no sense.
Just all at once it dissolved in the water.
"It wasn't strong," they said then,
Former and Shaper.
"It looks wet.
If it should just get wet,
it couldn't walk
And it couldn't be made to multiply.
So be it.
Its mind is dark there," they said.
And so they destroyed it.
They overthrew again
what they had formed,
they had shaped.[26]
And they said again,
"What are there that we can make
that may succeed then,
that may be intelligent then,
worshiping us,
and calling upon us?" they said.
Then they thought further
and just called upon
Xpiacoc and Xmucane,
Hunter Possum and Hunter Coyote.
"They can try again their divination,
their creation," they told each other,
the Former and Shaper.[27]
And so they spoke to Xpiacoc and Xmucane.
And indeed it was proposed to them,
The far seers,
The Grandmother of Day,
The Grandmother of Light.

---

26. This sharp contrast between the text of the *Popol Vuh* and the Biblical account probably caused a great surprise in both the Mesoamerican sages and the Spanish missionaries.

27. Here *Xpiacoc* and *Xmucane*, "the old man, the old woman," as well as Hunter Possum and Hunter Coyote, appear as different gods who are called precisely by the supreme Dual God. This can be probably understood as indicating that in the realm of the supreme divine being a form of dialogue is constantly entertained.

They were addressed by the Former and Shaper.
These are the names of Xpiacoc and Xmucane.

And there spoke also
One Leg
with Majesty and Quetzal Serpent.
Then they spoke to the Sun Priest.[28]
and the Shaper, the far seers,
"It must be sought
and it will just be found
so that then again we can shape man,
so that we can form man again then,
as a supporter and nourisher.
We shall be called upon,
and we shall be remembered.
Then there may be support in words,
Ancestress of Grandchildren,
Ancestor of Grandchildren,
our Grandmother,
our Grandfather,
Xpiacoc and Xmucane.
If you plow it
and it is then planted,
then it will brighten into
our being called upon,
our being supported,
our being remembered
by the formed people,
the shaped people,
the doll people,
the made-up people.
Do it then. So be it.
Manifest you, your names,
Hunter Possum, Hunter Coyote
Grandmother, Grandfather,

---

28. "The sun priest" (*ab q'ib*) was the title of the astrologers, the priests in charge of the books. The Dual Creator God speaks here as a deity who is a prototype of the priests of the Quiche.

Great Pig, Great Coati,
Gemcutter, Jeweller,
Carver, Sculptor,[29]
Green Plate Spirit, Blue Bowl Spirit,
Incense Maker, Craftsman,[30]
Grandmother of Day,
Grandmother of Light.
Be called upon by what we form,
what we shape.
Cast with the corn;
with the *tz'ite* beans operate,[31]
and it will just come to pass
that we elaborate
and that we chisel out his mouth
and his face for him,"
they declared to the Sun Priests.[32]
And then indeed was their throwing,
their divining,
that they cast with corn
and with *tz'ite*,
the Sun and Shaper.
And then spoke a Grandmother
and a Grandfather to them.
There was the Grandfather:
he was the *tz'ite* man.[33]
Xpiacoc was his name.

---

29. The Dual Creator God is here compared to various sorts of artists, those who are to shape the human beings able to remember, worship, and support the gods.

30. The word used in the *Popol Vuh* to express the idea of "craftsman" is a loan from the Nahuatl language, *toltecatl*. This is another proof of the influence received by the Maya from those inhabiting the highlands of central Mexico. In parts 3 and 5 of the present book several Nahuatl texts are included in which the term *toltecatl* connotes also the idea of craftsman and artist.

31. Now the creator gods cast lots to find out what they are going to use as the raw material to form the human beings. They cast with corn and with the *tz'ite* (divining beans). According to Munro S. Edmonson, these divining beans are the fruit of the *pito* tree, *Erythrina corallodentron*, a red bean. In the codices or pre-Columbian books there are representations of gods and men casting lots, using either seeds of corn or of red beans or both. See, for instance, page 21 of *Codex Borbonicus*.

32. As in the historical times of the Quiche-Mayas the sun priests were those performing the divinations, mention of them is made here, referring to some sort of divine prototypes of that religious hierarchy which was to exist in the future.

33. I believe this identification of the grandfather with the *tz'ite* man means prob-

There was the Grandmother,
Sun Priest, the Shaper,
at his feet,
Xmucane was her name.
And they said
as they began to divine,
"Just look around
and just find it,"
you say.
Our ear hears your speaking,
what may have been said.
Just find the wood to be worked
and to be carved
by the Former and Shaper.
Indeed this will be a nourisher
and supporter
when it is planted then,
when it brightens then.
O Corn, O *Tz'ite*,
O Sun, O Shaper,
join now and be coupled,"
they said to the corn and *tz'ite*,
the Sun Priest and Shaper.
"Blush up yonder,
O Heart of Heaven, and do not degrade
the mouth and face
of Majesty and Quetzal Serpent,"
they said.
And then they spoke the truth:
"It is turning out well, this doll
carved of wood.
It speaks.
Something on earth talks.
Then so be it," they said,
and as they spoke
at a stroke the dolls were made,
carved of wood.

---

ably that the creator god visualized his future creatures thanks to the *tz'ite*, the divining beans.

They looked like people
and they talked like people.
There were beings
on the face of the earth.
They existed; they multiplied.
They produced daughters;
they produced sons,
the dolls, carved of wood.
But they had no hearts
and they had no minds.
They did not remember their Former
and their Shaper.
In vain they walked
and crawled around.
They did not again recall the Heart of Heaven
and so they fell there.
It was just a preliminary effort,
and it was just a demonstration person.[34]
They spoke all right,
but their faces were dry.
Their legs were not filled out,
nor their arms.
They lacked blood and serum.
They lacked sweat and fat.
Dry their cheeks
and masks were their faces.[35]
They jerked their legs
and their arms.
One destroyed their bodies
because they did not know anything besides,
before Former and Shaper,
the Bearers of them,
the Hearteners of them.

---

34. This new attempt to create intelligent human beings is here described as a "preliminary effort." Edmonson interprets the expression *u vababexik chi vinag* as "the preparation, the demonstration of real persons."

35. To better understand the meaning of this sentence we must remember that for the Mesoamericans the face was a symbol for the moral physiognomy and the essence of a person. Now if the dolls carved of wood had masks instead of faces, it is meant that they were only fake persons.

They were the first numerous people
who came to be here on earth.

And so in fact they were finished off again.
They were destroyed
and they were broken up
and killed again,
the dolls carved of wood.
Then their flood was invented by the Heart of Heaven.
A great flood was made,
and descended on the heads
of those who were dolls,
who were carved of wood.
Of *tz'ite* was the body of the man,
when he was carved
by Former and Shaper.
Woman reed was the body of the woman
who was carved
by Former and Shaper.
They did not think, and they did not speak
before their Former,
their Shaper, the Maker of them,
the Creator of them,
and so they were killed;
they were overwhelmed.
There came a great rain of glue
down from the sky.
There came the Rippers of Eyes, as they are called,[36]
and tore their eyes from their sockets.
There came Killer Bats
and snatched off their heads.
There came Lurking Jaguar
and ate their flesh.
There came Aroused Jaguar
and tore them open,

---

36. "The Rippers of Eyes" and the other nocturnal beings that are mentioned immediately after can be considered as servants of the gods, whose obligation was to punish or to destroy the creatures who were not behaving properly. As it is stated a few lines later, this happened "because they (the human beings carved of wood) did not think...."

and shattered their bones
and their cartilage.
Ground up, crumbled fine
were their bones.
The grinding up of their faces was
because they did not think
before their Mother and before their Father,
The Heart of Heaven,
One Leg by name.
By them the face of the earth was darkened
and there began a rain of darkness,
daytime rain and nighttime rain.
There came out the little animals,
and the big animals.
Their faces were abused by the trees and rocks.
And there spoke up all their jars,
their griddles, their plates,
their pots, their dogs, their mortars,
however many things,
everything
abused their faces.[37]
"Pain you have caused us.
You have eaten us,
and now we are going to eat you back,"
said their dogs
and their chickens to them.
And then the grindstones:
"We have been shattered by you
every day, every day—
night and day, all the time,
Crunch! Crunch!
Scrape! Scrape!
On our faces you went.
If that was formerly our service to you,
when you were people,

---

37. As if the destruction caused by the various nocturnal beings, the Rippers of Eyes, the Killer Bats, and the Lurking Jaguar, were not enough, now the jars, griddles, plates, pots, dogs, mortars, as if awakening, decide to take vengeance of the stupid human beings carved of wood, who had caused them various forms of pain.

then you can now try our strength.
We shall grind up
and we shall scrape your flesh,"
their grindstones said to them.
And then it was their dogs
that said further
when they spoke:
"Why was it that you didn't give us our food?
We just looked on, and you just ate us up.
Whether we lay down here
or got up there,
we were beaten by you
while you ate.
You just used to lecture us then;
we couldn't talk,
and we got nothing from you
unless you didn't know about it,
and then when you found out later,
then we were lost.
So now you can try our bones
that are in our mouths:
we shall eat you,"
their dogs said to them,
and their face was destroyed.
And so their griddles
and their pots spoke further to them:
"Pain it was you inflicted on us.
Sooty our mouths,
sooty our faces.
Always we were dumped on the fire.
You burned us.
We felt no pain, so you try it,
we shall burn you,"
said all their pots,
and their face was destroyed.
And there were their rocks,
and their hearthstones stretched
and came from the fire,
pounding on their heads
and hurting them.

They tried to run away.[38]
They were forced to scatter completely then.
They tried to climb on the houses,
but the houses collapsed and down they fell.
They tried to climb the trees:
They were thrown off by the trees.
They tried to crawl in the holes,
but the holes closed in their faces.
And thus was the destruction of the formed people,
the shaped people.
They were destroyed.
They were overthrown as people.
They destroyed, they crushed
their mouths, their faces entirely.
And it is said that the remainder
are the monkeys that are in the forests today.
That must be the remainder
because their bodies were only fixed of wood
by Former and Shaper.
So the fact that the monkeys
look like people
is a sign of one generation of formed people,
of shaped people,
only puppets and just carved of wood.[39]

The Last Creation

And this is the beginning when man was invented,
and when that which would go into man's
body was sought.
Then spoke the Bearer and Engenderer,
who were Former and Shaper,
Majesty and Quetzal Serpent by name,

---

38. Humans carved of wood appear here alive again for a brief while. Trying to escape from complete destruction, they scattered and disappeared. Only a reminder of them, says our text, are the monkeys living in the forest today. A parallel account in the Nahuatl language, which we will transcribe in this same part, reads as follows: "Then . . . people were turned into monkeys; they were scattered over the mountains, and the monkey-men lived there. . . ."

39. Other creations and destructions of the human beings correspond to the succes-

"The dawn has already appeared;
the creation has already been made,
and there is clearly a nourisher appearing,
a supporter, born of light,
engendered of light,
man has already appeared,
the population of the surface of the earth," they said.
It was all assembled, and came
and went, their wisdom,
in the darkness, in the nighttime,
as they originated things,
and dissolved things.
They thought;
and they meditated there
and thus came their wisdom directly,
bright and clear.
They found and they maintained
what came to be man's body.
That was just a little later,
there not having appeared
the sun, moon, and stars
over the heads
of Former and Shaper.
In Cleft, in Bitter Water by name,
there came then yellow corn ears
and white corn ears.

And these are the names of the animals;
these were the bringers of the food:
wildcat, coyote,
parakeet, and crow.
They are the four animals
who told the news
of the yellow corn ears

---

sive "suns" or cosmic ages that had existed. The text that we will transcribe now deals with the last creation, "when man was invented, when our ancestors were created." This time, the gods went too far in their creative effort. Our ancestors in this last creation were exceedingly perfect. Then the gods had to correct the excess of perfection.

and white corn ears to them.[40]
There they went then to Cleft
to point out the Cleft road,
and there they found the food
whence came the flesh
of the formed people,
the shaped people.[41]
And water was their blood;
it became man's blood.
There came to Bearer
and Engenderer the corn ears
and they rejoiced then
over the discovery
of the marvelous mountain
filled with quantities and quantities
of yellow corn ears,
and white corn ears,[42]
and also loads of cacao and chocolate,
numberless mameys,
custard apples,
anonas, nances,
soursops, and honey.
It was full of the sweetest foods,
in the town
at Cleft and at Bitter Water by name.
There was food there
from the fruit of everything:
small vegetables, big vegetables,
small plants and big plants.

---

40. These four animals informed the gods about the corn ears with which they were going to shape the bodies of the first really intelligent human beings. In another mythical account preserved in the Nahuatl language, which will be also included in this part 2, a different animal, the red ant, is the one who tells the god Quetzalcoatl where the corn that is to be used as the basic food of man is located.

41. In the Quiche-Maya language the word *tiyohil* menas human flesh. In the Nahuatl language the equivalent word is *tonacayotl,* "our flesh," which is also a term meaning "corn."

42. The so-called Marvelous Mountain (*utzilah huyuv*), filled with a great quantity of corn, has its equivalent in the Nahuatl myth about which mention has been already made. In the referred-to Nahuatl text the Marvelous Mountain is called *Tonacatepetl,* a compound word whose meaning is "the Mountain of our flesh or our sustenance."

The road was pointed out
by the animals.
And then the yellow corn was ground
and the white corn,
and nine bushels
were made by Xmucane.
The food came
with water to create strength,
and it became man's grease
and turned into his fat
when acted upon by Bearer and Engenderer,
Majesty and Quetzal Serpent, as they are called.
And so then they put into words the creation,
the shaping
of our first mother and father.
Only yellow corn
and white corn were their bodies.
Only food were the legs
and arms of man.
Those who were our first fathers
were the four original men.
Only food at the outset
were their bodies.

These are the names of the first men who were made,
who were shaped:
the first man was Jaguar Quiche,
and the second in turn was Jaguar Night,
and the third in turn was Nought,
and the fourth was Wind Jaguar,
and these are the names of our first mothers
and fathers.
Only formed,
only shaped they were said to be.
They had no mother;
they had no father.
Just heroes by themselves we have said.[43]

---

43. "*Heroes*," in the Maya-Quiche language *achib*. According to Edmonson, this is a particularly clear example of the use of *achib* as opposed to *vinaq*. "Both mean 'man' but the first is the Latin *vir*, the second is *homo*."

No woman bore them;
nor were they engendered
by the Former and Shaper,
the Bearer and Engenderer.
Just power, just magic
was their forming, their shaping
by the Former and Shaper,
Bearer and Engenderer,
Majesty and Quetzal Serpent.
And when they looked like men,
they became men.
They spoke and they talked;
they saw and they heard;
they walked; they grasped;
they were fine men.
They were handsome.
Manly faces
were their features.
They had breath and existed.
And they could see too;
immediately their sight began.[44]
They came to see;
they came to know
everything under heaven
if they could see it.
Suddenly they could look around
and see around
in the sky, in the earth.
It was scarcely an instant
before everything could be seen.
They did not have to walk at first
so as to gaze at what was under heaven:
they were just there and looked.
Their understanding became great.
Their gaze passed over trees,

---

44. To speak, see, hear, walk, grow, to be handsome, to have a face with its particu-lar features, to breathe, are the traits this text underlines as essential attributes of man. But to see and to understand appear immediately after as that which particular-ly matters. Here precisely the gods discovered that they had now committed a mis-take, but this time by an excess of perfection in their creative action.

rocks, lakes,
seas, mountains, and valleys.
Truly, then,
they were the most beloved of men,
Jaguar Quiche, Jaguar Night,
Nought, and Wind Jaguar.

And then they were asked by the Former
and Shaper:
"How pleasant is your existence?
Do you know?
Can't you see? Can't you hear?
Isn't your language good
and your walking?
And look now
at what you see under heaven!
Aren't the mountains clear?
Do you see the valleys?
Then try it now!"
they were told.
And so then they came to see
everything under heaven
and so then they gave thanks
to Former and Shaper.
"Truly then twice thanks,
thrice thanks that we are created already,
and that we are mouthed and faced.
We can speak; we can hear;
we ponder; we move;
we think very well;
we understand far and near,
and we can see large and small,
what is in heaven,
what is on earth.
Thanks then to you
that we are created,
we are formed,
we are shaped,
we exist O our Grandmother,
O our Grandfather."

They said as they gave thanks
for their forming, their shaping.
They came to understand everything;
they saw it:
the four creations,
the four destructions,
the womb of heaven,
the womb of earth.
And not very happily
did they listen to this,
the Former and Shaper.
"It is not good
what they said,
our forming, our shaping:
*We know everything great
and small,"* they said.[45]

And so they took back again
their knowledge,
did Bearer and Engenderer.
"How shall we make them again
so that their sight reaches only nearby?
So that it will just be a little space
of the surface of the earth that they see?
It is not good what they say.
Aren't their names just formed and shaped?
But quite like gods will they become then
unless they begin to multiply
and begin to grow numerous

---

45. The reaction of the supreme Bearer and Engenderer was mysterious indeed in the eyes of the Maya-Quiche. In this last creation the Dual God and the other gods had finally succeeded in creating beings capable of understanding, worshiping, and giving thanks, but the fact that the human ancestors had confessed that they knew everything great and small displeased their creators very much. A parallel to this can perhaps be found in the Biblical account: Adam and Eve tasted the fruit of the tree of knowledge and, because of this, they lost their paradise. In Mesoamerica human beings, our ancestors, apparently did not violate any prohibition. It just happened to them that they could understand everything and, because of this, the supreme Dual God decided to alter their nature, to reduce their capacities—in a word, to expel them from the paradise of knowledge.

when it whitens, when it brightens:
unless it increases.
Then, so be it!
Let's just undo them a little more.
That's what is still needed.
It isn't good what we have found out.
Won't they just equate their deeds with ours[46]
if their understanding reaches too far
and they see everything?" they were told
by the Heart of Heaven, One Leg,
Dwarf Lightning, Green Lightning,
Majesty, Quetzal Serpent,
Bearer, and Engenderer,
Xpiacoc, Xmucane,
Former and Shaper, as they are called.
And then they made their life over
for their forming, their shaping.

And their eyes were chipped
by the Heart of Heaven.
They were blinded
like the clouding of the surface of a mirror;
their eyes were all blinded.
They could only see nearby then,
however clear things might be,
and thus they lost their understanding,
and all the wisdom of the four men
at the start, at the beginning.
And thus was the forming, the shaping
of our first grandfathers, our first fathers,
by the Heart of Heaven,
the Heart of Earth.
And then there were their mates;
and their wives came to exist.
Only the gods

---

46. To be like gods was the tempting invitation, according to the Biblical account. To be quite like gods, to equate human beings with the divine ones was also, according to the *Popol Vuh, Book of the Counsel*, of the Quiches, something that was not approved by the Bearer, the Engenderer.

invented them too.
Thus it was just in their sleep
that they brought them then.[47]
Truly they were beuatiful
and they were women
for Jaguar Quiche, Jaguar Night,
Nought, and Wind Jaguar.
When their wives were there,
they were properly brought to life;
at once their hearts rejoiced again over their mates.
And these are their names;
their wives were these:
Red Sea House was the name
of the wife of Jaguar Quiche;
Beauty House was the name
of the wife of Jaguar Night;
Hummingbird House was the
name of the wife of Nought;
Parrot House was the name
of the wife of Wind Jaguar.
And these were the names of their wives,
who became queens.
They were the bearers of the little tribes,
the great tribes,
and this was the root of us
who are Quiche people.
And the worshipers became many,
and the scarificers.
They came to be no longer four,
though four were the mothers of us,
Quiche people.
Different were their names
for each of them.

---

47. Accounts like this and others we have already underlined, which have a parallel in the Bible, have inclined some interpreters of the *Popol Vuh* to admit in it the presence of non-Mesoamerican elements derived or introduced through the teaching of the missionaries. In relation to this hypothesis it can be stated that the question remains open to further research taking into account other native testimonies of the Mayas.

Then they multiplied there
at the sunrise.
Many were their names.
They became the peoples:
majesties, ballplayers,
maskers,[48] children of Lords,
as they continued to be called,
the names of the peoples.
And there at the sunrise they multiplied
and there was known
the beginning too
of the branches, of the seers.
Together they came there
from the sunrise.
Jaguar Quiche was the grandfather
and father of the nine great houses
of the Kaveks.[49]
Jaguar Night was the grandfather
and father of the nine great houses
of the Great-Houses.[50]
Nought was the grandfather
and father of the four great houses
of the Lord Quiches.
Three divisions of the family
were created,
and the names of their grandfathers,
their fathers, were not lost.
They were the procreators and multipliers,
there at the sunrise.
But really there came then the branches, the seers,

---

48. As Edmonson has noted, the meaning of the word *k'obah* is not clear. Some have interpreted it as "maskers," or those who act or play with a mask. Other translators have suggested it is related to *corugar*, the American puma or panther, to evoke perhaps a rank of warrior.

49. According to Edmonson, "the leading lineage of the Quiche in the 15th century was called *gavek*. The meaning of this name is obscure but it may be related to *gav*, 'ancestor, kinsman' and perhaps also to the old man of the 19th day, *gavok*, associated with rain, lightning and thunder. The probable meaning of the name was something like 'fathers.' "

50. In this way the Quiches preserved the memory about the grandfathers and the fathers of those they considered the proceators of their various lineages.

with thirteen of the secondary tribes.
The thirteen were:
the Palaces (with the Rabinals),
the Fire Trees,
the Bird House People
(and with them the White Corns,
and also with them the Barriers),
Serpents,
Sweatbath House,
Speaker House,
the Star House People
(with the Chest House People),
the Ring House People,
the Beehive men,
Jaguar House,
Serpent Keepers,
Jaguar Guts.
For truly these are the greatest of the tribes
that made up the secondary tribes.
We are speaking only of the greatest,
which we have enumerated,
many more having come after
who were each one a division of the city.
We shall not write their names.
Nonetheless they went on multiplying
there at the sunrise.
Many peoples they became in the darkness
as they grew.
The sun was not yet born,
nor the light, as they were multiplying.[51]
They all remained together then,
and very numerous they became.
And they walked along there
at the sunrise.
There was no one to nourish them
and support them

---

51. "The sun was not yet born" is a sentence difficult to understand. In manifest contradiction of other accounts about the cosmic ages, here men appear already "multiplying" before the birth of the sun.

but they bowed their faces to heaven.
They did not know where to go.
For a long time they did that
while they were there in comfort,
black people,
white people.[52]
Many were the people's languages.
Scattered on the flanks
were the generations under heaven.
And there were mountain people
who did not show their faces
and had no houses.
They just wandered in the little mountains,
and big mountains.
"As though they were crazy," they said.
"Because mountain people are a menace," they said.
They watched for the sunrise there
and they all had the same language.
They did not yet call on wood and stone[53]
to remind them of the words
of Former and Shaper,
"The Heart of Earth," as they said.
Really they remembered about what was hidden
and turned bright.
Just praying was what they did.
They were lovers of the word;
they were adorers;
they were worshipers;
they were pious people
who bowed their faces to heaven
when they prayed,
for their daughters and their sons:[54]

---

52. Other translators have understood the meaning of these two lines as "men of the shadows, men of the dawn."

53. I understand the sentence "They did not yet call on wood and stone to remind them of the words of Former and Shaper" in the sense that they had not yet become worshipers of gods represented with such materials. Have we here a trace of the missionary's influence in terms of a condemnation of idolatry?

54. The following lines offer the text of a prayer that, as it is stated, was conceived when the Quiches were "lovers of the word, pious people. . . . "

"Hail, you Former,
you Shaper,
look upon us,
hear us.
Do not oppress us;
Do not turn on us,
Oh God in heaven and on earth!
Heart of Heaven, Heart of Earth!
Give us our sign, our word,
on the road of day,
on the road of light,
when it is whitened,
when it is brightened.
Great be the wealth of the path,
the wealth of the road.
Give us then tranquility and light,
tranquillity and peace;
perfect light
and perfect peace may there be.
Perfect life
and existence
give us then,[55]
you, One Leg,
Dwarf Lightning, Green Lightning,
Dwarf Quarter Gods,[56]
Green Quarter Gods,
Hawk, Hunter,
Majesty, Quetzal Serpent,
Bearer, Engenderer,
Xpiacoc, Xmucane,
The Grandmother of Day,
The Grandmother of Light,
as it has been whitened,

---

55. A divine word, tranquillity, light, peace, and life were the gifts the Quiches expected to receive from their gods.

56. Edmonson employs the word "quarter," in the sense of "a division or section in a town," to translate the term *Nanahuac*, probably a loan from the Nahuatl. I incline to a different meaning: "the four quadrants" (of the world). Thus the Dwarf gods mentioned here are to be described as the deities of the four quadrants of the world.

as it has been brightened," they said
when they worshiped
and they prayed.
They ruled watching for the dawn;
they just gazed there toward the sunrise
to watch and see the Sun Passer,
the Great Star,
when the sun would be born,
illuminator of what is in Heaven,
what is on earth,
the path of the formed people,
the shaped people.
Then spoke Jaguar Quiche,
Jaguar Night,
Nought, and Wind Jaguar:
"Let us wait now
for the dawn," they said.
They were great sages;
they were wise men;
they were sacrificers;
they were worshipers, as they are called.
For there was nothing as yet
either of wood or stone
to guard our first mothers and fathers.
And they just wore their hearts out there
in expectation of the sun.
They were already many and all of the tribes;
together with the Mexican people[57]
were worshipers and sacrificers.
"Let us go ourselves and search,
and we shall see for ourselves
whether there is something to guard our sign.
We will find what we should say before them,
and thus we shall live.
There are no guardians for us,"

---

57. In the Quiche text one reads *yaqui vinac,* which literally means "the departed people." Edmonson adds, as a commentary, that "it clearly means 'Mexican' in Quiche," that is the people who came from the highlands of central Mexico.

then said Jaguar Quiche,
Jaguar Night,
Nought, and Wind Jaguar.
They heard news of a city
and went there.[58]

---

58. The parts of the *Popol Vuh* included here, following the translation from the Quiche-Maya prepared by Munro S. Edmonson, were originally published in *The Book of Counsel: The Popol Vuh of the Quiche-Maya of Guatemala* (New Orleans: Middle American Research Institute, Tulane University, 1971 [Publication 35], pp. 3–31, 145–160.

Teotlatolli, Teocuilcatl:
Divine Words, Divine Songs

The Five Suns or Cosmic Ages: A Nahuatl-Aztec Version

Here is the oral account of what is known of how the earth was founded long ago.[59]

One by one, here are its various foundations [ages].[60]

How it began, how the first Sun had its beginning 2513 years ago—thus it is known today, the 22 of May, 1558.[61]

This Sun, 4-Tiger, lasted 676 years.[62]

Those who lived in this first Sun were eaten by ocelots. It was the time of the Sun 4-Tiger.

And what they used to eat was our nourishment,[63] and they lived 676 years.

And they were eaten in the year 13.

Thus they perished and all ended. At this time the Sun was destroyed.

It was on the year 1-Reed. They began to be devoured on a day [called] 4-Tiger. And so with this everything ended and all of them perished.

---

59. "The oral account (*tlamachilliztlatolzazanilli*) is derived from the word *tlamachi-liztli*, which means "wisdom" in the passive sense, "known wisdom or tradition"; and from the composite *tlatoltzatzanilli*, "the word which is repeated."

60. Each foundation corresponds to a cosmic age, "a sun."

61. The presence of this and other dates reflects the Mesoamerican concern for exactness. The date of the 22 of May, 1558, is the day in which this text was transcribed. Together with it one finds the year believed to be the beginning of the first cosmic age, that is 2,513 years from the above date.

62. Each sun or age receives the name of the element that will bring about its destruction. Here we have the name of the day-sign, according to the Pre-Columbian calendar, "tiger," preceded by the numeral 4.

63. According to another source, the *Historia de los Mexicanos por sus Pinturas*, during the time of the first sun, they "used to eat acorns." I use here the expression "our nourishment" to translate the Nahuatl word *tonacayotl*, which, as has been stated in note 41, means both "our flesh, and our corn." In describing what happened in the various cosmic ages the present text repeats the same expression: "What they used to eat was our nourishment." Thanks to the source we have quoted, we know that an evolution in the nature of food was taking place from one cosmic age to the next. Thus in the second cosmic age "water-corn" was the food consumed. In the third, man used to eat a seed similar to corn, which they called *cincocopi*. Concerning the fourth age, no specific mention is made about food. Finally, in the fifth or present age, "corn, *tonacayotl*," "our flesh," was the sustenance of the human beings.

This Sun is known as 4-Wind.

Those who lived under this second Sun were carried away by the wind. It was under the Sun 4-Wind that they all disappeared.

They were carried away by the wind. They became monkeys.[64]

Their homes, their trees—everything was taken away by the wind.

And this Sun itself was also swept away by the wind.

And what they used to eat was our nourishment.

[The date was] 12-Serpent. They lived [under this Sun] 364 years.

Thus they perished. In a single day they were carried off by the wind. They perished on a day 4-Wind.

The year [of this Sun] was 1-Flint.

This Sun, 4-Rain, was the third.

Those who lived under this third Sun, 4-Rain, also perished. It rained fire upon them. They became turkeys.

This Sun was consumed by fire. All their homes burned.

They lived under this Sun 312 years.

They perished when it rained fire for a whole day.

And what they used to eat was our nourishment.

[The date was] 7-Flint. The year was 1-Flint and the day 4-Rain.

They who perished were those who had become turkeys.

The offspring of turkeys are now called *pipil-pipil*.[65]

This Sun is called 4-Water; for 52 years the water lasted.

And those who lived under this fourth Sun, they existed in the time of the Sun 4-Water.

It lasted 676 years.

Thus they perished: They were swallowed by the waters and they became fish.

The heavens collapsed upon them and in a single day they perished.

And what they used to eat was our nourishment.

[The date was] 4-Flower. The year was 1-House and the day 4-Water.

---

64. As has been noted, this reference closely corresponds to what is recorded in the *Popol Vuh* of the Quiche-Maya.

65. *Pipil-pipil:* This Nahuatl expression is used to connote the turkeys. On the other hand, *pipil-tin* means also "children." Until the time of the narrator of this myth, the belief was still popular that turkeys were the descendants of the people who had lived in the third cosmic age.

They perished, all the mountains perished.
The water lasted 52 years and with this ended their years.
This Sun, called 4-Movement, this is our Sun, the one in which we now live.[66]
And here is its sign, how the Sun fell into the fire, into the divine hearth, there at Teotihuacan.[67]
It was also the Sun of our Lord Quetzalcoatl in Tula.
The fifth Sun, its sign 4-Movement, is called the Sun of Movement because it moves and follows its path.
And as the elders continue to say, under this sun there will be earthquakes and hunger, and then our end shall come.[68]

*The Cosmic Ages, the Rescuing of the Precious Bones
and the Discovery of Corn*

Thus it is told, it is said:
There have already been four manifestations
and this one is the fifth age.[69]

So the old ones knew this,
that in the year 1-Rabbit
heaven and earth were founded.
And they knew this,
that when heaven and earth were founded
there had already been four kinds of men,
four kinds of manifestations.
Also they knew that each of these
had existed in a Sun, an age.

And they said of the first men,
their god made them, fashioned them of ashes.

---

66. The contents of this text are in agreement with the carving of the famous "calendar stone," the so-called Aztec calendar, in which the central figure, with the day-sign 4-movement, represents the face of the sun.

67. An allusion is made here to the myth that speaks about the creation of the fifth sun in *Teotihuacan*. There one of the gods threw himself into the divine fire in order to reappear transformed as the sun, thus marking the beginning of a new age. Later on the Aztecs found in this account the inspiration for their mystic militarism: If only by an act of sacrifice could the sun exist, only through human sacrifice will life and existence be prolonged.

68. *Codice Chimalpopoca: Leyenda de los Soles,* fol. 76–77.

69. This text, which offers some variants when compared with the one previously transcribed, is taken from a different source: *The Annals of Cuauhtitlan.*

This they attributed to the god Quetzalcoatl,[70]
whose sign is 7-Wind;
he made them, he invented them.
The first Sun or age that was founded,
its sign was 4-Water,[71]
it was called the Sun of Water.
Then it happened
that water carried away everything.
The people were changed into fish.

Then the second Sun or age was founded.
Its sign was 4-Tiger.
It was called the Sun of Tiger.
Then it happened
that the sky was crushed,
the Sun did not follow its course.
When the Sun arrived at midday,
immediately it was night
and when it became dark,
tigers ate the people.
In this Sun giants lived.
The old ones said
the giants greeted each other thus:
"Do not fall down," for whoever falls,
he falls forever.
Then the third Sun was founded.
Its sign was 4-Rain-of-Fire.
It happened then that fire rained down,
those who lived there were burned.
And then sand rained down.
And they say that then
it rained down the little stones we see,
that the *tezontle* stone boiled[72]

---

70. This first forming of men, fashioned of ashes, can be correlated with the first creative attempt recorded in the *Popol Vuh*.

71. While in the previously quoted text the sign that presided over the first cosmic age was 4-Tiger, related to the element earth, here the calendar sign is 4-Water, as everything in it was related to said element.

72. *Tezontle* stone, a red volcanic stone.

and the big rocks became red.
Its sign was 4-Wind,
when the fourth Sun was founded.
It was called the Sun of Wind.
Then everything was carried away by the wind.
People were turned into monkeys.
They were scattered over the mountains,
and the monkey-men lived there.

The fifth Sun,
4-Movement its sign.
It is called the Sun of Movement
because it moves, follows its course.
And the old ones go about saying,
now there will be earthquakes,
there will be hunger
and thus we will perish.
In the year 13-Reed,
they say it came into existence,
the sun that now exists was born.
That was when there was light,
when dawn came,
the Sun of Movement that now exists.
for Movement is its sign.
This is the fifth Sun that was founded;
in it there will be earthquakes;
in it there will be hunger.[73]

This Sun, its name 4-Movement,
this is our Sun,
in which we now live,
and this is its sign,
where the Sun fell in fire
on the divine hearth,
there in Teotihuacan.
Also this was the Sun
of our prince of Tula,
of Quetzalcoatl.[74]

---

73. *Annals of Cuauhtitlan,* fol. 2.
74. *Codice Chimalpopoca,* "Manuscript of 1558," fol. 77.

The Rescuing of the Precious Bones

And as soon as the gods came together
they said: "Who shall live on the earth?
The sky has already been established,
and the earth has been established.
But who shall live on the earth, oh gods?"[75]
Citlalinicue, Citlaltonac,
Apantecuhtili, Tepanquizqui,
Quetzalcoatl, and Tezcatlipoca   .
were grieved.
Then Quetzalcoatl went to Mictlan,[76]
he approached Mictlantecuhtli and Mictlancihuatl[77]
and immediately said to them:
"I have come for the precious bones
that you keep here,
I have come to take them."
And Mictlantecuhtli said to him:
"What would you do with them, Quetzalcoatl?"
And Quetzalcoatl answered him:
"The gods are concerned
that someone shall live on the earth."
And Mictlantecuhtli replied:
"Very well. Sound my conch shell
and go four times around my domain."

But the conch shell had no holes;
therefore Quetzalcoatl called the worms;
they made holes in it and
then the bees and hornets went inside
and made it sound.
On hearing it sound, Mictlantecuhtli said again:
"Very well. Take the bones."
But Mictlantecuhtli said to those who served him:

---

75. As in the account of the *Popol Vuh*, here also the gods appear anxious to have people living on the earth from whom they will receive worship.
76. *Mictlan*, "The Place of the Dead."
77. *Mictlantecuhtli*: "Lord of the Place of the Dead"; *Mictlancihuatl*: "Lady of the Place of the Dead."

"People of Mictlan!
Oh gods, tell Quetzalcoatl
he must not take them."
Quetzalcoatl replied:
"Indeed, yes, I take possession of them."
And he said to his *nahual* [alter ego],[78]
"You go and tell Mictlantecuhtli I will not take them."
And his *nahual* said loudly, "I will not take them."

But then Quetzalcoatl went,
he gathered up the precious bones.
The bones of the man were together on one side
and the bones of the woman together on the other side
and Quetzalcoatl took them
and made a bundle.
Again Mictlantecuhtli said to those who served him:
"Gods, is Quetzalcoatl
really carrying away the precious bones?
Gods, go and dig a big hole."
They went and dug it.
And Quetzalcoatl stumbled, frightened by quail,
and fell into the hole.
He fell down as if dead
and the precious bones were scattered,
so that the quail chewed and gnawed upon them.

After a while Quetzalcoatl was revived;
he was grieved, and he said to his *nahual*:
"What shall I do now?"
His *nahual* answered him:
"Although the affair has started badly,
let it continue as best it may."
Quetzalcoatl gathered up the bones,
put them together, made again a bundle,
and carried them to Tamoanchan.[79]
As soon as he arrived,

---

78. *Nahual* or *Nahualli* is an "alter ego." Often a Nahual was symbolized by an animal, in one way or another related to the attributes of the person or the god of whom he was the Nahual.

79. *Tamoanchan:* a name for the mythical place of "the origins."

the goddess called Quilaztli,[80]
also called Cihuacoatl,
ground them up
and put them in a fine earthen tub.
Quetzalcoatl bled his male organ on them.
And immediately the gods named
Apantecuhtili, Huictolinqui, Tepanquizqui,
Tlallamanac, Tzontemoc,
and the sixth, Quetzalcoatl,
all did penance.
And they said:
"Oh gods, the *macehuales* are born."[81]
And thus we mortals owe our life to penance,
because for our sake the gods did penance.[82]

The Discovery of Corn

Once more the gods said:
"What shall they eat, O gods?
Let our sustenance, corn, come down."

And then the ant went to gather
shelled corn
from within the Mountain of our sustenance.[83]

Quetzalcoatl went to meet the ant.
He asked her:
"Where did you go to gather it? Tell me!"
But she does not want to tell him.
Quetzalcoatl insisted on asking.
Then she said:

---

80. *Quilaztli,* a name of the Mother young goddess. It literally means: "She who fosters vegetal life." (*Cihuacoatl,* another name of the same mother goddess, means 'She-Serpent."

81. *Macehuales,* in Nahuatl *Macehualtin,* literally means "those merited by the divine sacrifice." In a more general sense this word connotes the idea of "human being." Later on, it was applied to the commoners or people of the lower class.

82. *Codice Chimalpopoca, "Leyenda de los Soles,"* fol. 76–77.

83. "The Mountain of our sustenance," in Nahuatl *Tonacatepetl.* See footnote 42 of this same part 2.

"It is there!"
Whereupon she led him.

Promptly Quetzalcoatl changed himself into a black ant.
Then she guided him,
and thus introduced him.
Together they came to enter.
It is said that the red ant
guided Quetzalcoatl
to the foot of the Mountain
where they placed the corn.
Then Quetzalcoatl carried it.
on his back, to Tamoanchan.[84]

Whereupon, from it, the gods ate and ate
and later they put it into our mouths
so that we might become strong.

And then they said:
"What shall we do with the Mount of our sustenance?
For now it will only remain where it is."
Quetzalcoatl pulled at it,
But he could not move it.
Then Oxomoco[85]
drew lots,
and likewise Cipactonal,
the wife of Oxomoco, drew lots.
(For Cipactonal is a woman.)
Oxomoco and Cipactonal said:
"If only Nanahuac will send a bolt of lightning[86]
to the Mount of our sustenance,
because we drew lots."

Then the gods of rain were summoned:[87]

---

84. *Tamoanchan:* see footnote 79 of this same part 2.

85. *Oxomoco* and *Cipactonal* are the Nahuatl equivalents of Adam and Eve, that is the first human couple.

86. *Nanahuac* is the name of a god closely related to Quetzalcoatl. He was the one who threw himself into the divine fire in Teotihuacan in order to be transformed into the sun, the fifth, which rules the present cosmic age.

87. The gods of rain, the *Tlaloque,* were the attendants of *Tlaloc,* the God of Rain.

143

the blue-green gods of rain,
the white gods of rain, the yellow gods of rain,
the red gods of rain.
At once Nanahuac sent a lightning bolt.
Then our sustenance was stolen
by the gods of rain.
White, dark, yellow, red corn,
beans, blades, amaranth,
from us our sustenance was stolen.[88]

They are described as being of different colors in accordance with their presence in the different quadrants of the universe.

88. *Codice Chimalpopoca*, "Manuscript of 1558," fol. 5.

The Origins of the Mixtec People[89]

In the year and in the day
of obscurity and utter darkness,
before there were days and years,
the world being in deep obscurity,
when all was chaos and confusion,
the earth was covered with water,
there was only mud and slime
on the surface of the earth.
At that time . . .
there became visible
a god who had the name 1-Deer[90]
and the surname Snake of the Lion
and a goddess, very genteel and beautiful,
whose name was also 1-Deer
and whose surname was Snake of the Tiger.
These two gods are said to have been the beginning
of all the other gods. . . .
As soon as these two gods became
visible on the earth, in human form,
the accounts of our people relate
that with their power and wisdom
they made and established a large stone,
on which they built
a very sumptuous mansion,
constructed with the finest workmanship,
which was their seat and residence on earth.
And on top of the highest part
of the house and habitation of these gods
was a copper ax,
the blade turned upward,
above which were the heavens.
This large stone and the mansion

---

89. The Mixtecs are a people inhabiting parts of the present state of Oaxaca and adjacent regions of the states of Guerrero and Puebla. From a linguistic point of view they are distantly related to the Zapotecs, early settlers in central Oaxaca.

90 The name 1-Deer is derived from the astrological calendar in which twenty day-signs are combined with 13 numerals. Most of the gods, if not all of them, had a calendar name connoting a specific date in which their principal feast was celebrated.

were on a very high hill,
near the village of Apoala. . . .
This large stone was named
"the-place-where-the-heavens-were."
And there they remained many centuries
in complete tranquillity and contentment,
as in a pleasant and delightful place,
the world being
at that time in obscurity.
And these gods,
father and mother of all the gods,[91]
while in their mansion,
had two male children, very handsome,
prudent and wise in all the arts.
The first was called
Wind-of-Nine-Snakes,
taken from the name of the day he was born.
The second was called
Wind-of-Nine-Caverns,
which also was the name
of the day he was born.
These two children
were raised in great luxury.
The elder, when he wanted to amuse himself,
turned into an eagle,
which flew up very high.
The second transformed himself into a small animal,
in form of a serpent with wings,
which flew through the air
with such nimbleness and cunning
that he passed through large stones and walls,
and he made himself invisible. . . .
The two brothers, for their pleasure,
planted a garden;
they put there many kinds of trees,
flowers and roses
and trees with fruit

---

91. Here also, as in the *Popol Vub* of the Quiches and in other Maya and Nahuatl manuscripts, the supreme god is a dual entity, "father and mother of all the gods."

and many herbs.
After all this
began the creation of the heavens and the earth. . . .
Men were restored to life[92]
and in this way
began the Mixtec kingdom. . . . [93]

92. Although this account of the Mixtecs is brief indeed, if we compared it to that included in the *Popol Vub* or in other texts from central Mexico, explicit mention is made in it about the different creations and specifically about the restoration of human life on earth.

93. This text was transcribed in the work of Fray Gregorio Garcia, *Origen de los Indios del Nuevo Mundo e Islas Occidentales* (Madrid, 1729), pp. 137–138. A pictorial version of the same story is offered in the first pages of the Mixtec pre-Columbain book known as *Codex Vindobonensis*, which is preserved in the National Library in Vienna.

Part Three
THE STORY OF QUETZALCOATL

This is the story of Quetzalcoatl, who was a great sage, where he ruled and what he did when he went away. This Quetzalcoatl they considered as a god; he was thought a god; he was prayed to in olden times there at Tula.[1]

And there was his temple. It was very tall, very high, exceedingly high, exceedingly tall. Very many were its stair steps; verily they lay in a multitude, each one not wide but only very narrow. On each one the sole of one's foot could not lie.

It is said he just lay covered, he just lay with his face covered. And it is said he did not look as a human.

His face was like something monstrous, battered. There was no human creation in it. And his beard was very long, very lengthy. He was heavily bearded.[2]

And the Toltecs, his vassals, were highly skilled. Nothing was difficult when they did it, when they cut the green stone and cast gold, and made still other works of the craftsman, of the feather worker.[3] Very highly skilled were they. Indeed these crafts started, indeed these proceeded from Quetzalcoatl, all the crafts work, the learning.

And there stood his green-stone house, and his golden house, and his seashell house, and his snailshell house, and his house of beams, his turquoise house, and his house of precious feathers.

And for his vassals, the Toltecs, nothing was distant. Indeed,

1. This paragraph, a sort of introduction to the story of Quetzalcoatl, was written by Fray Bernardino de Sahagun. In it the Franciscan friar contrasts what the natives had informed him about Quetzalcoatl with his own personal interpretation. While the natives spoke of him as if he were a god, Sahagun reiterates that he was just a high pontiff and ruler of the Toltecs and that he had been a great wizard or, in the best of the cases, a sage. As we have seen in our Introduction to this book, it is necessary to distinguish between the god Quetzalcoatl, who probably was worshiped since the days of Teotihuacan, and the famous priest of Tula who derived his own name from that of the god. The present story obviously deals with the latter.

2. On the one hand this text, which is the transcript of an ancient oral tradition, recalls the belief about the high priest as a person heavily bearded. On the other, it also states that he was monstrous and that there was not "any human creation in it." By this our text probably refers either to the supernatural character of Quetzalcoatl or to what is mentioned later in this same story, that the aged priest, after so many years of retirement and penance, had his face completely emaciated.

3. Archaeology confirms that not until the beginnings of the Postclassic period, a time that coincides with the reign of Quetzalcoatl in Tula, was metal work a cultural reality in Mesoamerica. It is known that this took place as a consequence of a process of diffusion that originated in the Andean zone of high culture in South America.

they swiftly reached where they went. And so very quickly they went that they were called "those who walk the whole day."

And there was a mountain called Tzatzitepetl, "the Mountain of the Public Announcement." It is also just so named today. It is said that there the crier mounted. For what was required, he mounted there to cry out a proclamation. He could be heard everywhere. Indeed everywhere was heard what he said, what laws were made. Swiftly was there going forth; they knew what Quetzalcoatl had commanded the people.

And also the Toltecs were indeed rich. Of no value was food, all our sustenance. It is said that the gourds were each exceedingly huge; some were quite round. And the ears of maize were each indeed like hand grindstones, very long. They could be embraced only in one's arms. And the palm-tree-like amaranth plants: They could climb them, they could be climbed. And also the varicolored cotton grew: chili-red, yellow, pink, brown, green, blue, verdigris color, dark brown, ripening brown, dark blue, fine yellow, coyote-colored cotton. All of these came forth exactly so; they did not dye them.

And there dwelt all varieties of birds of precious feather: the lovely cotinga, the resplendent trogon, the troupial, the roseate spoonbill. And all the various birds sang very well; indeed gladdening one they sang. And all green stones and gold were not costly. Very much of this was kept. And also cacao grew, flowery cacao. In very many places there was cacao.

And these Toltecs were very rich; they were wealthy. Never were they poor. They lacked nothing in their homes. Never was there famine. The maize rejects they did not need; they only burned them to heat the sweat baths with them.[4]

And this Quetzalcoatl also did penances. He bled the calf of his leg to stain thorns with blood. And he bathed at midnight. And he bathed there where his bathing place was, at a place called Xippacoyan.[5] Him each of the fire priests imitated, as well as the offering priests. And the offering priests took their manner of conduct from the life of Quetzalcoatl. By it they established the law of Tula. Thus were also customs established here in Mexico.[6]

---

4. This description of the golden age of the Toltecs, attributed above all to the wisdom of Quetzalcoatl, coincides with what is related in other native accounts.

5. *Xippacoyan:* "the place of the bath of turquoise." Such designation has probably to be understood in a metaphorical sense as "the place of the sacred or ritual bath."

6. In many ways the Aztecs repeat that they had derived their traditions, laws,

Here is told how the glory of Quetzalcoatl came to an end and how three sorcerers came to him and what they did.

But at last Quetzalcoatl and all the Toltecs became continually neglectful. And then there arrived, there came as an evil omen, three wizards, Huitzilopochtli, Titlacauan, Tlacauepan. The three announced that Tula would be destroyed.[7]

This Titlacauan began what was prognosticated. It is said that he turned himself into a little old man. He represented, he appeared in the form of one who was much bent, whose hair was very white, who was small and very white-headed. Thereupon he went to the home of Quetzalcoatl.

When he had gone there, he thereupon said to the servants: "I wish to see the lord Quetzalcoatl."

Then they said to him: "Go hence, little old man. The lord is sick. You will vex him."

Then the little old man said: "Nay, but I will see him; but I will come to him."

They said to him: "It is well. Wait yet. Let us tell him."

And thereupon they informed Quetzalcoatl. They said to him: "My prince, some little old man has come to see you. He is like a snare for you, like a trap for you. When we turn him away he wishes in no way to go. He says: 'But I will see the lord.' "

Then said Quetzalcoatl: "Let him come; let him enter here. For I have awaited him for five, for ten days."

Then they brought him in to Quetzalcoatl.

The old man thereupon greeted him. He said: "My grandson, my lord, how do you feel as to your body? Here is a potion I have brought for you. Drink it."

And then Quetzalcoatl said: "Come here, O old one. You are fatigued; you are tired. For five, for ten days, I have awaited you."

And then the little old man said to him: "My grandson, how indeed do you feel as to your body?"

Then Quetzalcoatl said to him: "Much do I ail everywhere. No-

---

and customs, from those established by Quetzalcoatl and the Toltecs. In this context we can recall the fact that voluntarily they had received from the Culhuacans a prince of Toltecs lineage, Acamapichtli, who became their first supreme ruler.

7. It is remarkable that the names of the three wizards correspond to those of the tutelary deity of the Aztecs (Huitzilopochtli) and of Tezcatlipoca, the so much worshiped and feared "Smoking Mirror," here invoked as Titlacahuan, "He of Whom we are servants," and as Tlacahuepan, "The Strong Man."

where are my hands, my feet well. All tired is my body, as if undone."

And then the little old man said to him: "Here is the potion. It is very good, mellow, and it intoxicates one. If you shall drink of it, it will intoxicate you and it will refresh your body; and you will weep; you will be compassionate. You will think of your death. And also you will indeed think upon where you will go."

Then Quetzalcoatl said: "Where shall I go, old man?"

Then the little old man said to him: "You will just go there to Tollan-Tlapallan, "the metropolis of light and wisdom.[8] A man guards there, a man already aged. You will consult with one another. And when you will return here, you will once again have been made a child."

On this, Quetzalcoatl was stirred. And the little old man once again said to him: "Be of good cheer. Drink the potion. "

Then Quetzalcoatl said: "Old man, I will not drink it."

Then the little old man said to him: "Just drink of it. You will be in need. Just in truth, place it before you as your portion, your need. Taste just a little of it."

And Quetzalcoatl then tasted a little, and afterwards drank deeply of it.

Then said Quetzalcoatl: "What is this? It is very good. It has abated the sickness. Where went the pain? No longer am I sick."

Then the little old man said to him: "Drink of it once again; the potion is good. With it your body will gain strength."

And then once again he drank one vessel of it. Then be became drunk. Thereupon he wept; he was very sad. Thus, then, was Quetzalcoatl affected; his heart was then inflamed. No longer did he forget it. He only continued to reflect on that which he was reflecting. The wizard had indeed tricked him.

And the potion the little old man had given him, it is told, was

---

8. *Tollan* literally means "the place where reeds abound." Metaphorically it means an adequate place to settle because of the existence of water and its possibilities for agriculture and human life. With the passing of time it signified a large human settlement, a town, and finally, a metropolis. *Tlapallan* means "at the place of the red ink." This term, often paired with that of *Tlillan* ("at the place of the black ink"), signifies "writing and wisdom." In the present text *Tollan* and *Tlapallan*, appearing together, symbolize that place which Quetzalcoatl had to reach, "the metropolis of life and wisdom."

white *pulque*. And it is said that it was made of the sap of the yellow-leaved maguey.[9]

*   *   *

Here is told another portent the sorcerer Titlacauan brought about.

And here is still another thing that Titlacauan brought about in order to bode ill. He appeared in the form of, he represented a Huaxtec, an inhabitant of the hot and fertile lands to the east.[10] He just walked about with his virile member hanging; he sold green chilis. He went to sit in the marketplace at the palace entrance.[11]

And the daughter of Uemac, assistant to Quetzalcoatl,[12] was very fair. There were many Toltec lords who coveted her, who asked for her, who would marry her. But to none would Uemac give his consent; he gave her to none.

But this daughter of Uemac looked out into the marketplace. She saw the Huaxtec with virile member hanging.

And when she had seen him, then she went into the house. Thereupon she sickened. She became swollen, she became tumid. It was as if the Huaxtec's virile member tormented her.

And Uemac then learned that his daughter was already sick. He said to the women who guarded her: "What has she done? What is she doing? How began that which made my daughter tumid?"

Then the women who guarded her said to him: "It is he, the

---

9. *Pulque* is a word of uncertain origin. In Classical Nahuatl, the language in which the present text is written, the term *octli* is used. *Octli* is the fermented drink made, as is stated here, of the sap of the maguey, an agave also known as the "century plant."

10. The so-called *Huaxtecas*, "lands of the Huaxtecs," include parts of the modern Mexican states of Hidalgo, San Luis Potosí, Tamaulipas, and particularly some of the most fertile areas of Veracruz.

11. This account about the deeds of Tezcatlipoca, who had taken the form of a *Huaxtec*, deals really with the first within a series of portents that brought in all sort of disgraces to the Toltecs. The erotism that can be perceived in it has to be understood in terms of the antagonistic attitudes of the sage Quetzalcoatl and the gods who, much later, already in the days of the Aztecs, received a mystical-militaristic form of cult.

12. The personage mentioned here with the name of *Uemac*, according to some researchers, is no other than Quetzalcoatl himself. Nevertheless, there are various sources who describe him as an assistant to the sage and priest Quetzalcoatl, or as a dignitary in charge of the secular affairs of the Toltecs. See, for instance, Fray Juan de Torquemada, *Monarchia Indiana*, 3 v. (Madrid, 1723), t. II, p. 48. Our text agrees

Huaxtec, the seller of green chilis. He set her on fire; he tormented her. Thus it began; thus she already took sick."

And the lord Uemac thereupon commanded; he said: "O Toltecs, let the seller of green chilis, the Huaxtec, be sought out; he must appear."

Thereupon there was a search the world over. And when no one appeared, thereupon the town's crier, announced from Tzatzitepetl. He said: "O Toltecs, perhaps somewhere you see the seller of green chilis, the Huaxtec! Bring him here! The lord seeks him!"

Thereupon there was a search. They went everywhere. They went picking Tula to pieces as the search was made. And as they tired themselves out, as they saw no one, then they went to inform the ruler that nowhere had they seen him.

But later the Huaxtec showed himself of his own will in the same place where he had formerly come to sit, where he first showed himself.

And when he had been seen, then they went in haste to inform Uemac. They said to him: "The Huaxtec has appeared."

Then Uemac said. "Let him come quickly."

Then the Toltecs quickly went to seize the Huaxtec. They brought him before Uemac.

And when they had brought him, thereupon the lord said to him: "Where is your home?"

Then the other said to him: "I am a Huaxtec. I sell little chilis."

Then the ruler said to him: "Where had you gone, Huaxtec? Don your breech clout; cover yourself."

Then the other said to him: "But this is the way we are."

And the ruler then said to him: "You have tormented my daughter. You are the one who will heal her."

And then the Huaxtec said to him: "My noble old man, my nobleman, this may not be. Slay me, kill me, let me die. What are you telling me? Do I not just sell green chilis?"

But then the ruler said: "No. You shall heal her. Have no fear."

And thereupon they arranged his hair; they bathed him. When they had bathed him, thereupon they anointed him. They gave him a breech clout; they tied a cape on him.

---

with this last form of interpretation. We know, on the other hand, that, as in imitation of the dual nature of the supreme Deity, most often the Mesoamerican religious and political dignitaries existed by pairs.

And while they arrayed him, thereupon the lord said to him: "Look upon my daughter there where she is guarded."

And when he went there, he thereupon lay with her. Then the woman was well. Later he became the lord's son-in-law.

*   *   *

Here is told how the Toltecs were angered because of the marriage of the daughter of Uemac; and of still another portent that Titlacauan brought about.

And thereupon the Toltecs jested about Uemac; they jeered at him; they spoke maliciously of him. They said: "Well! The lord has taken the Huaxtec as son-in-law." Thereafter the lord summoned the Toltecs. He said to them: "I have heard that already jests are made of me, that already I am laughed at because I have made the Huaxtec my son-in-law. And this shall you do: by deceit abandon him while fighting at Zacatepec, at Coatepec."

And thereupon the Toltecs announced war. They all set out. Thereupon they went, that they might abandon the son-in-law.[13]

And when they had gone off to war, thereupon they entrenched the Huaxtec and all the dwarfs, the cripples.[14]

When they had entrenched them, thereupon the Toltecs went to capture men, to capture men from their foes, the Coatepecs.

And the Huaxtec said to all the dwarfs, the cripples: "Have no fear. Here we shall destroy them; here in our hands they will end."

And after this, thereupon their foes took after the Toltecs, who thought that here the foe would slay the Huaxtec whom thus they had gone abandoning deceitfully, they had gone leaving him to die.

And thereupon they came to inform Uemac. They said to him: "We have gone, abandoning the Huaxtec, who was your beloved son-in-law."

And Uemac rejoiced exceedingly as he thought it no doubt true,

---

13. I cannot resist seeing in this account a sort of parallel to the Biblical story of King David, who sent his captain Urias to the battlefield to liberate himself from his embarrassing presence.

14. We know from other Mesoamerican testimonies that often the native rulers had in their palaces some dwarfs and cripples who in various forms amused them. On the contrary, this is the only instance I know of in which dwarfs and cripples appear accompanying those sent to a battlefield.

no doubt so, because he was ashamed of the Huaxtec whom he had made his son-in-law.

But this Huaxtec, whom they had gone abandoning in battle, when their foes the Coatepecs, the Zacatepecs came up, thereupon commanded the dwarfs, the hunchbacks; he said to them: "Pay good heed! Be not terrified! Do not lose courage! Do not lose heart! Already I know all of you will take captives! In some manner we shall slay all of them!"

And when their foes came rising over them, when they came leaping over them, then verily they threw themselves upon them. They rose trampling over them. They slew them, they annihilated them, they destroyed them. Multitudes without number they slew of their foes.

And when Uemac heard of it, he was greatly bemused and saddened. Thereupon he summoned the Toltecs. He said to them: "Let us meet our beloved son-in-law."

And the Toltecs then broke out, burst forth. Thereupon they took the lord. They went scattered about him, they went circling about him to meet the Huaxtec. The Toltecs had their panoply with them, the quetzal-feather head devices and the turquoise mosaic shields. When they reached him, thereupon they gave them to him. They gave him the quetzal-feather head devices, the turquoise mosaic shields—all their array they had with them.

In this array he came dancing, he came dancing the captives' dance. He came showing disdain. He came vaunting himself. He came crouching. They came singing for him. The song came pouring out; the song came proclaiming. They came blowing flutes for him. The trumpets came blowing to superfluity; the shell trumpets came gurgling.

And when they went to reach the palace, then they pasted the Huaxtec's head with feathers and they anointed him with yellow ochre and they colored his face red. And all his friends were thus adorned.

And then Uemac said to his son-in-law: "Now are the hearts of the Toltecs satisfied that you are my son-in-law. Reach for the ground; rest your feet."

*   *   *

Here is related yet another portent the sorcerer brought about, by which the Toltecs died as they performed penances, as they danced.

A second portent this wizard brought about: When he had been pasted with yellow feathers, when he had overthrown his foes, he thereupon conceived that there should be dance and song, that they should intone a song.

Thereupon the herald made his cry, from the summit of Tzatzitepetl. He cried out to the people, he informed them the whole world over. Verily everywhere they heard the cry of the herald. And very swiftly there he was coming to Tula.

And when this was done, then the wizard went there to Texcalapan.[15] And every one of the commoners went with him. And when all the youths and maidens had gathered together, they could not be counted; they were very numerous.

Thereupon the wizard began to sing. There was the beating of the drum. He beat his drum. Thereupon there was dancing; they went as if leaping. There was the grasping of hands, there was the taking hold of each other from behind. There was much contentment as there was song. The song resounded with a crashing sound and remained proclaimed.

And the song that was chanted he only there had been inventing.

And when he intoned the song, right then they answered it. From his lips they took the song.

And when the singing and dancing began, it was dark. And when it ceased it was at the blowing of the flutes.

And when there was the dancing, as there was the greatest vibrancy of movements, as there was the greatest intensity of movement, very many threw themselves from the crags into the canyon. All there died. Then they were turned into rocks.

And as for the others at the craggy canyon, the wizard then broke the bridge. And the bridge was of stone. Indeed all fell there where they crossed the water. All were turned into rocks.

And how this was done, not then did the Toltecs understand. They were as if besotted.

And many times there was singing and dancing there at Texcalapan. And as many times as there was song and dance, so many times also there was death, there was falling from the crags.

When there was this falling, the Toltecs verily destroyed themselves.

---

15. *Texcalapan* means "at the stream surrounded by rocks." Later in this same text

Here is told of still another portent that same wizard brought about, whereby yet many more Toltecs died.

Behold yet another portent besides which the wizard brought about.

It is said that he took the form of a valiant warrior. He commanded the herald, the crier, that he should cry out to the people the world over that they come hither.

The herald said: "Let all men come! Let all the common folk come hither! You shall come to go to Xochitlan.[16] Gardens are to be planted; there is to be planting."

Thereupon came all the commoners. They came to Xochitlan. And as for naming it Xochitlan: They say it was the flower field of Quetzalcoatl.

And when there had been an assembling, when the Toltecs had assembled, when they had massed together, thereupon the valiant warrior slew people; he smote them repeatedly; he beat the backs of their heads repeatedly. In sooth, they were many, without number, who died at his hands, whom he slew.

And still others, who would only have fled, who would have run, who would have escaped his hands, who would have evaded his clutches when there was flight, when there was jostling, then died. And still others crowded on one another; they crushed one another. All died there.

* * *

Here is told of still another portent this same wizard brought about, by which very many more Toltecs perished.

Behold still another thing which the wizard did. He seated himself in the middle of the marketplace. He called himself Tlacauepan or Cuexcoch. There he caused to dance a figure like a child. They say it was the god Uitzilopochtli. In his hand he stood him as he made him dance.

And when the Toltecs saw this, thereupon there was a strong movement toward him; they pushed one another toward him in order to see it. Very many men were trampled there as they were crushed, as the crowd crushed them.

---

such a place, where another portent occurred, is described as "the craggy canyon."

16. *Xochitlan,* "the flowery place."

And when already many times it came to pass that many already died as they looked while he made the figure dance, this same wizard, as he shouted, said: "O Toltecs, what yet is this portent? Is it not a portent for us that he makes one dance? As for this one, let him die; let him be stoned!"

Then they stoned him. He fell under the stones. And when this was done, thereupon his body stank. Verily it terrified one as it stank; verily it wounded the head. And wheresoever the wind carried the stench, then the common folk died.

And when already many people had died of the stench, thereupon to the Toltecs this same wizard said: "let this corpse be cast away; let it be thrown out. For already its stench destroys. Let it be dragged away!"

And the Toltecs thereupon put a rope about it. Thereupon they pulled at it. But when already they heaved at it, they did not move it. Very heavy was it, this to which at first they had paid little heed, which they were disdaining.

Thereupon there was later shouting, and the herald said: "Let all men come! Bring here your heavy ropes that ye may go casting away the corpse!"

And when the Toltecs went to gather together, thereupon they fastened the corpse with many ropes. Thereupon the Toltecs raised a cry; they said to themselves: "O Toltecs! Along with it! Let it be pulled!"

But they did not in any way raise it; they could not move it. And when one of the ropes broke, then died all. As many as extended along the rope tumbled; they fell all mingled together; then they died.

And when they could in no way move it, when they could not face it, thereupon the wizard said to the Toltecs: "O Toltecs, he has need of his song."

Thereupon he intoned the song for the Toltecs. He intoned: "Drag away our beam, Tlacauepan, the wizard!"

And as he intoned, forthwith they moved the corpse; they came making it go forward; they proceeded shouting at it. When a rope again snapped, then on all of them the beam went as it ran over them, and many of them were indeed trampled. So were they crushed that they died.

And when all who were left had gone to cast away the corpse, Tlacauepan, thereupon they turned back. It was as if they paid no heed to all that had befallen them. No longer did they consider it an evil omen; they were as if besotted.

*   *   *

Here is told of still another portent which this same sorcerer brought about, by which he portended evil for Tula.

Behold how the wizard also portended evil for Tula.

It is said that a white plover, spent, went pierced by an arrow, went flying, went slowing down above the Toltecs not far from them as it went toward the earth, as it went slowing down. They could see it; upward they went looking toward it; they went looking upward at it.

Behold too yet another portent that became a portent for the Toltecs. It is said that a mountain called Zacatepetl burned. By night it was evident from afar how it burned. The flames rose high. When the Toltecs saw it, they became much agitated, troubled. There was general walking back and forth. There was a striking of their lips as they shouted; there was a shouting as they struck their lips. No longer was there living in peace; no longer was there being tranquil. And when they saw some portent, they said: "O Toltecs, this is all. For it is going, Toltec creations are perishing. We are forsaken. What shall we do? Whither shall we go? O unhappy we! Let us take heart!"

Behold yet another portent. It is said that stones rained upon the Toltecs. And when the stones rained, then from the heavens a large sacrificial stone fell; there at Chapoltepecuitlapilco[17] it came falling down. And afterwards a little old woman lived there. She sold paper flags. She walked about saying: "Here are your little flags." And those who wished to die said: "Buy me one." Thereupon one went where the sacrificial stone was. None asked: "What do you already do?" They were as if lost.

*   *   *

Here is told yet another portent this same sorcerer brought about, by which he mocked them, by which he ruined Tula, when he slew not a few Toltecs.

---

17. Chapoltecuitlapilco: "On the slopes of the mount of Chapultepec," that is, close to the foothills of the small mount located in what is at present Chapultepec Park in Mexico City.

Behold how evil was also portended for the Toltecs.

It is said that our sustenance became bitter. Very bitter, exceedingly bitter did it become. No longer was it placed in one's mouth. None at all of the Toltecs could eat our sustenance. In truth the Toltecs were mocked.

And a little old woman (they said it was thought that the wizard appeared as, took the form of, the little old woman) came to sit there at Xochitlan, "The Flowery place." There she toasted maize. And the hot maize, as she toasted it, spread its fragance the world over. Indeed it poured, it extended over the people the world over. Over the whole land extended the odor of the toasting maize.

And when they smelled the toasting maize, the Toltecs found the smell good; they found it agreeable, they found it good. And when they smelled it, quickly, swiftly they came here; in a very few moments they came here. It is said that the Toltecs thought no place distant; they thought nowhere remote. Though they lived far away, quickly, swiftly they arrived. Also quickly they returned whence they had departed.

And at that time, as many were gathered together, there she slew them all, she destroyed them completely. No more did they make their return, their turning back. Mocked indeed were the Toltecs as the wizard slew very many of them. It is said that in sooth he enjoyed the Toltecs.

*   *   *

This is the account about how Quetzalcoatl fled, took flight, when he went there to Tlapallan (The Place of Light and Wisdom), and of the many things he did on the way.

And still many more portents came upon the Toltecs until Tula was destroyed.

And when these were happening, Quetzalcoatl, who already was troubled, who already was saddened, was thereupon minded to go, to abandon his city of Tula.

Thereupon he made ready. It is said that he had everything burned, his house of gold, his house of seashells; and still other Toltec craft objects that were marvelous achievements, that were costly achievements, he buried, all; he hid all there in difficult places, perhaps inside a mountain or in a canyon.

And also the cacao trees he changed into mesquites. And all the precious birds, the resplendent trogons, the lovely cotingas, the roseate spoonbills, all of them he sent away beforehand.[18] They kept themselves before him; they went toward Anauac, the region close to the divine waters, the sea.

And when this was done, thereupon he departed; thereupon he followed the road.

Then he came to arrive elsewhere, at Quauhtitlan. A very thick tree stood there, and it was very tall. He stood by it. Thereupon he called forth for his mirror. Thereupon he looked at himself; he saw himself in the mirror; he said: "Already I am an old man." Then that place he named Ueuequauhtitlan, "The place of the old age's tree." Thereupon he stoned, he threw many stones at the tree. And as he threw the stones, the stones indeed went into it in various places, were stuck to the old tree in various places. Just the same has it continued to exist; thus is it seen. Beginning at the foot, the stones extend rising to its top.

And when Quetzalcoatl followed the road, they went blowing flutes for him.

Once again he came to rest elsewhere. Upon a stone he sat. He supported himself on it with his hands. Thereupon he looked toward Tula, and thereupon he wept. As one sobbing violently did he weep. Two hailstones fell as his tears; over his face did his tears spread; as they dripped, they indeed pierced holes in the stone.

*   *   *

Here are described the marks Quetzalcoatl left in place upon the stone with his hands when he rested himself there, when he sat there.

And as he supported himself on the rock by his hands, they sank deeply; as if in mud did the palms of his hands penetrate. Likewise his buttocks, as they were on the rock, likewise sank, submerged deeply. They are clearly visible, so deeply are they pierced in the rock. Hence the place was named Temacpalco, "The place where the human hands remained as if they were painted."

---

18. While we ignore how the splendor of the Classic Mesoamerican period came to an end, here, in the legendary story of Quetzalcoatl, we have a vivid representation of the destruction and abandonment of Tula, which in many respects was an heiress of the Classic metropolis of Teotihuacan.

And then he went off. When he came to reach a place named Tepanoayan, there was water. Water was coming forth; it was very wide, broad. Quetzalcoatl laid stones; he made a bridge. Then he crossed over it, and then he named it Tepanoayan, "The place of the bridge made of stone."

And once again he set forth. Then he went to arrive elsewhere, a place named Coaapan, "Where the Serpent's water is." And when he was there, wizards there would turn him back; they would send him back; they would stop him.

They said to him: "Where do you go? Where are you bound? Why already go you leaving the city? To whom do you go leaving it? Who will perform the penances?"

Then Quetzalcoatl said to the wizards: "In no way will it be possible to stop me. I shall only go on."

Then the wizards said to Quetzalcoatl: "Where are you going?"

Then Quetzalcoatl said to them: "I go there to Tlapallan; I go to learn."

And then they said to him: "What will you do there?"

Then Quetzalcoatl said: "I am called; the Sun called me."

Then they said to him: "It is well. Go, leaving all the works of craftsmanship, all the creations of the Toltecs."

Then he left there all the arts. The casting of gold, the craft of the lapidary, the carving of wood, sculpturing in stone, the art of the scribe, the art of feather working, they stripped all from him; they stole it all from him, they took it all away from him.

And when this was done, Quetzalcoatl thereupon scattered his jewels in the water; thereupon they swept away. Therefore he named the place Cozcaapan, "The place of the jewels in the water," which now is called Coaapan, "Where the Serpent's water is."

And thereupon he moved on. He went to arrive elsewhere, a place called Cochtocan, "Where one falls asleep." And there a wizard then came forth to meet him.

He said to him: "Where are you going?"

Then Quetzalcoatl said: "There to Tlapallan, I go to learn."

Then the wizard said to him: "It is well. Drink this, which I have taken hold of here.

Quetzalcoatl said: "In no way can it be that I drink it, even though it be a little that I taste."

Then once again the wizard said to him: "Neither can it be that you should not drink it, that you should not taste it. No one do I except, no one do I release, whom I do not give this drink, make drunk, make besotted. But come, be of good cheer! Drink it!"

Quetzalcoatl then drank it with a drinking tube.

And when he had drunk it, he quickly fell asleep in the road. He lay there rumbling as he slept, audible from afar as he snored. And when he awoke, thereupon he looked to one side and the other. He looked at himself. He arranged his hair. Then he named the place Cochtocan, "Where one falls asleep."

* * *

It is told here how Quetzalcoatl's vassals froze, died in the ice, as they passed between Iztactepetl and Popocatepetl, and of still others of his doings.

Then once again he set forth. As he went to climb between Popocatepetl and Iztactepetl, as he accompanied all the dwarfs, the hunchbacks, his servants, it snowed upon all of them. There they froze; they died of the cold.[19]

And Quetzalcoatl thereupon was affected; he wept to himself and he sang to himself. Much did he weep, did he sigh.

Thereupon he saw at a distance still another white mountain called Poyauhtecatl.[20] Once again he set forth. He passed by everywhere; he went forming villages everywhere. Thus, they say, he set down many things that were his signs, by which he is known.

Elsewhere, it is said, he took his pleasure on a mountain. He slid; to its foot he tottered.

And elsewhere he took maguey fibers from within the earth. Elsewhere he built a ball court all of stone. But in the middle, where the line was, it was cleft; it extended deep, so was it cleft. And elsewhere he shot as an arrow a silk cotton tree, such that he shot it likewise at another silk cotton tree; it penetrated into it. And elsewhere he built a house all underground at a place called Mictlan, "The Place of the Dead."

---

19. The *Popocatepetl* and *Iztac tepetl* (today called Iztaccihuatl), are two volcanic mountains marking the southern limits of the Valley of Mexico in its southern part. The first has an elevation of 17,888 ft. and the second of 16,960 ft. The rather abundant geographical references included in this text add to the vividness of the story of Quetzalcoatl.
20. *Poyauhtecatl*, the "Lord of the mist," is the Nahuatl name of the volcanic mountain known at present as "Peak of Orizaba" in the modern Mexican state of Veracruz. This is actually the highest altitude in the Mexican Republic: 18,701 ft.

And also still elsewhere he set in place a huge rock. It is said that one moved it with his little finger. It could move; from side to side it teetered. But it is said that when many pushed it, in no way could it move, even though many put themselves to it who wished to move it. They could not move it.

And still many other things he did everywhere in the towns. And it is said that he gave names to all the mountains. And everywhere he gave names here.

And when this was done, when he went to reach the sea coast, thereupon he made a raft of serpents. When he had arranged the raft, there he sat as if it were his boat. Thereupon he went off; he went swept off by the water. No one knows how he went to arrive there at Tlapallan, "The Place of Light and Wisdom."[21]

Here this account ends.[22]

---

21. According to other testimonies in Nahuatl, such as the *Annals of Cuauhtitlan*, Quetzalcoatl disappeared in a different form. These annals state that, once he reached the sea coast, he lighted a bonfire and threw thimself into it. The consequence of his voluntary sacrifice was that from his ashes his heart came forth and went up to the interior of the heaven. There it was transformed into the Morning Star.

22. *Florentine Codex*, book 3, chapters 3–14. This translation into English of the Story of Quetzalcoatl is the work of Arthur J. O. Anderson and Charles E. Dibble. I have introduced minor changes in it, keeping always an open eye on the original Nahuatl text, to facilitate the understanding of nonspecialists.

Another, Much Briefer, Account
About Quetzalcoatl, Our Prince

Year 1-Reed:
it is said, it is told,
in this year was born Quetzalcoatl,
he who was called Our Prince,
the priest 1-Reed, Quetzalcoatl.
It is said that his mother
was called Chimalman.
And thus it is told
how Quetzalcoatl was placed
in the womb of his mother:
she swallowed a precious stone. . . .
Years 2-Flint, 3-House,
4-Rabbit, 5-Reed,
6-Flint, 7-House,
8-Rabbit, 9-Reed.[23]
In 9-Reed, Quetzalcoatl asked about his father.
He was already nine years old,
he had reached the age of discernment.
He said:
"I would like to know my father,
to know his face."

They replied to him:
"He died; out there they buried him."
Forthwith Quetzalcoatl went
to dig in the earth;
he looked for the bones of his father. . . .

Year 2-Rabbit:
then arrived Quetzalcoatl
there in Tulancingo.
There he passed four years,

---

23. The *Annals of Cuauhtitlan* record in this form the passing of nine years, that is from 1-Reed to 9-Reed. In that last year Quetzalcoatl, still being a child, began to ask questions about his father.

he built his house of penance,
his house of green crossbeams.
Then he went out through Cuextlan,[24]
in that place he crossed a river;
for this he made a bridge.
They say that it still exists. . . .
In that year the Toltecs went to take
Quetzalcoatl,
that he should govern them
there in Tula
and also be their priest. . . .

And it is told, it is said,
that Quetzalcoatl invoked
Someone who was deified,
in the innermost of heaven:[25]
She of the starry skirt.
He who makes things shine;
Lady of our flesh, Lord of our flesh;
She who supports the earth,
He who covers it with cotton.
Toward that place he directed his plea,
thus it was known;
toward the Place of Duality,
above the nine levels of heaven.
And it was known that
he invoked the One who dwelt there,
made supplications,
living in meditation and retirement. . . .

They say that when Quetzalcoatl lived there,
often the wizards tried to trick him
into offering human sacrifices,

---

24. *Cuextlan*, the land of the Cuextecacs or Huaxtecas. In the previously transcribed text from the *Florentine Codex* other forms of relation of Quetzalcoatl to people from among the Huaxteca land were also mentioned.

25. Quetzalcoatl invokes the supreme deity as a being endowed with a dual countenance, Our Lord and Our Lady of the duality. In the form of a litany and by pairs, various titles of this supreme Dual God are also mentioned here, thus revealing the attributes Quetzalcoatl had discovered in him.

into sacrificing men.
But he never did, because he loved his people
who were the Toltecs. . . .
And they say, they relate,
that this angered the magicians
so that they began to scoff at him,
to make fun of him.
The magicians and wizards said
they wanted to torment him
so that finally he would go away,
as it really happened.
In the year 1-Reed, Quetzalcoatl died.
Truly they say
that he went to die there,
in the Land of the Black and Red Color.[26]

26. *Annals of Cuauhtitlan,* excerpts from pages 3–10 translated by M. Leon-Portilla. It is repeated here that Quetzalcoatl went to the "Land of the black and red colors," that is to the place where wisdom and knowledge exist. In this fragmentary text it is not clearly stated in which way he finally disappeared. As has been pointed out in note 21, another account also included in the *Annals of Cuauhtitlan* tells about a self-sacrifice by fire whose final consequence is Quetzalcoatl's transformation into the Morning Star.

Part Four

THE OFFICIAL DOGMA AND THE DOUBTS OF THE SAGES ABOUT THE AFTERLIFE

The Religious Doctrine

People here, the old men and the rulers, thus they thought about all who died: They went to one of three places when they died.[1]

The first place was there in the Place of the Dead, the one called *Mictlan.* And there, in the Place of the Dead, there dwelt, there were Mictlantecuhtli, Lord of the Place of the Dead, or Tzontemoc the One Who is descending, and Mictlancihuatl, Lady of the Place of the Dead, consort of Mictlantecuhtli.

And there to the Place of the Dead went all those who died on earth, who died only of sickness: the rulers, the commoners.[2]

And when one died—man, or woman, or child—and when they invoked him who had died, who died honored, they said to him as he still only was lying, as he still only was stretched out:[3]

"O my son, you have found your breath; you have suffered; Our Lord has been merciful to you. Truly our common abode is not here on earth. It is only for a little time, only for a moment that we have been warm.[4] Only through the grace of Our Lord have we come to know ourselves.

"But now Mictlantecutli has presented you, Acolnauacatl, Tzontemoc; as well as Mictecaciuatl. He has provided you a base; he has provided you a seat. For there is our common home, there is our common place of perishing; there, there is an enlarging of the earth where forever it has ended.

"You have arrived at the place of mystery, the place of the unfleshed, the place where there is arriving, the place with no smoke hole, the place with no fireplace.[5] No longer will you make your

---

1. This brief paragraph of introduction was most probably written by Fray Bernardino de Sahagun. He announces in it that the ancient Mesoamericans believed that in the beyond there were three possible different destinies. Nevertheless, it is important to add that what is to be presented in this text corresponds to the prevalent religious doctrine of the Aztecs. As we will see later, some of the sages had arrived at different conclusions in this matter.

2. To the Mesoamericans, one's destiny in the beyond is not the consequence either of being a noble or a commoner or of one's behavior during earthly life. The different causes of death are that which really determine one's destiny in the afterlife. On the other hand, the need for moral behavior is regarded in terms of what is "appropriate and righteous" for man and society on earth. See M. Leon-Portilla, *Aztec Thought and Culture,* pp. 152–154.

3. The following discourse constitutes another example of what we have called The Ancient Word.

4. Many are the Nahuatl testimonies in which the fugacity of life is a recurring theme. This is valid for texts in prose, such as the present, and also for poetical compositions of the sages.

5. These are the names that, not only here but also in other ancient Mesoameri-

way back, your return. No more will you bethink yourself of your life here, of your past. For some time you have gone leaving orphans, you have gone leaving people, your children, your grandchildren. No more will you bethink yourself how they will each perish. We shall go to reach you, we shall go to approach you after some time."

And here is that with which they entreated the mourner:

"O my son, grasp all; apply all your strength; force yourself; do not abandon the maize gruel, the half-tortilla. Strain yourself. Of what avail is it that we speak as we are accustomed? Does one therefore just feel ill will toward us? Does one therefore just mock us? Our Lord has willed it; He has spoken it: Here is his function, here is his time to die. How may you bring it about that he might borrow yet a little, yet a mere day, on earth?

"But well, then! Your heart, your body ache; they are in pain. Well, then! It is dark where he has gone, leaving things, where he awaited the word of Our Lord. Well, then! You must experience complete orphanhood!

"What can you do, you who are afflicted? O my son, apply all your strength! Do not once again hang your head as if in grief. Just now we have come to strengthen your heart, your body a little. Here have been devoted, have been satisfied motherhood, fatherhood.[6] Our Lord has destroyed it; your fathers, your mothers have gone, they who could pronounce, who could recount the weeping, the tearful words. Enough. Thus we, your mothers, we, your fathers, entreat you. Pay good heed!"

Then those skilled with paper, the old men who were experienced, ornamented them.[7] They kept on cutting, they kept on sundering, they kept on binding the paper. And when they had prepared the paper vestments, thereupon they arrayed the dead one; they sat him up; they poured water on his head.

They said to him: "Here is what you have come enjoying, what you have lived by on earth."

---

can testimonies, are given to the Land of the Dead. In essence, it is a place of mystery where, once someone has arrived in it, he has not any form of communication with the outside world.

6. Here, as in other texts, "motherhood, fatherhood" mean "the ancestors."

7. "They ornamented them," that is they prepared in the prescribed way the corpses, which were later to be burned. The description that follows is particularly rich in information related to this subject.

And then they placed a little water in a small vessel; they gave it to him. They said to him:

"Here is wherewith you will travel."[8]

They then put the bowl in with him. Thereupon they wrapped the dead one well, they wrapped him thoroughly, they bound him thoroughly, they bound him closely. Then they apportioned his paper vestments, and when they had apportioned them, then they gave him the assemblage; they laid them out before him. They said to him:[9]

"Here is wherewith you will pass where the mountains come together.

"And here is wherewith you will pass by the road which the serpent watches.

"And here is wherewith you will pass by the blue lizard, the *xochitonal*.[10]

"And here is wherewith you will travel the eight deserts.

"And here is wherewith you will cross the eight hills.

"Here is wherewith you will pass the place of the obsidian-bladed winds."

And in this place, the place of the obsidian-bladed winds, it was said that there was much suffering. By winds were all the obsidian blades and the stones swept along. And hence when men died, their kin burned with them all their baskets with insignia, their shields, their obsidian-bladed swords, and all the things they had wrested from their captives, and all their capes, and all that had been their various clothing.

Likewise, if it were a woman, all her baskets, her waist bands, her divided cords for holding up the textile, her skeins, her shuttles, her battens, her cane stalks, her combs, also all burned with her.

It was said that they would make themselves an enclosure with

---

8. Water, the precious element that makes life possible on earth, is also required to travel through the nine different levels, each one below the other, that lead finally to the Place of the Dead.

9. The following words are of the greatest interest in that they describe the places through which the dead person had to travel before reaching the abode of the Lord of the Dead.

10. *Xochitonal* literally means "the flowery destiny." It is difficult to give a satisfactory explanation of the relations existing between that blue lizard and such a destiny. It can at least be said that somehow, in terms of the astrological calendar of 260 days, such *tonalli*, destiny or divine attribute, determined the presence of that inhabitant on the road that led to the Place of the Dead.

these things; thus they would crouch protected from the obsidian-bladed winds; not much would they suffer. But he who had no wretched clothing, who went just as he was, endured much, suffered much as he passed the place of the obsidian-bladed winds.

And also they caused him to take with him a little dog, a yellow one; they fixed about its neck a loose cotton cord. It was said that it would take the dead one across the place of the nine rivers in the Place of the Dead.[11]

And when there was arrival with Mictlantecutli, the Lord of the Place of the Dead, he gave him the various things with which they had adorned the dead here on earth: the wooden figures, the pine incense; and the smoking tubes, and the loose cotton thread and the chili-red cotton thread they had bound up, or his capes, or his breech clouts. And a woman gave up her skirts, her shifts, and all her clothing she left as she departed, all of which they had bound up.

When it was the end of eighty days, then they burned all this. Also the like was done when it was the end of a year and when it was the end of two years and when it was the end of three years. But when it was the end of four years it was the last time they did it.

And this, it was said, all arrived with Mictlantecutli. And when the four years had ended, thereupon the dead one went to the nine places of the dead, where lay a broad river.

There dogs carried one across. It was said that whosoever went to pass looked over to a dog. And when it recognized its master, thereupon it threw itself into the water in order to carry its master across. Hence everybody here took care to breed dogs.

And it was said that a white dog and a black one, one that was black, it was said, could not carry one across to the Place of the Dead. It was said that the white one said: "I have just washed myself." And the one that was black said: "I have just stained myself black." Only the yellow one could carry one across.

And there in the nine places of the dead, in that place there was complete disappearance.[12]

---

11. The hairless dogs of the Aztecs, those named *itzcuintli*, were companions of man not only on earth but also in the afterlife. Such a belief explains perhaps the great love most Mesoamericans felt for their dogs.

12. When four years had passed since the death of a person, and when he or she had finally reached the abode of the Lord of the Dead, nothing more could be said about the one who had disappeared. It is not clear whether or not the statement about

And when it came to pass that the old men had ornamented the dead one, then they took him to the fire. And the little dog they first slew; thereupon the dead one and the dog burned.

Two sextons took great care of the dead one. And some of the sextons were gathered singing. And when the body of the dead one already was burning, they took great pains with it; they kept packing it down. And the body crackled and popped and smelled foul. And when it had come to pass that they burned it, thereupon they placed in a heap, they piled up, the embers. And they said: "Let him be bathed"; thereupon they bathed him, they threw water on him, they kept wetting him, they made a slush. When it cooled, once again they placed the charcoal in a heap. Thereupon they dug a round hole in which to place it: a pit. This they called a cave. Thereupon they put the charcoal in. There they covered the pit.

And likewise was it done with the noblemen as well as the commoners.

When they had burned the body, they sorted out, they gathered up all his bones. Into an earthen vessel, into a pot, they put them. Upon the bones they placed a green stone. They buried the pot in the home, in the *calpulli*, the quarter, of the dead one.

And where they buried them, they always made offerings to them.

And when the rulers and the noblemen died, they put green stones in their mouths. And if they were only commoners, they used only greenish stones or obsidian. It was said that they became their hearts.[13]

And they bedizened the rulers with many things, their paper adornment that they made was a noble paper streamer either four fathoms or three fathoms in length, of paper glued together. And upon it they hung various feathers, heron feathers, troupial feathers, dark yellow parrot feathers, scarlet macaw wing feathers, motmot feathers, hawk feathers, and still other feathers.

"a complete disappearance" has to be understood as a sort of annihilation. Our text, instead of providing any further commentary about this, returns to the subject of how they ornamented the corpses and how finally they burned them.

13. The noblemen put *chalchihuitl* stones, jades, in the mouths of their dead. The commoners made use of cheap substitutes described here as greenish stones or obsidians. Such stones symbolize the vital energy attached to the heart. Obviously the putting of the stones in the mouths of the dead implied the belief in a further existence, close perhaps to the abode of the Lord and Lady of the Dead who after all were nothing but manifestations of the supreme Dual God.

And some became the companions of the dead one, the beloved slaves, perchance a score of the men as well as so many of the women.[14] Thus they said: As they had taken care of their lord, they yet made chocolate for him, they yet prepared food for him. And the man who had served them as messengers just so would care for them in the Place of the Dead.

And when the ruler already burned, they thereupon slew the slaves; they only drove bird arrows in their throats. They did not burn with the ruler. Only apart they buried the slaves; quite alone the ruler burned.[15]

The second place they went to was there in Tlalocan, the paradise of Tlaloc, the God of Rain. And in Tlalocan there was great wealth, there were great riches. Never did one suffer. Never did the ears of green maize, the gourds, the squash blossoms, the heads of amaranth, the green chilis, the tomatoes, the green beans, the yellow flowers, fail.[16]

And there dwelt the tlaloques, assistants to the God of Rain, who were like the offering priests, those of the long, disordered hair; who were like the fire priests.

And there went those who had been struck by thunderbolts, and those who had been submerged in water, and those who had drowned, and those who suffered from the "divine sickness," and those afflicted by pustules, and those afflicted by hemorrhoids, and those afflicted by skin sores, and those afflicted by festering, and those afflicted by the gout, and those whom swellings overcame, those swollen by dropsy, who died of it.

These, when they died, did not burn; they only buried them.[17]

---

14. The practice of killing or sacrificing the slaves of the dead nobles and rich men, so that they could keep on being the servants of them in the afterlife, existed, as it is well known, in several other high cultures of the antiquity. In this respect what is stated in the present text, including the obligation to prepare a chocolate drink in the afterlife, has to be taken as the Mesoamerican version of a more general attitude related to the beliefs about the afterlife.

15. *Codex Florentine*, book 3, appendix, chapter 1. The translation of this text and of the following, dealing also with the official religious doctrines about the destinies of those who died, has been prepared by Arthur J. O. Anderson and Charles E. Dibble.

16. The Tlalocan, a place of abundance and happiness in the afterlife, the paradise of the God of Rain, was the object of pictorial representations in some of the ancient books and also in mural paintings. One example of this is offered by the fifth-century mural painting that is still preserved in a palace of Teotihuacan.

17. Only the corpses of those who had one of the above-mentioned forms of death

They applied liquid rubber to their faces, and they put fish amaranth paste on their cheeks; and they colored their foreheads blue, and they gave them each a paper lock of hair at the back of the head. Figurines of the gods who dwell in the mountains were placed before them. And they placed a paper cape over each one, and in their hands they put large wooden staves.

So they said that in Tlalocan there is always the putting forth of young shoots, there is always sprouting, it is always spring, it is continually springtime.

The third place to which they went was there to the home of the Sun, in heaven. Those went there who died in war, who perhaps right there indeed died in battle, in the warring place, where they despoiled them, where their breathing ceased, where they laid down their cares, or only were taken in, those who were to die later. Perchance one was slain in gladiatorial sacrifice, or cast into the fire, or pierced by darts or offered up on the barrel cactus, or shot by arrows, or encrusted and burned with pieces of resinous wood: all went to the home of the Sun.[18]

It was said that they lived together where there was a place like a vast open space. When the Sun appeared, when it came forth, then they made a din, they howled; shields were struck together. And he whose shield was pierced by arrows in perhaps two places or three places could there see the Sun, but he whose shield was nowhere pierced by arrows could not see the Sun; he could not look into its face. And where the war dead were, there were the magueys, the prickly plants, the mesquite groves. And all the offerings that the living offered them they could see; these could reach them.

And when they had passed four years there, then they changed into precious birds—hummingbirds, orioles, yellow birds, yellow

---

were buried in Pre-Columbian Mesoamerica. This explains the scarcity of burials within the geography related to this cultural context. For the most part the corpses were disposed of in the traditional form, which our text has already described in detail.

18. As has been mentioned in the Introduction to this book, besides those mentioned here as the privileged ones who, on account of their death in the battlefield, became companions of the Sun, women who died in childbirth also had a similar destiny. The reason was that they had also terminated their existence on earth with a prisoner in their wombs. These "divine women" accompanied the sun in its heavenly travel from the zenith to the sunset. This explains why the west is described in many religious texts as "the region of the women."

birds blackened about the eyes, chalky butterflies, feather-down butterflies; gourd-bowl butterflies; they sucked honey from the flowers there where they dwelt. And here upon earth they came to suck honey from all the various flowers. . . . [19]

---

19. *Florentine Codex*, book 3, appendix, chapter 2.

The Thought of the Sages[20]

Sorrowful Certainty of Death

Meditate upon it, O princes of Huexotzinco;
although it be jade, although it be gold,
it too must go to the place of the fleshless.
It too must go to the region of mystery;
we all perish, no one will remain!

We came only to be born.
Our home is beyond:
In the realm of the defleshed ones.
I suffer:
Happiness, good fortune never comes my way.
Have I come here to struggle in vain?
This is not the place to accomplish things.
Certainly nothing grows green here:
Misfortune opens its blossoms.[21]

It is true that we leave, truly we part.
We leave the flowers, the songs, and the earth.
It is true that we go; it is true that we part![22]

May your heart open!
May your heart draw near!
You bring me torment,
you bring me death.
I will have to go there
where I must perish.
Will you weep for me one last time?
Will you feel sad for me?

---

20. The compositions included in this section convey more personal feelings in relation to death and the possibility of an afterlife. All of them are part of the contents of the collections of poems and songs in Nahuatl already described in the Introduction. Their translation has been prepared by Miguel Leon-Portilla.

21. *Collection of Mexican Songs,* manuscript preserved in the National Library of Mexico, fol. 14 v. and 4 v.

22. *Ibid.*, fol. 61 v.

Really we are only friends,
I will have to go,
I will have to go.[23]

Let us consider things as lent to us, O friends;
only in passing are we here on earth;
tomorrow or the day after,
as Your heart desires, Giver of Life,
we shall go, my friends, to His home.

Meditate, remember the region of mystery;
beyond is His house; truly we all go
to where the fleshless are, all of us men;
our hearts shall go to know His face.
What are you meditating?
What are you remembering, O my friends?
Meditate no longer!
At our side the beautiful flowers bloom;
so does the Giver of Life concede pleasure to man.
All of us, if we meditate, if we remember,
become sad here.[24]

I shall have to leave the precious flowers;
I shall have to descend to the place where those,
     in one way or another, live.[25]

To the Region of Mystery

This song accompanies the march
To the region of mystery!
You are fêted,
You have spoken divine words,
But you have died . . . ![26]

---

23. *Ibid.*, fol. 26 r.
24. *Ibid.*, fol. 14 v.
25. *Ibid.*, fol. 62 r.
26. The deeds of a great warrior are here recalled. He had spoken divine words and accomplished extraordinary things but one has to accept that now he is dead.

MESOAMERICAN SPIRITUALITY

So when I remember Itzcoatl,[27]
Sadness invades my heart.
Is it that you were tired?
Or did laziness defeat the Lord of the house?
The Giver of Life resists no one. . . .
So the cortege continues:
It is the universal march![28]

Anguished Doubts[29]

Where do we go, oh! where do we go?
Are we dead beyond, or do we yet live?
Will there be existence again?
Will the joy of the Giver of Life be there again?[30]

Do flowers go to the region of the dead?
In the Beyond, are we dead or do we still live?
Where is the source of light, since that which gives life hides
    itself?[31]

Perchance, are we really true beyond?
Will we live where there is only sadness?
Is it true, perchance is it not true . . . ?
How many can truthfully say
that truth is or is not there?
Let our hearts not be troubled.[32]

Given over to sadness
we remain here on earth.

---

27. *Itzcoatl*, the well-known Aztec ruler, reigned from 1428 to 1440. For more information about him see the general Introduction to this book.
28. This poem is included in the already quoted *Collection of Mexican songs*, fol. 30 r.
29. In the already transcribed poems, the sages' expression is directly concerned with the sorrowful certainty of death. Now the examples I will present are testimonies of their anguished doubts about what we can expect to experience beyond our earthly reality.
30. *Collection of Mexican Songs*, National Library of Mexico, fol. 61 v.
31. *Ibid.*, fol. 61 r.
32. *Ibid.*, fol. 62 r.

Where is the road
that leads to the Region of the Dead,
the place of our downfall,
the country of the fleshless?

Is it true perhaps that one lives
there, where we all go?
Does your heart believe this?
He hides us
in a chest, in a coffer,
the Giver of Life,
He who shrouds people forever.

Will I be able to look upon,
able to see perhaps, the face
of my mother, of my father?
Will they loan me
a few songs, a few words?
I will have to go down there;
nothing do I expect.
They leave us,
given over to sadness.[33]

Where shall I go?
Where shall I go?
Which is the path to the God of Duality?

Perchance, is Your Home
in the place of the fleshless?
In the innermost of heaven?
Or is the place of the fleshless
only here on earth?[34]

Are we to live a second time?
Your heart knows it:
Only once have we come to live![35]

---

33. *Ibid.*, fol. 14 r.
34. *Ibid.*, fol. 14 v.
35. *Ibid.*, fol. 12 r.

Am I going to disappear,
Like the withered flowers?
How will my heart do it?
Nothing will remain of me?
At least poetry: flower and song![36]

Let Us Enjoy Ourselves Here and Now[37]

For only here on earth
shall the fragrant flowers last
and the songs that are our bliss.
Enjoy them now![38]

One day we must go,
one night we will descend into the region of mystery.
Here, we only come to know ourselves;
only in passing are we here on earth.
In peace and pleasure let us spend our lives; come, let us
    enjoy ourselves.[39]

Let us have friends here!
It is the time to know our faces.
Only with flowers
can our song enrapture.
We will have gone to His house,
but our word
shall live here on earth.
We will go, leaving behind
our grief, our song.
For this will be known,
the song shall remain real.
We will have gone to His house,

---

36. *Ibid.*, fol. 10 r.
37. The following compositions convey the feelings and ideas of some of the sages, those in particular who had adopted a sort of "Epicurean attitude" in their lives. If we have to disappear from the earth, and if we are ignorant about our destiny, "let us enjoy ourselves now, for as long we can. . . . "
38. *Collection of Mexican Songs*, fol. 61 v.
39. *Ibid.*, fol. 25 v.

but our word
shall live here on earth.[40]

I weep, I feel forlorn;
I remember that we must leave flowers and songs.
Let us enjoy ourselves now, let us sing now!
For we go, we disappear.[41]

Remove trouble from your hearts, O my friends.
As I know, so do others:
Only once do we live.
Let us in peace and pleasure spend our lives;
come, let us enjoy ourselves!
Let not those who live in anger join us,
the earth is so vast.
Oh! that one could live forever!
Oh! that one never had to die![42]

Beyond is the Place Where One Lives[43]

Truly earth is not the place of reality.
Indeed one must go elsewhere;
beyond, happiness exists.
Or is it that we come to earth in vain?
Certainly some other place is the abode of life.[44]

Beyond is the place where one lives.
I would be lying to myself were I to say,
"Perhaps everything ends on this earth;
here do our lives end."

---

40. *Romances de los Señores de Nueva España,* Library of the University of Texas, Austin, fol. 27 v.

41. *Collection of Mexican Songs,* fol. 35 r.

42. *Ibid.,* fol. 25 v. and 26 r.

43. Followers of a different trend of thought were the sages who, while being persuaded that "earth is not the place of reality," accepted the idea that "one must go elsewhere," to that place, in the beyond, where happiness really exists. Otherwise, they said, we would have to admit that man had come to live in vain.

44. *Collection of Mexican Songs,* fol. 1 v.

No, O Lord of the Close Vicinity,
it is beyond, with those who dwell in Your house,
that I will sing songs to You, in the innermost of heaven.
My heart rises;
I fix my eyes upon You,
next to You, beside You,
O Giver of Life![45]

Thus the dead were addressed,
when they died.
If it was a man, they spoke to him,
invoked him as a divine being,
in the name of pheasant;
if it was a woman, in the name of owl;
and they said to them:

"Awaken, already the sky is tinged with red,
already the dawn has come,
already the flame-colored pheasants are singing,
the fire-colored swallows,
already butterflies are on the wing."

For this reason the ancient ones said,
he who has died, he becomes a god.
They said: "He became a god there,"
which means that he died.[46]

---

45. *Ibid.*, fol. 2 r.
46. *Codex Matritensis*, fol. 195 r.

Part Five

ANONYMOUS RELIGIOUS POETRY AND OTHER RELATED TEXTS

The Sacred Hymns[1]

Song of Huitzilopochtli[2]

Huitzilopochtli, the young warrior,
he who acts above, moving along his way.

"Not in vain did I take the raiment of yellow plumage,
for it is I who made the Sun appear."[3]

Portentous one, who inhabits the region of clouds,
you have but one foot!
Inhabiter of the cold region of wings,
you have opened your hand!

Near the wall of the region that burns,
feathers come forth.
The Sun spreads out,
there is a war cry....

My god is called Protector of Men.
Oh, now he advances, comes well adorned with paper,
he who inhabits the region that burns,
in the dust, in the dust, he gyrates.

Our enemies are those of Amantla;[4]
come adhere to us!
War is made with combat,
come adhere to us!

---

1. Our presentation of the anonymous religious poetry in the Nahuatl language begins with the translation I have prepared of five of the old sacred hymns. Several archaisms that can be detected in the original text confirm that, in one way or another, the composition of these hymns took place several centuries before the Spanish arrival.

2. As has been shown in the Introduction to this book, Huitzilopochtli was the tutelary deity of the Aztecs. He was also, and above all, conceived as a god of war.

3. With the passing of time, and probably as a result of a process of religious syncretism, Huitzilopochtli became identified with the Sun.

4. *Amantla* is a place-name that corresponded to a mythical site and was also applied later to a place in the city of Mexico where a temple was built. In relation to the mythical site it can be said that in *Amantla* Huitzilopochtli had defeated some semidi-

Our enemies are those of Pipiltlan:[5]
come adhere to us!
War is made with combat,
come adhere to us!

Song of the warrior of Huitznahuac[6]

Oh, where the darts are kept
there is my captain.
Thus I hear
the man who taunts me.

I know I am the portentous,
I know I am a warrior.

When it is said,
"Where the darts are kept
there is my captain,"
they are taunting my lineage.

The warrior, the one of Tocuillan,[7]
has ornamented his eagle cape with thorns.

Oh, among the young people of Oholman
my captive is dressed in feathers.
I am feared, I am feared,
my captive is dressed in feathers.

---

vine beings who had attacked him immediately after his portentous birth. In this same part an epic poem is included in which, with an abundance of details, the birth of Huitzilopochtli is recalled.

5. *Pipiltlan:* "the place of the nobles." This is another place-name with a mythical connotation and a further application to a sacred site in the city of Mexico. See note 4.

6. "The warrior of Huitznahuac," that is, of "the place of the thorns" (the south), is no other than the same tutelary deity of the Aztecs, Huitzilopochtli. Here again his portentous birth and his early victories are recalled.

7. *Toucillan,* and the other place-names mentioned in this poem (Oholman, Huitznahuac, and Tzicotlan), have mythical connotations and, at least in one case—that of Tzicotlan—correspond to some of the buildings erected close to the great temple of Huitzilopochtli in the heart of Mexico City.

Oh, among the young people of Huitznahuac,
my captive is dressed in feathers.
I am feared, I am feared,
my captive is dressed in feathers.

Oh, among the young people of Tzicotlan
my captive is dressed in feathers.
I am feared, I am feared,
my captive is dressed in feathers.

The god enters in Huitznahuac,
the portentous sign has descended,
now he is born,
the day has dawned,
the day has dawned.

The god enters in Tocuillan,
the portentous sign has descended,
now he is born,
the day has dawned,
the day has dawned.

Song of Tlaloc, God of Rain[8]

Choir:
In Mexico we beg a loan from the god.[9]
There are the banners of paper
and at the four corners
men are standing.

[*The verse is repeated, probably by the people, and then the priest himself addresses the divinity, imploring rain. The priest of Tlaloc mentions the victims to be offered in the festival. They are small children*

---

8. In this hymn, addressed to the God of Rain, a dialogue is easily perceivable. The participants in it are a priest of Tlaloc and two choirs, one who speaks for the people, and another who speaks for the God of Rain. This hymn was probably intoned in some of the public celebrations related to the cult of this god.

9. Rain is precisely the loan that is being begged from the god.

MESOAMERICAN SPIRITUALITY

whose weeping, when they are sacrificed, will be an omen of heavy rain. These children, whose crying is awaited, are symbolically referred to as bundles of blood-stained ears of corn.]

Priest of Tlaloc:
Now it is time for you to weep![10]
Alas, I was created
and for my god
festal bundles of blood-stained ears of corn
I carry now
to the divine hearth.

You are my Chief, Prince and Magician,
and though in truth
it is you who produce our sustenance,
although you are the first,
we cause you only shame.

[*Again the choir of students or perhaps another group of priests replies in the name of Tlaloc. The god exhorts the people and the priesthood to venerate him and recognize his power:*]

Tlaloc:
If anyone
has caused me shame,
it is because he did not know me well;
you are my fathers, my priesthood,
Serpents and Tigers.

[*Then the priest of the Rain God begins to chant another song, mentioning the mansion of Tlalocan and asking the god to spread out over all parts to make the beneficent rain fall.*]

Priest of Tlaloc:
In Tlalocan, in the turquoise vessel,[11]

---

10. The priest of Tlaloc addresses himself to the children whose weeping will anticipate the divine gift of water. Later he will speak with the God of Rain, invoking him as a prince.

11. See the description of the Tlalocan in the text included in part 4 of this book.

it is wont to come forth, but now is not seen
Acatonal.[12]
Spread out in Poyauhtlan,
in the region of mist!
With timbrels of mist
our word is carried to Tlalocan. . . .

[*The choir, now speaking in the name of the victim, the little girl dressed in blue who will be sacrificed to the Rain God, chants several verses of deep religious significance. The victim will go away forever. She will be sent to the Place of Mystery. Now is the time for her crying. But perhaps in four year's time there will be a transformation, a rebirth, there in the region-of-the-fleshless. He who propagates men may send once more to this earth some of the children who were sacrificed. In veiled form this hints at a kind of reincarnation, which is very seldom mentioned in the ancient texts. Now the choir speaks once more for the child:*]

Choir [speaking in the name of the victim]:
I will go away forever,
it is time for crying.
Send me to the Place of Mystery,
under your command.
I have already told
the Price of the Sad Omen,
I will go away forever,
it is time for crying.
In four years
comes the arising among us,
many people
without knowing it;
in the place of the fleshless,
the house of quetzal feathers,
is the transformation.
It is the act of the Propagator of Men.[13]

---

12. This is a calendric name that means "the one born in a day *acatl*, that is, reed." It can also be understood probably as "the one whose destiny is related to the sustenance of man," represented here by the reed of corn. In any way this name belongs either to Tlaloc himself or one of his attendants, the *Tlaloque*.

13. In these lines there is a vague allusion to a sort of "arising" in the beyond.

[*The priest of Tlaloc repeats the invocation to the God of Rain. He begs him once more to be present in all parts, to make fertile the land sown with seed, to spread out and make the rain fall.*]

Priest of Tlaloc:
Go to all parts,
spread out
in Poyauhtlan,[14]
in the region of mist.
With timbrels of mist
our word is carried to Tlalocan.

Song of the Mother of the Gods[15]

Yellow flowers opened their corollas,
she is Our Mother,
She, the one with the thigh
painted on her face.[16]
She has left Tamoanchan,
the Place-of-our-origin.

Yellow flowers are your flowers,
She is Our Mother,
She the one with the thigh
painted on her face.

Four years had passed, and in the place of the fleshless a transformation occurs. See in this context the text included in part 4 of this book about what happened to those existing in the Place of the Dead once four years had elapsed after their disappearance from earth.

14. *Poyauhtlan*, "the region of mist," is a place-name that can be related to the *Poyautecatl*, the name of the highest mountain in the Mexican territory. In this hymn it is probably mentioned as one place essentially related to the God of Rain. It is important to remember here that Tlaloc and his attendants, the Tlaloque, were thought of as the deities residing and exercising their favorable influence in the mountains," "where the clouds are formed."

15. The Mother goddess was revered and invoked with different names. In this hymn he receives the title of *Teteu Innan*, which literally means "the Mother of the gods."

16. Facial painting, which occurs in a great variety of forms, is one of the basic elements that characterize the different divine beings. The Mother of the gods is mentioned here as "the one with the thigh painted on her face." I confess that I have not been able to identify the symbolism attached to this particular form of painting.

She has left Tamoanchan,
the Place-of-our-origin.

White flowers opened their corollas,
She is Our Mother,
She, the one with the thigh
painted on her face.
She has left Tamoanchan,
the Place-of-our-origin.

White flowers are your flowers,
She is Our Mother,
She, the one with the thigh
painted on her face.
She has left Tamoanchan,
the Place-of-our-origin.

She sits upon the melon cactus,
Our Mother, Itzpapalotl,[17]
O let us see her
in the nine plains,
she feeds herself
with deers' hearts,
Our Mother, Lady of the earth!

With new chalk, with new feathers
she is painted, she is covered.
In the four directions of the world
darts are broken.

You have turned to deer
in the land of the vast plains,

---

17. *Itzpapalotl*, "Flint-butterfly," or "the butterfly black as flint," is another advocation of the Mother goddess. To call her with such a name implies a recalling of her deeds in the vast plains of the north when she accompanied the Aztecs in their pilgrimage to Central Mexico. In the last line of this hymn two personages are mentioned, Xiuhnel and Mimich, who in other sources appear in association with Itzpapalotl. They are described as two deers, inhabiting the land of the vast plains. See in this respect *Codex Chimalpopoca*, translated into Spanish and edited by Primo F. Velazquez, 2nd edition (Mexico: National University Press, 1975), pp. 5–7.

they come to see you,
Xiuhnel and Mimich!

Song of Ixcozauhqui, God of Fire[18]

In Tzonimolco, my fathers,[19]
may you not be ashamed.
In Tetemocan, my fathers,
may you not be ashamed,
Oh, in Macatlan, my lords,
the drums of Chicueyocan are resounding.
House of magicians, the magician descends.

In Tzonimolco there is singing; we have begun.
In Tzonimolco there is singing; we have begun.
Behold, it is time to go out with masks.
Behold, it is time to go out with masks.
In Tzonimolco . . . a man
is about to be offered!

Oh, the Sun has come out; oh, the Sun has come out,
that a man may be offered to him!
In Tzonimolco the song of the servants
resounds again and again:
"With deeds the princes enrich themselves,
make themselves worthy of glory."
Oh Little Mother, call together the people;
you who inhabit the House of Mist, the House of Rains;
call together the people.

Song of Chicomecoatl, Our Mother Goddess[20]

Oh Seven Cobs of Corn . . . arise now,
awaken. . . . You are Our Mother!

18. *Ixcozauhqui* literally means "the one of the yellow face." As it is clearly stated in this hymn, this was one of the names of *Xiuhtecuhtli*, the god of fire, often identified with *Huehueteotl*, "the old god."
19. *Tzonimolco* is the name of the temple of the God of Fire, close to that of *Huitzilopochtli* in Mexico City.
20. *Chicomecoatl* is one of the calendar names of the Mother goddess. It literally

You would leave us orphans;
go now to your house, Tlalocan.

Oh Seven Cobs of Corn . . . arise now,
awaken. . . . You are Our Mother!
You would leave us orphans;
go now to your house, Tlalocan.[21]

---

means "Seven-serpent." The Mother goddess, invoked here as "Seven cobs of corn," appears closely related to the God of Rain. It is said of her that her house is also in the Tlalocan, paradise of Tlaloc.

21. The text in Nahuatl of these sacred hymns is included in the *Codex Matritensis*, preserved in the Library of the Royal Spanish Academy of History. The translation is due to M. León-Portilla.

The Ideal Image
of the Nahuatl Sage[22]

The wise man: a light, a torch, a stout torch that does not smoke.

A perforated mirror, a mirror pierced on both sides.[23]

His are the black and red ink, his are the illustrated manuscripts, he studies the illustrated manuscripts.

He himself is writing and wisdom.

He is the path, the true way for others.

He directs people and things; he is a guide in human affairs.

The wise man is careful (like a physician) and preserves tradition.

His is the handed-down wisdom; he teaches it; he follows the path of truth.

Teacher of the truth, he never ceases to admonish.

He makes wise the countenances of others; to them he gives a face [a personality]; he leads them to develop it.

He opens their ears; he enlightens them.

He is the teacher of guides; he shows them their path.

One depends upon him.

He puts a mirror before others; he makes them prudent, cautious; he causes a face [a personality] to appear in them.

He attends to things; he regulates their path, he arranges and commands.

He applies his light to the world.

He knows what is above us [and] in the region of the dead.

He is a serious man.

Everyone is comforted by him, corrected, taught.

Thanks to him people humanize their will and receive a strict education.

He comforts the heart, he comforts the people, he helps, gives remedies, heals everyone.[24]

---

22. *Tlamatini*, "the one who knows something," is the Nahuatl equivalent of the "sage" in Western culture.

23. The meaning of this sentence is an allusion to a kind of scepter with a pierced mirror at its upper end. This object was part of the equipment of various gods and it was used by them to scrutinize the earth and human affairs. Applied to the sage, it conveys the idea that he himself is a living medium of contemplation.

24. *Codex Matritensis*, fol. 118 r.–v.

About the Supreme Dual God[25]

And the Toltecs knew
that many are the heavens.
They said there are twelve superimposed divisions.
There dwells the true god and his consort.
The celestial god is called the Lord of Duality.
And his consort is called the Lady of Duality, the celestial
    Lady;
which means
he is king, he is Lord, above the twelve heavens.[26]

In the place of sovereignty, in the place of sovereignty, we
    rule;[27]
my supreme Lord so commands.
Mirror which illumines things.[28]
Now they will join us, now they are prepared.
Drink, drink!
The God of Duality is at work,
Creator of men,
mirror which illumines things.[29]

Mother of the gods, father of the gods, the old god[30]
spread out on the navel of the earth,

---

25. The following compositions have in common that they are directly related to Ometeotl, the supreme Dual God. Some of them include specific references to the Toltec period. It can be asserted that probably the belief in such a deity went back at least to that golden age. There are also various expressions in these poems indicating relations and even a sort of identity between the supreme Dual God and other divine beings worshiped in ancient Mexico. An example of this is offered by the text in which the Dual God is also invoked as "the old god," Huehueteotl, which, as we have seen, was also a title of the God of Fire. In other instances the Dual God appears also identified with Quetzalcoatl.

26. *Codex Matritensis*, fol. 175 v.

27. This is a poem that, it is said, was composed some time after the fall of the metropolis of Tula. See in this context the Introduction to the present book.

28. Here the supreme Dual God is related to Tezcatlipoca, the "Smoking Mirror." *Tezcatlipoca* appears here as *Tezcatlanextia*, the "Mirror that illuminates things." Tezcatlipoca and Tezcatlanextia are two aspects of the Dual God, conceived here as Lord of day and night.

29. *Historia Tolteca-Chichimeca*, fol. 33.

30. Here the Dual God is identified with Huehueteotl, "the old god." In a poeti-

within the circle of turquoise.
He who dwells in the waters the color of the bluebird, he
   who dwells in the clouds.
The old god, he who inhabits the shadows of the land of the
   dead,
the lord of fire and of time.[31]

It was said that in the twelfth heaven
our fates were determined.
When the child is conceived,
when he is placed in the womb,
his fate comes to him there;
it is sent to him by the Lord of Duality.[32]

And it is told, it is said[33]
that Quetzalcoatl would invoke, deifying something in the
   innermost of heaven:
she of the starry skirt, he whose radiance envelops things;
Lady of our flesh, Lord of our flesh;
she who is clothed in black, he who is clothed in red;
she who endows the earth with solidity, he who covers the
   earth with cotton.
And thus it was known, that toward the heavens was his plea
   directed,
toward the place of duality, above the nine levels of heaven.[34]

Lord, our master:
she of the jade skirt,
he who shines like a sun of jade.
A male has been born,
sent here by our mother, our father,
Lord of Duality, Lady of Duality,

---

cal form his omnipresence is described by saying that he is on the navel of the earth,
that he dwells in the heavens and in the inferior levels of the Land of the Dead.

31. *Florentine Codex*, book 6, chapter 17.
32. *Ibid.*
33. This text is a part of the one we have included at the end of part 3 of the present book. See in relation to it note 25, part 3. I have transcribed it once again here because of its meaning in relation to the prevalent ideas about the Dual God.
34. *Annals of Cuauhtitlan*, fol. 4.

he who dwells in the nine heavens,
he who dwells in the place of duality.[35]

You live in heaven;
you uphold the mountain,
Anahuac is in your hands.
Awaited, you are always everywhere;
you are invoked, you are prayed to.
Your glory, your fame is sought.
You live in heaven;
Anahuac is in your hands.[36]

Our Master, the Lord of the Close Vicinity,[37]
thinks and does what He wishes; He determines, He amuses
    himself.
As He wishes, so will it be.
In the palm of His hand He has us; at His will He shifts us
    around.
We shift around, like marbles we roll; He rolls us around
    endlessly.
We are but toys to Him; He laughs at us.[38]

Rise, array yourself, stand on your feet,
partake of the pleasure of the beautiful place,
the home of your mother, your father, the Sun.
Good fortune, pleasure and happiness are there.
Go forth, follow your mother, your father, the Sun.[39]

---

35. *Florentine Codex*, book 6, chapter 22.
36. *Collection of Mexican Songs*, fol. 21 v.
37. The Lord of the Close Vicinity is Tloque Nahuaque, an expression to invoke
the supreme God, which we have also translated as "Lord of the Near and Close." He
is the one who determines the existence of men on the earth. Implicitly an affirma-
tion is made in this text about the philosophical question of what is the possible free-
dom of men vis-à-vis the inscrutable designs of God.
38. *Florentine Codex*, book 6, chapter 17.
39. *Ibid.*

Icnocuicatl,
Songs of Reflection[40]

Where is your heart?[41]
If you give your heart to each and every thing,
you lead it nowhere: you destroy your heart.
Can anything be found on earth?[42]

Who am I?[43]
As a bird I fly about,
I sing of flowers;
I compose songs,
butterflies of song.
Let them burst forth from my soul!
Let my heart be delighted with them![44]

Our priests, I ask of you:[45]
From whence come the flowers that enrapture man?
The songs that intoxicate, the lovely songs?

Only from His home do they come, from the innermost part
    of heaven,
  only from there comes the myriad of flowers. . . .

---

40. In these *icnocuicatl*, "sorrowful songs," or, perhaps better, "songs of reflection," the Nahuatl sages often expressed their doubts and concerns. Among other things they asked themselves about the possibility of finding satisfaction in earthly things, or about a way or path that will lead to where songs and flowers forever exist. Here some of these poems, which reveal another aspect of Mesoamerican spirituality, will be transcribed.

41. In Nahuatl the term *yollotl* (the heart) is derived from the same root as *ollin* (movement). The heart is the dynamic element inherent in the human being. That is why, according to the Mesoamerican sages, "to have a face and to have a heart" (*ixe, yolle*) was the essential attribute of a person.

42.. *Collection of Mexican Songs*, fol. 2 v.

43. The sage who composed this brief poem looks for an answer to the old question about the ultimate meaning of his own self. With a metaphorical expression he speaks of "the butterflies of song" born in himself.

44. *Collection of Mexican Songs*, fol. 11 v.

45. Here the sage appears asking the priests about the origin of flowers and songs, the universe of poetry and art. The native Mesoamericans tried indeed several paths in their search for true words on earth.

Where the nectar of the flowers is found
the fragrant beauty of the flower is refined. . . .
They interlace, they interweave;
among them sings, among them warbles the quetzal bird.

The flowers sprout, they are fresh, they grow;
they open their blossoms,
and from within emerge the flowers of song;
among men You scatter them, You send them.
You are the singer![46]

My fine master, I have come; I am here to laugh.[47]
I'm a rascal. My singing is a flower;
it gets mixed up, then it gets untangled.
Oh, I'm a master in the house.

Now let us begin. Already there has come
the sweet-smelling flower; may it please you.
It is going to rain flowers;
may they please you!

I am scattering many different flowers.
I come to offer songs, intoxicating flowers.
Oh, I'm a rascal, who comes from there,
where the water flows.
I come to offer songs, intoxicating flowers.

I who come am the Deer-Two-Rabbit,
the Rabbit bleeds,
the Deer with big horns. . . .
My fine master, my friends, we open
his book of flowers, his book of songs.
Whose?
His.

---

46. *Collection of Mexican Songs*, fol. 34 r.
47. In a different tone the poet who composed this song shows himself here as a "rascal," and, as an actor, disguises himself in various forms. But penetrating reflection accompanies his jokes. He confesses that he is in reality a beggar of wisdom. That is why he describes himself as a "stealer of songs," true words to overcome his misery.

Erect is the Flowery Tree,
it has many branches,
it has grown large; now it is scattering flowers.
We have come to listen at your threshold,
on the branches you are walking, Precious Pheasant.
You are singing. . . .

I'm a rascal.
I am the thrush with a red breast,
now I shrill my song: jojojojon.

I come to make paintings
where the courtyard spreads out;
I am the thrush with a red breast;
shrill, shrill, my song: jojojojon.

I wink my eyes,
as I go laughing;
from within the court I come,
into a flower I am changing myself,
I am the Rabbit who suffers. . . .

I am the chattering Parrot,
I go to catch it, I throw it. . . .
Now I begin, now I can sing.
From there I come, from the interior of Tula;
now can I sing; my voice bursts forth,
the flower has opened.
Listen to my song:
"Stealer of songs, oh my heart,
where can you find them?
You are in need. But like a painting
grasp firmly the black and red ink,
then perhaps you will no longer be a beggar."[48]

---

48. *Collection of Mexican Songs*, fol., 67 r.

About the Ancient Toltecs[49]

A Skillful People

The Toltecs were a skillful people;
all of their works were good, all were exact,
all well made and admirable.

Their houses were beautiful, with turquoise mosaics,
the walls finished with plaster,
clean and marvelous houses, which is to say
Toltec houses, beautifully made,
beautiful in everything. . . .

Painters, sculptors, carvers of precious stones,
feather artists, potters, spinners, weavers,
skillful in all they made, they discovered
the precious green stones, the turquoise;
they knew the turquoise and its mines, they found
its mines and they found the mountains hiding
silver and gold, copper and tin,
and the metal of the moon.

The Toltecs were truly wise;
they conversed with their own hearts. . . .
They played their drums and rattles;
they were singers, they composed songs
and sang them among the people;
they guarded the songs in their memories,
they deified them in their hearts.[50]

---

49. These compositions are a sort of complement to the Story of Quetzalcoatl. They describe for us some of the spiritual creations of the Toltecs, that extraordinary people.

50. *Codex Matritensis*, fol. 172 v. The translation of this and the following texts is due to M. León-Portilla.

The Artist[51]

The artist: disciple, abundant, multiple, restless.
The true artist, capable, practicing, skillful,
maintains dialogue with his heart, meets things with his mind.

The true artist draws out all from his heart;
works with delight; makes things with calm, with sagacity;
works like a true Toltec; composes his objects; works
    dexterously; invents;
arranges materials; adorns them; makes them adjust.

The carrion artist works at random; sneers at the people;
makes things opaque; brushes across the surface of the face of
    things;
works without care; defrauds people; is a thief.[52]

Love of Truth

These Toltecs were very religious men,
great lovers of the truth;
they were not liars.
Their speech was sincere.
They said:
—God, older brother.
—God, younger brother.
They said:
—It is true, it is thus,
Because this is the truth; yes, no.

Toltec Calendar

These Toltecs were very wise;
it was their custom to converse with their own hearts.

51. The word *Toltecatl* was often used with the connotation of "artist" by Nahuatl-speaking peoples such as the Aztecs. Here an ideal image of the Toltecatl-artist
is given.
52. *Codex Matritensis*, fol. 115 v.

They began
the year count,
the counting of days and destinies.
They learned the omens given by the day and the night,
which signs of the day were good, propitious,
and which were not,
calling those the terrible signs.
They created a whole system,
The Book of Dreams.

Astronomical Knowledge

And so were they wise;
they were experienced in the knowledge of the stars
that are in the skies.
They gave each its name.
They understood their influence;
they knew how the sky moves,
how it turns;
this they saw in the stars.[53]

53. *Codex Matritensis,* fol. 175 r.

About the Arts Inspired
in the Toltec Legacy

Amantécatl: the feather artist.
He is whole; he has a face and a heart.[54]

The good feather artist is skillful,
is master of himself; it is his duty
to humanize the desires of the people.[55]
He works with feathers,
chooses them and arranges them,
paints them with different colors,
joins them together.

The bad feather artist is careless;
he ignores the look of things,
he is greedy, he scorns other people.
He is like a turkey with a shrouded heart,
sluggish, coarse, weak.
The things that he makes are not good.
He ruins everything that he touches.[56]

He who gives life to clay:[57]
his eye is keen, he molds
and kneads the clay.

The good potter:
he takes great pains with his work;
he teaches the clay to lie;[58]

---

54. "Face and heart" is an expression often repeated in the Nahuatl texts. The face appears linked to the internal physiognomy of man, and the beating of the heart symbolizes the source of dynamism in the human being. To be in possession of a face and a heart is presented here as a sine qua non condition for becoming an artist.

55. If the good artist is master of himself and possesses a face and a heart, he will be able to achieve what is the end of the art-creations: "to humanize the desires of the people," that is, to help others to understand things human and divine, and to behave in a truly human way.

56. *Codex Matritensis,* fol. 116 r.

57. "He who gives life to clay," the potter or ceramist.

58. "He who teaches clay to lie," that is, he who makes clay to take countless

he converses with his heart;
he makes things live, he creates them;
he knows all, as though he were a Toltec;
he trains his hands to be skillful.

The bad potter:
careless and weak,
crippled in his art.[59]

The good painter is a Toltec, an artist;
he creates with red and black ink,
with black water. . . .

The good painter is wise,
God is in his heart.
He puts divinity into things;
he converses with his own heart.[60]

He knows the colors, he applies them and shades them;
he draws feet and faces,
he puts in the shadows, he achieves perfection.
He paints the colors of all the flowers,
as if he were a Toltec.[61]

Toltec Crafts[62]

They were stonemasons, stonecutters,
artists with feathers,

---

shapes. To achieve this the potter has to converse with his own heart, to become as skillful as if he were a Toltec.

59. *Codex Matritensis*, fol. 124 r.

60. The painters had a very important role in Mesoamerican culture. They painted the sacred books and also the great murals in the temples and other monuments. They were masters of the symbolism that had to be expressed with the red and black inks. They had to learn how to converse with their own hearts. In this way they would become a *Yolteotl*, "one with God in his heart." They would then attempt to transfer the symbols of the divine into their paintings, in the books and murals: "He puts divinity into things."

61. *Codex Matritensis*, fol. 117 v.

62. A study on the nature of Mesoamerican art can be based on texts such as this and those transcribed above. Here a brief description of various creative professions is given.

fastening them together,
potters, spinners, weavers.

They were very experienced in these things,
they discovered, they knew
the green stones and the turquoises,
they knew the mines of turquoise,
they discovered the cave and the mountain of silver,
of gold and of copper,
of tin, of the moon metal,
of the stone of the moon,
they were experienced in it,
they searched for the cave of amber,
of crystal and of amethysts.
They set great value on pearls,
those of many colors.
Thanks to their knowledge
there are now necklaces and bracelets.

Of some of these precious things
some are forgotten, others were destroyed. . . .
Many were the houses in Tula,
there the Toltecs buried many things.
But there is not only this,
as a reminder of the Toltecs,
also their pyramids, their mounds,
where it is called Tula Xicocotitlan.
Everywhere can be seen,
everywhere are to be discovered remains of pottery vessels,
of their bowls, of their figures,
of their dolls, of their figurines,
of their bracelets.
Everywhere there are vestiges,
truly the Toltecs were living there together.

The Toltecs were experienced people,
it is said they were artists of feathers,
of the art of fastening them together.
From ancient times they guarded it,
it was truly their invention,

the art of feather-mosaics.
From ancient times they were entrusted
with the shields, the insignias,
those which were called *apanecayotl.*
This was their heritage,
thanks to which the insignias were granted.
They made them beautifully,
they fastened the feathers.
The artists knew how to place them,
truly they put their deified heart into them.[63]
What they made was marvelous, precious,
worthy of admiration.[64]

Goldsmiths

Here is told
how a work was cast
by the smiths of precious metals.
They designed, created, sketched it
with charcoal and wax, in order
to cast the precious metal,
the yellow or the white;
thus they began their works.

If they began the figure of a living thing,
if they began the figure of an animal,
they searched only for the similarity;
they imitated life
so that the image they sought
would appear in the metal.

Perhaps a Huaxtec,
perhaps a neighbor
with a pendant hanging from his nose,
his nostrils pierced, a dart in his cheek,
his body tattooed with little obsidian knives;

---

63. The idea of transforming the raw materials into art by putting a deified heart
into them is repeated here.
64. *Codex Matritensis,* fol. 173 r.–v.

213

thus the charcoal was fashioned,
was carved and polished....

Whatever the artist makes
is an image of reality;
he seeks its true appearance.

If he makes a turtle,
the carbon is fashioned thus:
its shell as if it were moving,
its head thrust out, seeming to move,
its neck and feet
as if it were stretching them out.

If it is a bird
that is to be made of the precious metal,
then the charcoal is carved
to show the feathers and the wings,
the tail-feathers and the feet.

If it is a fish,
then the charcoal is carved
to show the scales and fins,
the double fin of the tail.
Perhaps it is a locust or a small lizard;
the artist's hands devise it,
thus the charcoal is carved.

Or whatever is to be made,
perhaps a small animal, or a golden neckpiece
with beads as small as seeds
around its border,
a marvelous work of art,[65]
painted and adorned with flowers.

---

65. To create an image of life, to imitate nature but at the same time transform it into a universe of symbols related to the ultimate realities, appears to be at the core of the artistic creations. The texts I have transcribed here are indeed an introduction to some of the most interesting aspects of Mesoamerican spirituality. This last text is taken from *Codex Matritensis*, fol. 44 v.

What We Know about
Our Gods . . .[66]

From our ancestors,
from them have we inherited
our pattern of life,
which in truth did they hold;
in reverence they held,
they honored, our gods.
They taught us
all their rules of worship,
all their ways of honoring the gods.
Thus before them do we prostrate ourselves;
in their names we bleed ourselves;
our oaths we keep,
incense we burn,
and sacrifices we offer.

It was the doctrine of the elders
that there is life because of the gods;
with their sacrifice, they gave us life.
In what manner? When? Where?
When there was still darkness.[67]

It was their doctrine
that they [the gods] provide our subsistence,
all that we eat and drink,
that which maintains life: corn, beans,
amaranth, sage.
To them do we pray
for water, for rain,
which nourishes things on earth.

---

66. In 1524, six years after the surrender of the Aztecs to the Spaniards, a dialogue took place between some of the surviving native sages and the twelve Franciscan missionaries recently arrived in Mexico. The paragraphs I have translated and included here convey the answer given by the Aztecs to the Spanish missionaries about their ancestral knowledge on the subject of religion.

67. "When there was still darkness," that is in the ancient times, perhaps in the beginnings of the present cosmic age, when the gods sacrificed themselves to give life to the sun, the moon, and the human beings.

215

They themselves are rich,
happy are they,
things do they possess;
so forever and ever,
things sprout and grow green in their domain . . .
there "where somehow there is life," in the place of Tlalocan.
There, hunger is never known,
no sickness is there,
poverty there is not.
Courage and the ability to rule
they gave to the people. . . .

And in what manner? When? Where were the gods invoked?
Were they appealed to; were they accepted as such;
were they held in reverence?

For a long time has it been;
it was there at Tula,
it was there at Huapalcalco,
it was there at Xuchatlapan,
it was there at Tlamohuanchan,
it was there at Yohuallichan,
it was there at Teotihuacan.[68]

Above the world
they had founded
their kingdom.
They gave the order, the power,
glory, fame.

And now, are we
to destroy
the ancient order of life?

---

68. This is a list of the most ancient religious and cultural centers where, according to tradition, the gods were invoked and accepted as such. Tula was the metropolis of Quetzalcoatl. *Xuchatlapan* and *Tlamohuanchan* are two designations referred to the mythical place of the cultural origins. *Yohuallichan* was a sanctuary of the Totonac people. Archaeology has discovered its remains in the northeastern part of the present state of Puebla. Teotihuacan, "the city of the gods," was the greatest metropolis of central Mexico during the Classic period.

Of the Chichimecs,
of the Toltecs,
of the Acolhuas,
of the Tecpanecs?[69]

We know
on Whom life is dependent;
on Whom the perpetuation of the race depends;
by Whom begetting is determined;
by Whom growth is made possible;
how it is that one must invoke,
how it is that one must pray.[70]

---

69. Well-known peoples are mentioned here as those in possession of the ancient order of life: the Chichimec nomads and the civilized Toltecs, as well as the famous allies of the Aztecs, the Acolhuas of Texcoco and the Tecpanecs of Azcapotzalco.

70. *Colloquies and Christian Doctrine*, manuscript preserved in the Vatican Library, fol. 36.

Songs of War[71]

There, where the darts are dyed,
where the shields are painted,
are the perfumed white flowers,
flowers of the heart.
The flowers of the Giver of Life
open their blossoms.
Their perfume is sought by the lords:
this is Tenochtitlan.[72]

Death is here among the flowers,
in the midst of the plain!
Close to the war,
when the war begins,
in the midst of the plain;
the dust rises as if it were smoke,
entangled and twisted round
with the flowery strands of death. . . .
Be not afraid, my heart!
In the midst of the plain
my heart craves death
by the sharpness of the obsidian blades.
This is all my heart craves:
death in war . . .[73]

From where the eagles rest,
from where the ocelots are exalted,
The Sun is invoked.

Like a shield that descends,
so does the Sun set.

71. Compositions conceived in a very different tone are these I will include here.
They have also to do with Mesoamerican spirituality inasmuch as they are closely related to what I have described as the mystical militarism of the Aztecs. See in this
context what has been said about the attitude of the Aztecs in the Introduction to this
book.
72. *Collection of Mexican Songs*, fol. 18 r.
73. *Ibid.*, fol. 66 r.–v.

In Mexico night is falling,
war rages on all sides.
O Giver of Life!
war draws near . . .

Proud of itself
is the city of Mexico-Tenochtitlan.
Here no one fears to die in war.
This is our glory.
This is Your command,
O Giver of Life!
Keep this in mind, O princes,
do not forget it.
Who could conquer Tenochtitlan?
Who could shake the foundation of the heavens?
Through our arrows,
through our shields,
the city exists.
Mexico-Tenochtitlan remains.[74]

Even though we may offer the Giver of Life[75]
jade and precious ointments,
if with the offerings of necklaces
You are invoked,
with the strength of the eagle and of the ocelot
[with the force of the warriors],
it may be that on earth
no one speaks the truth.[76]

---

74. *Ibid.*, fol. 19 v.–r.
75. This poem contradicts the mystical-militaristic attitude so much proclaimed in the previously quoted chants. Jades, ornaments, necklaces, other offerings—including those resulting from the strength of the eagle and the ocelot, that is, from the warriors—are not the way to speak the truth on earth. As we will see in part 6 of the present book, other poems are preserved in which some sages whose names and deeds are known to us speak in a tone very similar to the one of this "critical composition."
76. *Collection of Mexican Songs*, fol. 13 r.

The Birth of Huitzilopochtli,[77]
Patron God of the Aztecs

The Aztecs greatly revered Huitzilopochtli;
they knew his origin, his beginning,
was in this manner:

In Coatepec, on the way to Tula,
there was living,
there dwelt a woman
by the name of Coatlicue.
She was mother of the four hundred gods of the south
and their sister
by name Coyolxauhqui.

And this Coatlicue did penance there,
she swept, it was her task to sweep,
thus she did penance
in Coatepec, the Mountain of the Serpent.
And one day,
when Coatlicue was sweeping,
there fell on her some plumage,
a ball of fine feathers.
Immediately Coatlicue picked them up
and put them in her bosom.
When she finished sweeping,

---

77. This is a *teocuitatl,* "divine song," a sort of epic poem in which the birth of Huitzilopochtli is recalled. The portentous patron god of the Aztecs was the son of Coatlicue, "she of the skirt of serpents," a title of the Mother goddess. This text has been the object of various forms of interpretation. According to some reserachers, the myth has to do with an astral primeval confrontation. Huitzilopochtli is the Sun who is born from Cuatlicue, the earth. His sister, Coyolxauhqui, the moon, incites her four hundred brothers, the innumerable stars, to attack the Sun. In the astral struggle the moon and the four hundred stars are defeated. The triumph of the Sun, the patron god of the Aztecs, anticipates the destiny of the latter. This idea leads to a different or complementary interpretation. If the destiny of Huitzilopochtli has been to defeat his enemies and to deprive them of their possessions, the Aztec people, by siding with their patron God, will become "the people of the Sun," those chosen to impose their rule on many other nations in the four quadrants of the universe.

she looked for the feathers
she had put in her bosom,
but she found nothing there.
At that moment Coatlicue was with child.

The four hundred gods of the south,
seeing their mother was with child,
were very annoyed and said:
"Who has done this to you?
Who has made you with child?
This insults us, dishonors us."
And their sister Coyolxauhqui
said to them:
"My brothers, she has dishonored us,
we must kill our mother,
the wicked woman who is now with child.
Who gave her what she carries in her womb?"

When Coatlicue learned of this,
she was very frightened,
she was very sad.
But her son Huitzilopóchtli, in her womb,
comforted her, said to her:
"Do not be afraid,
I know what I must do."
Coatlicue, having heard
the words of her son,
was consoled,
her heart was quiet,
she felt at peace.

But meanwhile the four hundred gods of the south
came together to take a decision,
and together they decided
to kill their mother,
because she had disgraced them.
They were very angry,
they were very agitated,
as if the heart had gone out of them.
Coyolxauhqui incited them,

she inflamed the anger of her brothers,
so that they should kill her mother.
And the four hundred gods
made ready,
they attired themselves as for war.

And those four hundred gods of the south
were like captains;
they twisted and bound up their hair
as warriors arrange their long hair.

But one of them called Cuahuitlicac
broke his word.
What the four hundred said,
he went immediately to tell,
he went and revealed it to Huitzilopochtli.
And Huitzilopochtli replied to him:
"Take care, be watchful,
my uncle, for I know well what I must do."

And when finally they came to an agreement,
the four hundred gods were determined to kill,
    to do away with their mother;
then they began to prepare,
Coyolxauhqui directing them.
They were very robust, well equipped,
adorned as for war,
they distributed among themselves their paper garb,
the *anecúyotl* [the girdle], the nettles,
the streamers of colored paper;
they tied little bells on the calves of their legs,
the bells called *oyohualli*.
Their arrows had barbed points.

Then they began to move,
they went in order, in line,
in orderly squadrons,
Coyolxauhqui led them.
But Cuahuitlicac went immediately up onto the mountain,

so as to speak from there to Huitzilopochtli;
he said to him:
"Now they are coming."
Huitzilopochtli replied to him:
"Look carefully which way they are coming."
Then Cuahuitlicac said:
"Now they are coming through Tzompantitlan."
And again Huitzilopochtli said to him:
"Where are they coming now?"
Cuahuitlicac replied to him:
"Now they are coming through Coaxalpan."
And once more Huitzilopochtli asked Cuahuitlicac:
"Look carefully which way they are coming."
Immediately Cuahuitlicac answered him:
"Now they are coming up the side of the mountain."
And yet again Huitzilopochtli said to him:
"Look carefully which way they are coming."
Then Cuahuitlicac said to him:
"Now they are on the top, they are here,
Coyolxauhqui is leading them."

At that moment Huitzilopochtli was born,
he put on his gear,
his shield of eagle feathers,
his darts, his blue dart-thrower.
He painted his face
with diagonal stripes,
in the color called "child's paint."
On his head he arranged fine plumage,
he put on his earplugs.
And on his left foot, which was withered,
he wore a sandal covered with feathers,
and his legs and his arms
were painted blue.

And the so-called Tochancalqui
set fire to the serpent of candlewood,
the one called Xiuhcoatl
that obeyed Huitzilopochtli.

MESOAMERICAN SPIRITUALITY

With the serpent of fire he struck Coyolxauhqui,
he cut off her head,
and left it lying there
on the slope of Coatepetl.
The body of Coyolxauhqui
went rolling down the hill,
it fell to pieces,
in different places fell her hands,
her legs, her body.

Then Huitzilopochtli was proud,
he pursued the four hundred gods of the south,
he chased them, drove them off
the top of Coatepetl, the mountain of the snake.
And when he followed them
down to the foot of the mountain,
he pursued them, he chased them like rabbits,
all around the mountain.
He made them run around it four times.
In vain they tried to rally against him,
in vain they turned to attack him,
rattling their bells
and clashing their shields.
Nothing could they do,
nothing could they gain,
with nothing could they defend themselves.
Huitzilopochtli chased them, he drove them away,
he humbled them, he destroyed them, he annihilated them.

Even then he did not leave them,
but continued to pursue them,
and they begged him repeatedly, they said to him:
"It is enough!"

But Huitzilopochtli was not satisfied,
with force he pushed against them,
he pursued them.
Only a very few were able to escape him,
escape from his reach.
They went toward the south,

224

and because they went toward the south,
they are called gods of the south.
And when Huitzilopochtli had killed them,
when he had given vent to his wrath,
he stripped off their gear,
their ornaments, their *anecuyotl;*
he put them on, he took possession of them,
he introduced them into his destiny,
he made them his own insignia.[78]

And this Huitzilopochtli, as they say,
was a prodigy,
because only from fine plumage,
which fell into the womb of his mother, Coatlicue,
was he conceived,
he never had any father.
The Aztecs venerated him,
they made sacrifices to him,
honored and served him.
And Huitzilopochtli rewarded
those who did this.
And his cult came from there,
from Coatepec, the Mountain of the Serpent,
as it was practiced from most ancient times.[79]

---

78. The meaning of these last lines is particularly eloquent. When Huitzilopochtli defeated and killed his brothers, he took possession of their insignia and attributes, and he introduced them into his own destiny. For the Aztecs this was an anticipation of their own future. They too had to take possession of the riches of others to introduce them into their own destiny.

79. *Florentine Codex*, book 3, chapter 1. Translation by M. Leon-Portilla.

MESOAMERICAN SPIRITUALITY

Songs about the Spanish Conquest[80]

Broken Spears

Broken spears lie in the roads;
we have torn our hair in our grief.
The houses are roofless now, and their walls
are red with blood.

Worms are swarming in the streets and plazas,
and the walls are splattered with gore.
The water has turned red, as if it were dyed,
and when we drink it,
it has the taste of brine.

We have pounded our hands in despair
against the adobe walls,
for our inheritance, our city, is lost and dead.
The shields of our warriors were its defense,
but they could not save it.

We have chewed dry twigs and salt grasses;
we have filled our mouths with dust and bits of adobe;
we have eaten lizards, rats and worms. . . .

The Fall of Tenochtitlan[81]

Our cries of grief rise up
and our tears rain down,
for Tlatelolco is lost.

---

80. The following compositions are a different kind of testimony. They are true elegies composed by postconquest Aztec poets, most probably by individuals who contemplated the destruction of their own metropolis and the ruin of their culture. Thus, in close relation with the first of the following testimonies, we find this statement written in Nahuatl: "And all these misfortunes befell us. We saw them and wondered at them; we suffered this unhappy fate."

81. This text is taken from the *Historical Annals of the Mexican Nation*, Mexican Manuscript 22, National Library, Paris, France, fol. 33.

226

The Aztecs are fleeing across the lake;
they are running away like women.

How can we save our homes, my people?
The Aztecs are deserting the city:
the city is in flames, and all
is darkness and destruction.

Motelchiuhtzin the Huiznahuacatl,
Tlacotzin the Tlailotlacatl,
Oquitzin the Tlacatecuhtli
are greeted with tears.[82]

Weep, my people:
know that with these disasters
we have lost the Mexican nation.
The water has turned bitter,
our food is bitter!
These are the acts of the Giver of Life. . . .
Ah, it is true: The kings are prisoners now!"[84]

Flowers and Songs of Sorrow

Nothing but flowers and songs of sorrow
are left in Mexico and Tlatelolco,
where once we saw warriors and wise men.

We know it is true
that we must perish,
for we are mortal men.

---

82. The three mentioned individuals were prominent chiefs in the Aztec army.

83. Doña Isabel was one of the daughters of Montezuma. She was married to Cuauhtemoc, the young Aztec prince who directed the defense of Mexico City. At the death of Cuauhtemoc she lived with Hernando Cortez from whom she had a daughter. Later on she became the wife of the former conqueror Alonso de Grado. Doña Isabel was married two times more, as she lost her successive husbands, becoming finally the wife of Juan Cano de Saavedra; she had from him five children, the origin of the well-known Cano-Montezuma family.

84. *Collection of Mexican Songs*, fol. 54 r.

You, the Giver of Life,
You have ordained it.

We wander here and there
in our desolate poverty.
We are mortal men.
We have seen bloodshed and pain
Where once we saw beauty and valor.

We are crushed to the ground;
we lie in ruins.
There is nothing but grief and suffering
in Mexico and Tlatelolco,
where once we saw beauty and valor.

Have you grown weary of your servants?
Are you angry with your servants,
O Giver of Life?[85]

The Imprisonment of Cuauhtemoc[86]

The Aztecs are besieged in the city;
the Tlatelolcas are besieged in the city![87]

The walls are black,
the air is black with smoke,
the guns flash in the darkness.
They have captured Cuauhtemoc;
they have captured the princes of Mexico.

---

85. *Ibid.*, fol. 54 v.

86. Various chroniclers wrote about the defeat of the Aztecs, the destruction of their city, and the imprisonment of Cuauhtemoc. From both the Spanish chronicles and the Aztec annals we know that the prince who led the native armies surrendered to the Spaniards on August 13, 1521.

87. The Tlalelolcas were the people living in an inlet to the north of Mexico-Tenochtitlan. The Tlalelolcas, although closely related to the Aztecs, existed for many years as an independent people. About fifty years before the arrival of the Spaniards they were subdued by the Aztecs. It is interesting to recall here that when the city was besieged by the Spaniards, the Tlalelolcas resisted to the last moment.

MESOAMERICAN SPIRITUALITY

The Aztecs are besieged in the city;
the Tlatelolcas are besieged in the city!

After nine days, they were taken to Coyoacan:[88]
Cuauhtemoc, Coanacoch, Tetlepanquetzaltzin.[89]
The kings are prisoners now.

Tlacotzin consoled them:
"O my nephews, take heart!
The kings are prisoners now;
they are bound with chains."

The king Cuauhtemoc replied:
"O my nephew, you are a prisoner;
they have bound you in irons.

"But who is that at the side of the Captain-General?
Ah, it is Doña Isabel, my little niece! [83]
Ah, it is true: The kings are prisoners now!

"You will be a slave and belong to another:
the collar will be fashioned in Coyoacan,
where the quetzal feathers will be woven."[90]

---

88. Coyoacan, a town situated in the southern part of the Valley of Mexico. To-day Coyoacan is a suburb of greater Mexico City.

89. Coanacoch ruled in the allied chiefdom of Texcoco. Tetlepalquezaltzin ruled in the also allied puppet-state of Tlacopan.

90. *Collection of Mexican Songs*, fol. 55 r.

Yucatec-Maya Songs[91]

You are singing, little dove,
on the branches of the silk-cotton tree.
And there also is the cuckoo,
and many other little birds.
All are rejoicing,
the songbirds of our god, our Lord.
And our goddess
has her little birds,
the turtledove, the redbird,
the black and yellow songbirds, and the hummingbird.
These are the birds of the beautiful goddess, our Lady.
If there is such happiness
among the creatures,
why do our hearts not also rejoice?
At daybreak all is jubilant.
Let only joy, only songs,
enter our thoughts![92]

Only Thee[93]
do I trust entirely,
here where one dwells.
For thou, O great Kin,
providest that which is good,
here where one dwells,
to all living beings.
Since Thou abidest to give reality to the earth,
where all men live.
And Thou art the true helper
who grants that which is good.[94]

---

91. Religious poetry flourished also among the various groups of Maya language. Unfortunately the Maya compositions that have come down to us are not so abundant as those existing in Nahuatl. Here I present three songs from the Yucatec-Maya. They are included in the so-called *Book of Songs of Dzitbalche.*
92. *Book of Songs of Dzitbalche,* p. 80. This translation into English derives from the Spanish version prepared by Alfredo Barrera Vazquez.
93. This is a composition addressed to *Kin,* the solar deity.
94. *Op. cit.* p. 46–47.

MESOAMERICAN SPIRITUALITY

O watcher, watcher from the trees,[95]
with one, with two,
we go to hunt at the edge of the grove,
in a lively dance up to three.
Raise your head high,
do not mistake,
instruct well your eyes
to gather the prize.

Make sharp the tip of your arrow,
make taut the cord
of your bow; now you have good
resin of *catsim* on the feathers
at the end of the arrow's rod.
You have rubbed well
the fat of a male deer
on your biceps, on your muscles,
on your knees, on your twin muscles,
on your shoulders, on your chest.

Go nimbly three times round
about the painted stone column,
where stands that virile lad,
unstained, undefiled, a man.
Go once, on the second round
take up your bow, put in the arrow,
point it at his chest; you need not
use all your strength
so as to kill him,
or wound him deeply.
Let him suffer
little by little,

---

95. Human sacrifice was also practiced by the Maya. Although they did not offer to their gods as many human victims as the Aztecs, we have various testimonies describing their various forms of sacrificial rituals. This song is precisely related to the so called "arrow-sacrifice." The chant is addressed to the bowman who, dancing around the victim, had to instruct his eyes to point its arrows to the chest of the one impersonating a deity whose blood had to be offered to fertilize the earth. The strange form of mysticism implicit in this song of the bowman inevitably has to be included as another aspect of what has been described here as Mesoamerican spirituality.

as He wishes it,
the magnificent Lord God.

The next time you go round
this stony blue column, the next time
you go round, shoot another arrow.
This you must do without
stopping your dance, because
thus it is done by well-bred
men, fighters, those who
are sought after, pleasing
in the eyes of the Lord God.

And as the Sun appears
over the forest to the east,
the song of the bowman begins.
These well-bred men, fighters,
do their utmost.[96]

---

96. *The Book of Songs of Dzitbalche*, p. 77–78.

The Creation of the
Twenty-Day Cycle[97]

Thus it was recorded
by the first sage . . .
The first prophet, *Napuctun*,[98]
the priest, the first priest.
This is a song of how the *uinal,*
the twenty-day cycle,
came to be created
before the creation of the world.
Then he began to march
by his own effort alone. . . .
Then said his maternal grandmother,
then said his maternal aunt,
then said his paternal grandmother,
then said his sister-in-law:
"What shall we say when we see man on the road?"
These were their words
as they marched along,
when there was no man as yet.
Then they arrived there in the east
and began to speak.
"Who has passed here?
Here are footprints.
Measure it off with your foot."
So spoke the mistress of the world.
Then he measured the footstep
of our Lord, God the Father.
This was the reason it was called
counting off the whole earth.

---

97. The following composition is taken from the *Book of the Chilam Balam of Chumayel.* In it an account is given of what happened when for the first time a twenty-day period (a Mesoamerican "month") was integrated and thus this basic unit of time was born.

98. Napuctun was the name of one of the *ah kinob,* "the priests of the sun," who probably lived in a community close to Chumayel in the Yucatec peninsula before the Spanish arrival.

233

This was the count,
after it had been created by the day 13-*Oc*,
after his feet were joined evenly,
after they had departed there in the east.

Then he spoke its name,
when the day had no name,
after he had marched
along with his maternal grandmother,
his maternal aunt,
his paternal grandmother, and his sister-in-law.
The *uninal*,
twenty-day cycle,
was created,
the day, as it was called,
was created,
heaven and earth were created,
the stairway of water,
the earth, rocks, and trees;
the things of the sea
and the things of the land
were created.

On 1-*Chen* he raised himself to his divinity,[99]
after he had made heaven and earth.
On 2-*Eb* he made the first stairway.
It descended from the midst of the heavens,
in the midst of the water,
when there were neither earth,
rocks, nor trees.
On 3-*Ben* he made all things,
as many as there are,
the things of the heavens,
the things of the sea,
and the things of the earth.

---

99. The names of the days in the Maya language are given here in an orderly form preceded by the numerals, from one to thirteen. Once the appearance in succession of the twenty days has been described, then, according to our text, "occurred the invention of the word of Our Lord God. . . . " Then everything was created.

On 4-*Ix* sky and earth were tilted.
On 5-*Men* he made everything.
On 6-*Cib* the first candle was made;
it became light,
when there was neither sun nor moon.
On 7-*Caban* honey was first created,
when we had none.
On 8-*Edznab* his hand and foot
were firmly set,
then he picked up small things on the ground.
On 9-*Cauac* the lower world was first considered.
On 10-*Ahau* wicked men went to the lower world
because of God the Father,
that they might not be noticed.
On 11-*Imix* rocks and trees were formed;
this he did within the day.
On 12-*Ik* the breath of life was created.
The reason it was called *Ik*
was because there was no death in it.
On 13-*Akbal* he took water
and watered the ground.
Then he shaped it
and it became man.
On 1-*Kan* he first created anger
because of the evil he had created.
On 2-*Chicchán* occurred the discovery
of whatever evil he saw
within the town.
On 3-*Cimi* he invented death;
it happened that our Lord God
invented the first death.
On 5-*Lamat* he established
the seven great waters of the sea.
On 6-*Muluc* all valleys were submerged,
when the world was not yet created.
Then occurred the invention
of the word of our Lord God,
when there was no word in Heaven,
when there were neither rocks nor trees. . . .

The *uninal* [the twenty-day cycle]
was created,
the earth was created;
sky, earth, trees, and rocks
were set in order;
all things were created
by our Lord, God the Father.
Thus He was there in His divinity,
in the clouds, alone and by His own effort,
when He created the entire world,
when He moved in the heavens in His divinity.
Thus He ruled in His great power.

Every day is set in order
according to the count,
beginning in the east,
as it is arranged. . . . [100]

---

100. *The Book of the Chilam Balam of Chumayel*, edited and translated by Ralph L. Roys, Carnegie Institution of Washington, publication 438, 1933, pp. 116–119.

The Four Cosmic Trees

The red flint stone
is the stone of the red *Mucencab.*[101]
The red ceiba tree of abundance
is his arbor,
which is set in the east.
The red bullet-tree is their tree.
The red zapote . . .
The red-vine . . .
Reddish are their yellow turkeys.
Red toasted corn is their corn.

The white flint stone
is their stone in the north.
The white ceiba tree of abundance
is the arbor of the white *Mucencab.*[102]
White-breasted are their turkeys.
White Lima-beans are their Lima-beans.
White corn is their corn.

The black flint stone
is their stone in the west.
The black ceiba tree of abundance
is their arbor.
Black speckled corn is their corn.
Black tipped camotes are their camotes.
Black wild pigeons are their turkeys.
Black *akab-chan* is their green corn.[103]

---

101. This text, taken also from the *Book of the Chilam Balam of Chumayel,* brings us close to the symbolism attached to the four quadrants of the earth. Following the sacred order east-north-west-south, we know about the primeval stones, birds, seeds, cosmic ceibas, and other realities corresponding to each quadrant.

102. *Mucencab,* according to Ralph L. Roys, in his commentary to this text, is a term that connotes "a class of supernatural bees dwelling at Cobac" in the Yucatec peninsula.

103. Roys quotes here another source of information and says that such a term may also mean the name of two gods in the form of large bees who governed all the bees. Akab-chan, according to Roys, "is probably a dark variety of maize."

Black beans are their beans.
Black Lima-beans are their Lima-beans.

The yellow flint stone
is the stone of the south.
The ceiba tree of abundance,
the yellow ceiba tree of abundance,
is their arbor.
The yellow bullet-tree is their tree.
Colored like the yellow bullet-tree are their camotes.
Colored like the yellow bullet-tree
are the wild pigeons which are their turkeys.
Yellow green corn is their green corn.
Yellow-backed are their beans. . . . [104]

---

104. *The Book of the Chilam Balam of Chumayel*, p. 64.

Part Six

THE POETRY OF NEZAHUALCOYOTL (1402–1472) AND OF OTHER PRIESTS AND SAGES KNOWN TO US

The Poetry of Nezahualcoyotl
(1402–1472)[1]

The starting point for Nezahualcoyotl seems to have been his keen awareness of time and change, *cahuitl* in Nahuatl, or "that which leaves us." Everything in *tlalticpac*, "on the earth," is transitory. It appears here for a while but then withdraws and vanishes forever. Here is the way Nezahualcoyotl expressed it:

I, Nezahualcoyotl, ask this:
Is it true one really lives on the earth?
Not forever on earth,
only a little while here.
Though it be jade it falls apart,
though it be gold it wears away,
though it be quetzal plumage it is torn asunder.
Not forever on earth,
only a little while here.[2]

If jade and gold fall apart and wear away, then faces and hearts, more fragile, will have to die and to be erased like paintings.

I comprehend the secret, the hidden:
O my lords!

---

1. Information about the life of the sage king Nezahualcoyotl is offered in the Introduction to this book. Here I include the translations of the Nahuatl compositions attributed to him, included in the native manuscripts preserved in the National Library of Mexico and in the Library of the University of Texas, Austin. A sort of sequence of thought can be perceived in these texts that doubtless convey to us something of the penetrating insights of Nezahualcoyotl. Thus, instead of reserving for the footnotes the required precisions that probably can help to reconstruct such sequence, I have intercalated some paragraphs between the various compositions in order to make their intrinsic relations more apparent. In this way I hope the core of Nezahualcoyotl's reflections will seem more evident. This I will do in respect to ten of his poems, those that can be considered particularly meaningful in terms of his ideas about the instability of human existence and the mysteries that surround the supreme Giver of Life. Immediately after, I will present, without further commentaries, other poems that somehow echo the same ideas and preoccupations previously analyzed.

2. *Collection of Mexican Songs*, National Library of Mexico, fol. 17 r. The translation of this and of the rest of the poems in this part 6 are due to M. Leon-Portilla.

Thus we are,
we are mortal,
men through and through,
we all will have to go away,
we all will have to die on earth.
Like a painting,
we will be erased.
Like a flower,
we will dry up
here on earth.
Like plumed vestments of the precious bird,
that precious bird with the agile neck,
we will come to an end . . .
Think on this, my lords,
eagles and ocelots,
though you be of jade,
though you be of gold
you also will go there,
to the place of the fleshless.
We will have to disappear,
no one can remain.[3]

The conviction that faces and hearts meet only for a brief time on earth was the cause of Nezahualcoyotl's sadness but it was also the beginning of his personal trend of thinking:

I am intoxicated, I weep, I grieve,
I think, I speak,
within myself I discover this:
indeed, I shall never die,
indeed, I shall never disappear.
There where there is no death,
there where death is overcome,
let me go there.
Indeed I shall never die,
indeed, I shall never disappear.[4]

---

3. *Romances de los Senores de Nueva Espana,* manuscript preserved in the Latin American Collection of the Library of the University of Texas, Austin, fol. 36 r.
4. *Collection of Mexican Songs,* fol. 17 v.

Nezahualcoyotl, recalling ancient beliefs, probably of Toltec origin, expressed his doubt and wondered where one had to go or what wisdom must be acquired in order to arrive at *Quenonamican*, "Where-in-some-way-one-lives," at *Can avac micohua*, "Where death does not exist."

> Where shall we go
> where death does not exist?
> But should I live weeping?
> May your heart find its way:
> Here no one will live forever.
> Even the princes will die,
> people are reduced to ashes.
> May your heart find its way:
> Here no one will live forever.[5]

Nezahualcoyotl found his own way. He says he has discovered the meaning of flower-and-song, the Nahuatl metaphor for art and symbolism.

> At last my heart knows it:
> I hear a song,
> I contemplate a flower . . .
> May they never fade![6]

When the heart at last has found its way, it seeks out the flowers and songs that never perish. Nezahualcoyotl is anxious to find the flowers and songs that will not come to an end:

> My flowers will not come to an end,
> my songs will not come to an end,
> I, the singer, raise them up;
> they are scattered, they are bestowed.
> Even though flowers on earth
> may wither and yellow,
> they will be carried there,

---

5. *Ibid.*, fol. 70 r.
6. *Romances de los Senores de Nueva Espana*, fol. 19 v.

to the interior of the house
of the bird with the golden feathers.[7]

Nezahualcoyotl believes that he whose heart has discovered flowers and songs can indeed approach the mystery that surrounds the Giver of Life. *Tloque Nahuaque*, The Lord of the Near and Close, also has a book of paintings. [In it with flowers and songs, he draws and shades whatever exists on the earth.]

With flowers You write,
O Giver of Life;
With songs You give color,
with songs You shade
those who must live on the earth.

Later You will destroy eagles and ocelots;
we live only in Your book of paintings,
here, on the earth.

With black ink You will blot out
all that was friendship,
brotherhood, nobility.

You give shading
to those who must live on the earth.
We live only in Your book of paintings,
here on the earth.[8]

The faces and hearts of men on earth are close and yet far from the Giver of Life. Nezahualcoyotl's thought, immersed in mystery, reaches out toward Him but expresses the impossibility of unveiling the mystery.

There, alone, in the interior of heaven
You invent Your word,
Giver of Life!
What will You decide?

---

7. *Collection of Mexican Songs,* fol. 16 v.
8. *Romances de los Senores de Nueva Espana,* fol. 35 r.

Do You disdain us here?
Do You conceal Your fame
and Your glory on the earth?
What will You decide?
No one can be intimate
with the Giver of Life ...
Then, where shall we go?
Direct yourselves,
We all go to the place of mystery.[9]

In spite of the statement that no one can say He is "intimate
with the Giver of Life," Nezahualcoyotl continued his search. Now
we find a series of questions as to the reality and roots of He Who invents His own word and brings us into being in His book of paintings:

Are You real, are You rooted?
Only You dominate all things,
the Giver of Life.
Is this true?
Perhaps, as they say, it is not true?

May our hearts
be not tormented;
All that is real
all that is rooted,
they say that it is not real,
that it is not rooted.
The Giver of Life
only appears absolute.

May our hearts
be not tormented,
because He is the Giver of Life.[10]

Above and beyond the doubts and the mystery that surround
the Giver of Life, it is necessary to accept His reality. This is the

---

9. *Collection of Mexican Songs,* fol 13 v.
10. *Romances de los Senores de Nueva Espana,* fol. 19 v–10 r.

only thing that can bring peace to the heart. This appears to be Nezahualcoyotl's conclusion in his effort to comprehend the mystery
of divinity. Invoking and paying homage to the Giver of Life, one
exists and feels better on earth.

> In no place can be the house of He who invents Himself,
> In no place can be the house of He who invents Himself,
> but in all places He is venerated.
> His glory, His majesty is sought throughout the earth.
>
> It is He who invents things,
> it is He who invents Himself; God.
> In all places He is invoked,
> in all places He is venerated.
> His glory, His majesty, is sought throughout the earth.
>
> No one here is able,
> no one is able to be intimate
> with the Giver of Life;
> only is He invoked,
> at His side,
> near to Him,
> one can live on the earth.
>
> He who finds Him
> knows only one thing: He is invoked,
> at His side, near to Him,
> one can live on the earth.
>
> In truth no one
> is intimate with You,
> O Giver of Life;
> Only as among the flowers
> we might seek someone,
> thus we seek You,
> we who live on the earth,
> we who are at Your side.
>
> Your heart will be troubled

only for a short time,
we will be near You and at Your side.

The Giver of Life enrages us,
He intoxicates us here.
No one is at His side
to be famous, to rule on earth.[11]

---

11. *Ibid.*, fol. 4 v.–5 v.

Other Poems of Nezahualcoyotl

(Song of the Flight Composed by Nezahualcoyotl While Fleeing from the Lord of Azcapotzalco.)[12]

In vain was I born,
in vain have I come forth
to the earth from the house of the Lord,
I am sorely lacking!
Better far I had not come forth,
truly better I had not come to the earth.
I cannot express it,
but what must I do,
O princes who are come here?
Must I live in the sight of the people?
What can I become?
Think on it!

Must I stand up straight on the earth?
What is my destiny?
I am sorely lacking,
my heart is faint,
You have scarcely befriended me
here, on the earth.

How should one live beside the people?
Acts perhaps at random
he who sustains and lifts the people?

Live peacefully,
pass life calmly!
I am bent over,
I live with my head bowed
beside the people.

---

12. As has been recalled in the Introduction to this book, Nezahualcoyotl's father, King Ixtlilxochitl of Texcoco, was murdered around 1419 by the ruler of Azcapotzalco who, in this way, laid hold of that chiefdom. Young Nezahualcoyotl had to flee to escape from the hands of the lord of Azcapotzalco. In the present composition he describes his sufferings while fleeing from his enemy.

For this I am mortified,
I am wretched;
I have remained alone
beside the people on earth.

How has Your heart decided,
Giver of Life?
Withhold Your displeasure;
Grant Your compassion,
I am at Your side, You are God.
Perhaps You would bring death to me?

Is it true that we are happy,
that we live on the earth?
It is not certain that we live
and have come on earth to be happy.
We are all sorely lacking.
Destiny brings sorrow
here, beside the people.

Let my heart be not afflicted.
Do not think any more now.
Truly, I scarcely
pity myself here on earth.

Sorrow has sprung up
near You and at Your side, Giver of Life.
Only I am searching,
I remember our friends.
Perhaps they will come once more,
perhaps they will live again?
Only once we perish,
only once here on the earth.
Let not our hearts suffer
near and at the side of the Giver of Life![13]

13. *Romances de los Senores de Nueva Espana*, fol. 21 r.–22 v.

MESOAMERICAN SPIRITUALITY

Stand Up

My friends, stand up!
the princes have gone away,
I am Nezahualcoyotl,
I am the singer,
the bird with a large head.
Take up your flowers and your fans.
With them go out to dance!

You are my child,
you are Yoyontzin.
Now take up your chocolate,
flower of the cacao tree,
may you drink all of it!
Do the dance.
Begin the exchange of songs!
Not here is our home,
we do not live here,
you also will have to go away.[14]

I Am Sad

I am sad, I grieve,
I, Nezahualcoyotl.
With flowers and with songs
I remember the princes,
those who went away,
Tezozomoctzin, Quahquauhtzin.

Truly they live,
there Where-in-some-way-one-exists.

Oh, that I might follow the princes,
and take them our flowers!
If I could but make my own
the songs of Tezozomoctzin!

---

14. *Ibid.*, fol. 3 v.–4 r.

Never will your name perish,
oh my lord, you, Tezozomoctzin!
Thus your songs fulfill a need.
I am grieving,
alone I remain saddened,
I have withdrawn from myself.

I have become saddened, I grieve.
No longer you are here, no longer,
but in the region Where-in-some-way-one-exists,[15]
you have left us without sustenance on earth,
for this I have withdrawn from myself.[16]

Song of Springtime[17]

In the house of paintings
the singing begins,
song is intoned,
flowers are spread,
the song rejoices.

Above the flowers is singing
the radiant pheasant;
his song expands
into the interior of the waters.
To him reply
all manner of red birds;
the dazzling red bird
sings a beautiful chant.

---

15. "The-region-where-in-some-way-one-exists." With this long expression I have tried to render in English the Nahuatl term *Quenonamican*, one of the forms adopted by some sages to convey the idea they had about the afterlife. Obviously this concept had a very different connotation than that of the *Mictlan* or "Place of the Dead" accepted by the official religion. I refer the reader to the texts in part 4 of this same book.

16. *Collection of Mexican Songs*, fol. 25 r. v.

17. *Xopan cuicatl:* "Song of the springtime." The compositions that can be considered as pertaining to this sort of literary genre are chants of happiness in which what is good on earth is exalted.

Your heart is a book of paintings,
You have come to sing,
to make Your drums resound.
You are the singer.
Within the house of springtime,
You make the people happy.

You alone bestow
intoxicating flowers,
precious flowers.
You are the singer.
Within the house of springtime,
You make the people happy.[18]

I Am Wealthy

I am wealthy,
I, Nezahualcoyotl.
I join together the necklace,
the large quetzal plumage;
from experience I recognize the jade,
they are princes, friends!
I look into their faces,
eagles and ocelots everywhere,
from experience I recognize the jade,
the precious bracelets . . .[19]

He Alone

He alone,
the Giver of Life.
Empty wisdom had I,
perhaps no one knew it,
perhaps no one?
I was not content at the side of the people.

---

18. *Romances de los Senores de Nueva Espana*, fol. 38 v.–39 r.
19. *Collection of Mexican Songs*, fol. 16 r.

Precious truths You distribute,
from You comes joy,
Giver of Life;
Sweet-smelling flowers, precious flowers,
with eagerness have I longed for them,
empty wisdom had I . . .[20]

Be Joyful

Be joyful with the flowers that intoxicate,
those that are in our hands.
Now put on
the necklaces of flowers.
Our flowers from the season of rain,
fragrant flowers,
now open their corollas.

There flies the bird,
he chatters and sings,
he has known the house of the Lord.
Only with our flowers
are we happy.
Only with our songs
does sadness disappear.

Oh lords, in this way
your sorrow is put to flight.
The Giver of Life invents them,
He has sent them down,
the Inventor of Himself,
the joyous flowers,
with these your sorrow is put to flight.[21]

---

20. *Romances de los Senores de Nueva Espana*, fol. 20 r.
21. *Ibid.*, fol. 19 r.

The Poem of Tlaltecatzin[22]

In my solitude I sing
to Him Who is my god.
In the place of light and warmth,
in the place where the lords command,
the flowering chocolate drink is foaming,
the one that intoxicates men with its flowers.

I yearn,
my heart has tasted,
my heart has been inebriated,
my heart already knows it:
O red songbird of the agile neck!
Fresh and burning,
you show your garland of flowers,
woman, mother,
sweet, delightful creature,
precious flower of toasted maize . . .

Here you have come
before the lords,
you, marvelous being,
inviting to pleasure.
Upon the mat of yellow and blue feathers,
here you stand proudly.
But, precious flower of toasted maize,
you only lend yourself,
soon you will have to be abandoned,
you will have to go away,

---

22. For information about the life of Tlaltecatzin, see the Introduction to this book. Here I will recall only that the following poem attributed to Tlaltecatzin is a composition addressed by him to an *ahuiani*, a poem of love to a gladdening companion, that is, a public woman. To look for pleasure did not mean for Tlaltecatzin to forget "Him who is my god." The idea of death had not disappeared from his consciousness and, in looking for pleasure, he kept his heart open to reflection: She, he himself, all, will have to go to the region of mystery. What really matters is that everything will happen as the Giver of Life has determined it, and as we mortals wish it to be, that is, without violence.

you also will become fleshless,
yours will be the abode of the dead.

The flowering chocolate drink is foaming,
tobacco flowers are passed round,
if my heart tastes them,
I will be intoxicated . . .
Listen, I am alone and tormented,
may I not go to the place of the fleshless . . .
Alone I must go,
my own self shall become lost . . .
I will go alone,
my heart covered with flowers . . .
Thus let it be,
but let it be without violence![23]

---

23. *Collection of Mexican Songs,* fol. 30 r.–v. The same text is included in *Romances de los Senores de Nueva Espana,* fol. 7 r.–8 r.

Poems of Tochihuitzin[24]

So has it been said by Tochihuitzin,
so has it been said by Coyolchiuhqui:
It is not true, it is not true
that we come to this earth to live.
We come only to sleep, only to dream.
Our body is a flower.
As grass becomes green in the springtime,
so our hearts will open, and give forth buds,
and then they wither.
So did Tochihuitzin say.[25]

You have lived the song,
you have unveiled the flower,
you, oh princess;
I, Tochihuitzin, I am only a weaver of twigs:
The garlands of flowers
fall out there.[26]

---

24. In the Introduction I give some information about the life of Tochihuitzin.
25. *Collection of Mexican Songs*, fol. 14 v.
26. *Ibid.*, fol. 15 r.

The Poems of Ayocuan[27]

Let the earth forever remain!
Let the mountains unchanged exist!
Thus spoke Ayocuan Cuetzpaltzin,
in Tlaxcala, in Huexotzinco.
Flowers of toasted maize, flowers of the chocolate tree,
may they be scattered.
Let the earth forever remain!

From within the heavens they come,
the beautiful flowers, the beautiful songs.
Our longing spoils them,
our inventiveness makes them lose their fragrance.
But not those of the Chichimec prince Tecayehuatzin.
With his, rejoice!

Friendship is a shower of precious flowers.
White tufts of heron feathers
are woven with precious red flowers,
in the branches of the trees
under which stroll and sip
the lords and nobles.

Your beautiful song
is a golden wood thrush
most beautiful, you raise it up.
You are in a field of flowers.
Among the flowery bushes you sing.
Are you perchance a precious bird of the Giver of Life?
Perchance you have spoken with God?

---

27. The author of the two following poems was a well-known sage who lived in the highlands of Central Mexico during the second half of the fifteenth century. More information about his life is given in the Introduction to this book. The second of his compositions quoted here has reached us as a part of "the dialogue of flower and song," which took place in Huexotzinco at the turn of the fifteenth century. The version I include here differs somewhat from that of the text of the dialogue. It is offered as a different attempt to convey the richness of meaning inherent in the poetry in the Nahuatl language.

As soon as you saw the dawn,
you began to sing.

Make an effort, let my heart desire
the flowers of the shield,
the flowers of the Giver of Life.

What can my heart do?
In vain have we come,
have we blossomed forth on the earth.
Thus alone will I have to go
like the flowers that perish?
Will nothing remain of my name?
Nothing of my fame here on earth?
At least my flowers, at least my songs!
What can my heart do?
In vain have we come,
have we blossomed forth on the earth.

Let us enjoy, O friends,
here we can embrace.
We stroll now over the flowery earth.
No one here can do away
with the flowers and the songs,
they will endure in the house of the Giver of Life.

Here on earth is the region of the fleeting moment.
Is it also thus in the place
Where-in-some-way-one-lives?
Is one happy there?
Is there friendship?
Or is it only here on earth
we came to know our faces?[28]

---

28. *Collection of Mexican Songs*, fol. 10 r. and 14 v.

The Poem of Macuilxochitzin[29]

I raise my songs,
I, Macuilxochitl,
with these I gladden the Giver of Life,
may the dance begin!

There Where-in-some-way-one-exists,
to His house,
may these songs be carried?
Or only here
remain your flowers?
May the dance begin!

The Matlatzincas
are your prey, Lord Itzcoatl.[30]
Axayacatzin, you have conquered
the city of Tlacotepec!
There turned in spiral
your flowers, your butterflies.
With this you brought happiness.
The Matlatzincas are in Toluca, in Tlacotepec.

Slowly he makes offerings
of flowers and feathers
to the Giver of Life.
He puts the eagle shields
on the arms of the men,
there where the war rages,
in the midst of the plain.
Like our songs,
like our flowers,
thus you, warrior of the tonsured head,
give pleasure to the Giver of Life.

---

29. Macuilxochitzin was a poetess born in Mexico City during the second half of the fifteenth century. Some information about her life and the circumstances in which she composed this poem is offered in the Introduction to this book.

30. As has been mentioned, Itzcoatl ruled the Aztecs from 1428 to 1440.

The flowers of the eagle
remain in your hands,
Lord Axayacatl.
With divine flowers,
with flowers of war
you are covered,
with these becomes intoxicated
he who is on our side.

Above us open
the flowers of war,
in Ehcatepec, in Mexico,
with these become intoxicated
he who is on our side.

They have shown themselves fearless,
the princes,
those of Acolhuacan,
you, the Tepanecs.[31]
On every side Axayacatl
made conquests,
in Matlatzinco, in Malinalco,
in Ocuillan, in Tequaloya, in Xohcotitlan.[32]
From here he went forth.

There in Xiquipilco was Axayacatl
wounded in the leg by an Otomi,
his name was Tlilatl.
That one went in search of his women,
he said to them:
"Prepare a breech cloth, and elegant cloak,
give these to him, you who are courageous."

---

31. Here Macuilxochitzin suggests that Itzcoatl had defeated already, during his reign, the Matlatzinca people.
32. These are the names of various towns situated in the Valley of Toluca, close to the Valley of Mexico. Some of them still exist and are inhabited by the descendants of the Pre-Columbian Matlatzinca.

And Axayacatl called out:
"Bring the Otomi
who wounded me in the leg!
The Otomi was afraid;
he said:
"Now truly they will kill me!"
Then he brought a large piece of wood
and a deer skin,
with these he bowed before Axayacatl.
He was full of fear, the Otomi.
But then his women
made supplication for him to Axayacatl.[33]

---

33. *Collection of Mexican Songs,* fol. 33 v.

MESOAMERICAN SPIRITUALITY

A Poem of Tecayehuatzin[34]

Now let us sing,
let us follow our songs
in the midst of the light and warmth,
O my friends!
Who are you?
I go out to meet you.
Where shall I look for you?
Here, in the place of the drums.
I invent only flowery songs,
I, your friend,
I am the Chichimec lord,
Tecayehuatzin.

Perhaps one of us,
why not all of us,
will give you,
will gladden
the Inventor of Himself?

In Tlaxcala, in good season,
may my flowery intoxicating songs be there.
May the songs that inebriate,
those of Xicohtencatl, of Temilotzin,
of the prince Cuitlizcatl be there.

The Tamoanchan of the eagles,
the House of Night of the tigers
are in Huexotzinco.
There is the place of death in Tlacahuepan,
prince rich in merits.

---

34. Tecayehuatzin, ruler of *Huexotzinco* in the modern state of Puebla, was well known both as a clever politician and as a poet. He was the one who, by the end of the fifteenth century, organized a famous dialogue in which various sages and poets participated to elucidate the meaning of "flowers and songs." In the Introduction to the present book more information is given about him.

MESOAMERICAN SPIRITUALITY

There are happy the flowers,
community of the nobles,
in their springtime houses.
With flowers of cacao
he calls out and comes quickly,
there with the flowers he is joyful
in the midst of the waters.
He comes quickly with his golden shield.
So with fans,
with staffs of red flowers,
with banners of quetzal feathers
let us come to be happy
in the interior of the springtime houses.

The kettle drums color of jade resound,
brilliant dew
has fallen over the earth.
In the house of yellow feathers
it pours down with force.
His son has come down,
descended there in the springtime.
He is the Giver of Life.
His songs make flourish,
he adorns himself
in the place of the drums.

Now they come forth from there,
the intoxicating flowers,
With them rejoice![36]

---

36. *Collection of Mexican Songs*, fol. 9 v.

A Dialogue on Poetry:
Flower and Song[37]

Tecayehuatzin:

Invitation to the Poets

Where have you been, oh poet?
Make ready the flowered drum
that is girded with quetzal feathers
intertwined with golden flowers.
You will delight the nobles,
the Eagle Knights and the Jaguar Knights.

Their Arrival at the Place of Music

Surely he went down to the place of the kettledrums,
surely the poet is there,
unfolding his precious songs,
offering them one by one to the Giver of Life.

"Flower and Song": the Gift of the Rattlesnake-bird

The rattlesnake-bird responds to him.
It sings, it offers flowers,
it offers our flowers.
I hear its voices there,
truly it responds to the Giver of Life,
the rattlesnake-bird responds,
it sings, it offers flowers,
it offers our flowers.

---

37. For information about the circumstances in which this dialogue took place, see
the Introduction to this book.

MESOAMERICAN SPIRITUALITY

The Poetry of Prince Ayocuan

Your words rain down
like emeralds and precious feathers.
Ayocuan Cuetzpaltzin also speaks in this way,
surely he knows the Giver of Life.
That famous lord
also came here to speak in this way,
the lord who delighted the one God
with bracelets of quetzal feathers
and with perfumes.

Is Poetry the Only Truth?

Might it not be pleasing to the Giver of Life?
Might it not be the only true thing on earth?

Invitation to the Poets and Praise of Them

For a brief moment,
for the time being,
I have the princes here on loan:
bracelets, precious stones.
I surround the nobles only with flowers.
I bring them together with my songs
in the place of the kettledrums.
I have called this meeting here in Huexotzinco.
I, the lord Tecayehuatzin,
have brought the princes together:
precious stones, quetzal feathers.
I surround the nobles only with flowers.

Ayocuan's Reply; Origin of "Flower and Song," Praise of Tecayehuatzin and of Friendship

Ayocuan:

The beautiful flowers, the beautiful songs
come from the interior of heaven.

MESOAMERICAN SPIRITUALITY

Our eagerness disfigures them,
our ingenuity destroys them,
when they are not those
of the Chichimeca prince, Tecayehuatzin.
Let us rejoice in those of the prince!

Friendship is a rain of precious flowers.
White tufts of heron feathers
are intertwined with precious red flowers.
The lords and nobles
walk about, sipping,
under the boughs of the trees.

Do the Princes Speak to the Giver of Life Through Flowers and Songs?

Your beautiful song
is a golden rattlesnake-bird,
you send it aloft most beautifully,
you sing from the flowering branches.
Are you by chance a precious bird
of the Giver of Life?
Have you by chance spoken with the God?
You have seen the daybreak
and you have been moved to sing.

Eagerness to Find Flowers and Songs

Exert yourself,
wish for the flowers of the shield,
the flowers of the Giver of Life.
What can my heart do?
We have come here in vain,
we have sprung up on earth in vain.

"Flower and Song": Memento of Man on the Earth

Must I depart only in this way,
like the flowers that perish?

Will nothing remain in my name?
Nothing of my fame here on earth?
Flowers, at least, and songs!
What can my heart do?
We have come here in vain,
We have sprung up on earth in vain.

"Flowers and Songs" Also Remain with the Giver of Life

O friends, let us rejoice,
let us embrace one another.
We walk the flowering earth.
Nothing can bring an end here
to flowers and songs,
they are perpetuated in the house
of the Giver of Life.

Expression of Doubt; Earthly Things Are Transitory; What of the Beyond?

The Region of the Fleeting Moment
is here on earth.
Is it also like this in the place
where one lives in a different way?
Is one happy there,
are there friendships there?
Or have we learned to know our faces
only here on earth?

Aquiauhtzin Replies

Aquiauhtzin:[38]

---

38. Aquiauhtzin, a noble born in Ayapanco, close to Amecameca in the present state of Mexico, left us other compositions of great interest. I have published one of them entitled "The Chalca cihuacuicatl," that is, the song of the women of Chalco, another village in the vicinity of Ayapanco. See M. León-Portilla, "The Chalca cihuacuicatl of Aquiauhtzin, erotic poetry of the Nahuas," *The New Scholar*, University of San Diego, vol. 5, num. 2, pp. 235–266.

MESOAMERICAN SPIRITUALITY

I have heard a song,
I am listening to it,
King Ayocuan is playing his flute,
a garland of flowers.
Now Aquiauhtzin, lord of Ayapanco,
responds to your song, he answers you.

The Search for the Giver of Life

Where do you dwell, O God,
oh Giver of Life?
Although, as a poet,
I am sometimes unhappy for You,
I succeed only in gladdening You.

The Giver of Life is Sought among Flowers and Paintings

Here where it rains white flowers,
precious white flowers,
here in the midst of spring,
in the house of paintings,
I succeed only in gladdening You.

Everyone Awaits the Word of the Giver of Life

Oh you that have come from Tlaxcala
to sing your songs to the beat
of the brilliant drums,
here in the place of the kettledrums;
oh fragment flowers,
Xicotencatl, lord of Tizatlan,
and Camazochitzin, and all those
who delight themselves with songs and flowers:
Wait for the word of the God.

MESOAMERICAN SPIRITUALITY

Invocation to the God

Your house is everywhere,
O Giver of Life.
The princes invoke you
on the flowered carpet
that I wove for you with flowers.

The Rattlesnake-bird, Symbol of the God, Appears
to Them, Singing; Flowers Rain Down

The many flowering trees stand straight
in the place of the kettledrums.
You are there:
Beautiful flowers are scattered there,
intermingled with precious feathers.
The rattlesnake-bird
walks upon the carpet of flowers,
it walks singing,
responding only to the God,
delighting the Eagles and Jaguars.

Now it is raining flowers.
The dance begins, O friends,
in the place of the kettledrums!

A Question

Who is awaited here?
Our heart is afflicted.

The God Arrives among the Flowers and Songs

Hear, now hear,
only the God has come down
from the interior of heaven,
He has come here singing.
The princes answer him now,
they came here to play their flutes.

Cuauhtencotzli:[39]

I, Cuauhtencotzli, am here, suffering.
My flower-decked drum
is adorned with my sorrow.

Questions about the Truth of Men and of Songs

Are men true?
Will our song be true tomorrow?
What remains standing by mere chance?
What will come out well?
We are here, we are living here,
but we are only beggars, O my friends.
If you are taken there,
there you will stand erect.

Motenehuatzin Addresses Them

Motenehuatzin:[40]

I have come here only to sing.
What are you saying, O my friends?
What are you discussing here?
Oh princes, here is the flower-filled patio,
the maker of rattles
comes weeping, comes singing,
here in the midst of spring.
Dissimilar flowers,
dissimilar songs:
Everything in my house is affliction.

---

39. Cuauhtencoztli was a poet from the already mentioned town of Huexotzinco in the present state of Puebla.
40. Metenehuatzin was a noble and poet from Tlaxcala. Apparently he witnessed the arrival of the Spaniards and the fall of the Aztecs.

MESOAMERICAN SPIRITUALITY

Flowers and Song Dispel Sorrow

The truth is, we scarcely live,
for we are embittered by sorrow.
I weave my songs like quetzal feathers
for the lords, for those that rule,
I, Motenehuatzin.
Oh Telpolohuatl, oh Prince Telpolohuatl,
we all live,
we all walk in the midst of spring.
Dissimilar flowrs,
dissimilar songs:
Everything in my house is affliction.

He Too Has Heard an Inspired Song

I have heard a song,
I have seen, in the flowering waters,
the one who walks there in spring,
the one who speaks with the dawn,
the bird of fire, the bird of the cornfields,
the right red bird: Prince Monencauhtzin.

The Host Again Exhorts Everyone To Be Happy

Tecayehuatzin:

My friends,
you that are here in the flower-filled house
of the bird of fire, which was sent by the God:
Come take the quetzal-feather crest,
I wish to behold
those who fill the flute with laughter,
those who speak with the flower-decked drums,
the princes and lords
who cause the turquoise-inscrusted drums
to sound and resound
within the house of flowers.

Hear,
sing,
speak from the branches of the flowering tree,
hear how the precious rattlesnake-bird
shakes its flower-decked golden rattles:
Hear the prince Monencautzin.
He opens his wings
as if they were golden fans,
he hovers among the flower-decked drums.

Flower and Song: Wealth and Joy of Princes

· Monencautzin:[41]

The flowers burst open, burst open,
the flowers burst open their buds
to the face of the Giver of Life.
He responds to you.
The precious bird of the god,
for which you sought.
How many have been enriched with your songs,
you have given them much delight.
The flowers move!

I walk everywhere,
I converse in all places,
I am a poet.
Fragrant, precious flowers have rained down
in the flower-filled patio,
in the house of butterflies.

Flower and Song: Means of Intoxicating One's Heart

Xayacamach:[42]

---

41. Monencauhtzin was another poet of the region of Huexotzinco.

42. Xayacamach, born around 1450, was the son of the ruler of Tizatlan, one of the chiefdoms of Tlaxcala. He is mentioned as a well-known poet in other native compositions.

MESOAMERICAN SPIRITUALITY

All have come from the place
where the flowers stand erect,
the flowers that confuse the people,
that cause their hearts to whirl.
They have come to delight themselves,
they have come to make it rain
garlands of flowers,
intoxicating flowers.
Who stands
on the carpet of flowers?
Surely your home is here,
in the midst of paintings:
So says Xayacamach, intoxicated
with the heart of the cacao flower.

A beautiful song resounds,
Tlapalteuccitzin lifts up his song.
The flowers are beautiful,
the flowers sway,
the cacao flowers.

Salutation by the Late Arrival

Tlapalteuccitzin:[43]

O friends, I have come seeking you,
crossing the flowering fields,
and here, at last, I have found you.
Be happy,
tell your stories!
O friends, your friend has arrived.

He Too Wishes to Speak of Flowers

I have not come
to mingle less beautiful flowers,

---

43. Tlapalteuccitzin is a poet about whose life no information has reached us. We can infer from his words that he was indeed a Nahuatl sage.

those of the burdock and the indigo plant,
with the precious flowers.
I am invited also,
O my friends,
I, the needy one.

Description of Himself

Who am I?
I live flying,
I compose hymns,
I sing the flowers:
butterflies of song.
They leap forth from within me,
my heart relishes them.
I have arrived among the people,
I have come down,
I, the bird of spring.
I have spread my wings over the earth
in the place of the flower-decked drums.
My song arises over the earth,
my song bursts out.

His Origins and Life: Flower and Song

I repeat my songs here, O friends.
I have sprung up among songs,
for songs are still made.
I bind my precious jar
with golden cords,
I, your impoverished friend.
I examine only flowers,
I, your friend,
and the opening of full buds.
I have roofed my hut with colored flowers.
Thus I gladden my heart,
for the sowings of the God are many.

MESOAMERICAN SPIRITUALITY

Invitation To Be Joyful

Let there be joy!
Be truly joyful
here in the place of flowers,
O lord Tecayehuatzi, you
that are adorned with collars.

Life Is a Unique Experience

Is it true that we return to life again?
Your heart knows the answer:
We come here to live only once.

Reply: Flowers and Songs Give Pleasure to Man and Bring Near the Giver of Life

I have reached the boughs
of the flowering tree,
I, the flower-decked hummingbird.
I delight in the fragrance of flowers,
I sweeten my lips with them.
Oh Giver of life,
you are invoked with flowers.
We abase ourselves here,
we give You delight
in the place of the flower-decked drums,
lord Atecpanecatl!
The drum awaits you,
it is kept in the house of spring,
your friends await you there,
your friends Yaomanatzin,
Micohuatzin, Ayocuatzin.
The princes are sighing with flowers.

Eulogy of Huexotzinco: It Is not a Warlike City

Ayocuan:

The city of Huexotzinco
would be hated, would be attacked,
if it were circled with darts
and ringed with arrows.[44]

Huexotzinco, House of Drums and Paintings, of the Giver of Life

The kettledrum and the tortoise shell
distinguish your house,
they are here in Huexotzinco
Tecayekuatzin is here,
the lord Quecehuatl,[45]
he plays the flute and sings
in his house, which is Huexotzinco.
Hear me:
the God our Father comes down to us,
this is His house,
here where the jaguar drum is played,
where the songs are sung
to the beat of kettledrums.

The cloaks of quetzal feathers
open like flowers
in the House of Paintings.
Thus the One God is worshiped
in the land and on the mountain.
Your precious houses rise up
like flowered darts.
My gilded House of Paintings,
O One God, is Yours also!

---

44. The final expression of Ayocuan about Huexotzinco means indeed a great praise. That famous town, from which so many poets originated, deserved, according to Ayocuan, to be forever kept away from war.

45. "Lord Quecehuatl," appears to be a title of Tecayehuatzin, meaning probably "the one exalting his old blood."

Tecayehuatzin:

And now, O friends,
hear the dream of a word:
Each spring gives us life,
the golden ear of corn refreshes us,
the tender ear of corn becomes a necklace for us.
We know that the hearts
of our friends are true.[46]

46. *Collection of Mexican Songs*, fol. 9 v.–11 v.

Bibliography

Sources, Editions, and Translations

Ancient Word (The). See *Huehuetlatolli.*

Annals of Cuauhtitlan, manuscript in the Nahuatl language from Central Mexico. A copy of the sixteenth-century original is in the Archive of the National Museum of Anthropology, Mexico City.

    Editions and translations: Codice Chimalpopoca, study and translation into Spanish by Primo F. Velazquez, second edition, Mexico: National University of Mexico Press, 1975. *Die Geschichte der Königreiche von Culhuacan und Mexico,* Introduction and translation into German by Walther Lehmann, second edition, Stuttgart, 1976.

Annals of the Mexican Nation (also known as *Anales de Tlatelolco*), Mexican manuscript number 22, National Library, Paris.

    Editions and translations: Facsimile reproduction in *Corpus Codicum Americanorum Medii Aevi,* v. II, edited by Ernst Mengin, Copenhagen, 1945. *Anales de Tlatelolco,* edited and translated into German by Ernst Mengin, *Baessler Archiv,* Teil I–II, Berlin, 1939–1940. *Andes de Tlatelolco y Códice de Tlatelolco,* translated into Spanish by H. Berlin, México: Editorial Robredo, 1948.

Book of Chilam Balam of Chumayel, a manuscript in the Yucatec-Maya language. A copy of the sixteenth-century original is in the Berendt Linguistics Collection, Museum of the University of Pennsylvania.

    Editions and translations: The Book of Chilam Balam of Chumayel, edited and translated into English by Ralph L. Roys, new edition published by the University of Oklahoma Press, 1967. *El Libro de los libros de Chilam Balam,* edited by Alfredo Barrera Vasquez, Mexico: Fondo de Cultura, 1948

Book of Songs of Dzitbalche, a manuscript in the Yucatec-Maya language in the Archive of the National Museum of Anthropology, Mexico City. It is apparently an eighteenth-century copy of an older compilation.

    Edition and translation: El libro de cantares de Dzitbalche, edited and translated into Spanish by Alfredo Barrera Vasquez, Mexico: Instituto Nacional de Antroplogía e Historia, 1965.

Codex Borbonicus, a sixteenth-century Aztec book of calendrical and religious content preserved at the Library of the French Chamber of Deputies (Palais Bourbon).

BIBLIOGRAPHY

Edition: Codex Borbonicus, Kommentar van Karl Anton Nowotny, Graz: Akademische Druck-und Verlaganstalt, 1974.

Codex Borgia, a pre-Columbian Nahuatl book of calendrical and religious content, preserved at the Vatican Library.

Editions: Codice Borgia, edicion facsimilar y comentarios de Eduard Seler, 3 v., Mexico: Fondo de Cultura, 1963. *Codex Borgia*, Kommentar von Karl Anton Nowotny, Graz: Akademische Druck-und Verlaganstalt,1976.

Codex Dresden, a pre-Columbian Maya book of calendrical and religious content, preserved at the Public Library of Dresden.

Editions and commentaries: E. W. Forstemann, *Die Mayahandschrift der Koniglichen offentlichen Bibliothek Zu Dresden*, Leipzig, 1880. J. Eric S. Thompson, *A Commentary on the Dresden Codex, a Maya Hieroglyphic Book, with a Facsimile Reproduction of the Codex*, Philadelphia: American Philosophical Society, 1972.

Codex Florentinus (Florentine Codex), a sixteenth-century manuscript in 4 v., containing the Nahuatl text of the native informants of Fray Bernardino de Sahagun, distributed in twelve books, a Spanish free translation of them and numerous drawings in which European influence is evident. The original manuscript is preserved at the Laurentian Library, Florence, Italy.

Editions and translations: Francisco del Paso y Troncoso, *Codice Florentino* (illustrations only), Madrid, 1905. *Florentine Codex*, edited and translated into English by J. O. Anderson and Charles E. Dibble, 11 v., Santa Fe, N. Mex.: School of American Research and the University of Utah, 1950–1969.

Codices Matritenses, sixteenth-century transcriptions of the texts in Nahuatl of the sages and elders, native informants of Fray Bernardino de Sahagun. Preserved, the first part (*Memorials*) at the Library of the Royal Palace, Madrid, and the second part at the Library of the Spanish Royal Academy of History.

Editions and translations: Francisco del Paso y Troncoso, editor, *Codices Matritenses (Historia general de las cosas de Nueva Espana)*, a facsimile reproduction, 3 v., Madrid, 1906–1907. Eduard Seler, *Einige Kapitel aus dem Geschichtwerk des P. Sahagún*, aus dem Aztekischen überstz von . . . , Stuttgart, 1927. Miguel León-Portilla, editor, *Ritos, Sacerdotes y Atavíos de los dioses*, Textos de los informantes de Sahagún 1 (*Códices Matritenses*), Mexico: Universidad Nacional, 1958 and 1969. Angel Ma. Garibay K., *Veinte*

BIBLIOGRAPHY

Himnos Sacros de los Hanuas, Textos de los informantes de Sahagún 2 (Codices Matritenses), Mexico: Universidad Nacional, 1958.

Codex Vindobonensis, a pre-Columbian Mixtec book of religious (mythological) and historical content, preserved at the National Library, Vienna.

Edition: *Codex Vindobonensis Mexicanus 1*, Introduction by O. Adelhofer, Graz: Akademische Druck-und Verlaganstalt, 1974.

Collection of Mexican Songs, a sixteenth-century manuscript in Nahuatl, preserved in the National Library, Mexico.

Edition and translation: Antonio Peñafiel, editor, *Colección de cantares mexicanos*, a facsimile reproduction, Mexico, 1904. *Poesía Nahuatl*, v. 2 and 3, with an introduction, paleography, and translation into Spanish by Angel Ma. Garibay K., Mexico: Universidad Nacional, 1965–1967. Numerous compositions taken from this manuscript, translated into English, are included in Miguel León-Portilla, *Pre-Columbian Literatures of Mexico*, Norman: University of Oklahoma Press, 1968 and several reprints.

Cuilapa Mixtec Text, is a mythical account about the divine origins of the world and of man, preserved by the vicar of the Monastery of Cuilapa, Oaxaca.

Edition: Fray Gregorio García, *Origen de los indios del Nuevo Mundo e Indias Occidentales*, Madrid, 1729.

Florentine Codex. See *Codex Florentinus*.

Huehuetlatolli. There are several collections of *Huehuetlatolli*, The Ancient Word: those preserved in the National Library of Mexico: The Bancrof Library, Paris; the National Library, Madrid; to which the texts that form book 6 of the *Florentine Codex* have to be added.

Editions and translations: Fray Juan Bautista, Huehuetlatolli, Pláticas de los viejos, Mexico, 1600. Angel Ma. Garibay. "*Huehuetlatolli*, Documento A," *Tlalocan* (a magazine on the native cultures and languages of Mexico), v. I, num. 1, (1943–1944), pp. 31–33 and 81–107. The paleography and translation into Spanish of other *Huehuetlatolli* have been included in v. 10–13 of *Estudios de Cultura Nahuatl*, Mexico: National University, 1972–1978.

Popol Vuh, The Book of Counsel, a Quiche-Maya text transcribed with the Spanish alphabet in the sixteenth century. It was discovered by Fray Francisco Ximenez, parish priest of Chichicastenango,

BIBLIOGRAPHY

Guatemala, in the eighteen century. Copies derived from the one prepared by Ximenez have survived. Reference has to be made in particular to the one preserved in the Ayer Collection, Newberry Library, Chicago.

Editions and translations; The *Popol Vub* has been translated into Spanish, French, German, English, and Japanese. Available editions with commentaries and translation into English: *Popol Vub: The Sacred Book of the Ancient Quiche Maya*, English version by D. Goetz and S. Morley, from the translation of Adrian Recinos, Norman: University of Oklahoma Press, 1950. *The Book of Counsel: The Popol Vub of the Quiche Maya of Guatemala*, edited and translated into English by Munro S. Edmonson, New Orleans: Middle American Research Institute, Tulane University, 1971.

Ritual of the Bacabs, a Yucatec-Maya manuscript with incantations, prayers, songs, and native medical prescriptions, probably an eighteenth-century copy from an older text, is preserved in the Princeton University Library.

Edition: Ritual of the Bacabs, translated into English and edited by Ralph L. Roys, Norman: University of Oklahoma Press, 1965.

Romances de los Señores de Nueva Espana, a manuscript in Nahuatl included in The Latin American Collection, Library of the University of Texas, Austin.

Edition: Poesia Nahuatl I, introduction, paleography, and translation into Spanish by Angel Ma. Garibay K., Mexico, National University, 1963. Several compositions from this manuscript have been translated into English: Miguel León-Portilla, *Pre-Columbian Literatures of Mexico,* Norman: University of Oklahoma Press, 1968 and several reprints.

Studies

Andrews, Richard. *Introduction to Classical Nahuatl.* Austin: University of Texas Press, 1975.

Barrera Vásquez, Alfredo. *The Maya Chronicles.* Publication 585 of the Carnegie Institution of Washington. Washington, D. C., 1949.

Carmack, Robert M. *Quichean Civilization: The Etnographic and Archaeological Sources.* Berkeley: University of California Press, 1973.

BIBLIOGRAPHY

Cline, Howard F., ed. "Guide to Ethnohistorical Sources." *Handbook of Middle American Indians*, v. XII–XIV. Austin: University of Texas Press, 1972–1974.

Edmonson, Murno S., ed. *Sixteenth Century Mexico: The Work of Sahagun*. A School of American Research Book. Albuquerque: University of New Mexico Press, 1974.

Eschmann, Anncharlott. *Das Religiose Geschichtsbild der Azteken*, edited by Gerdt Kutscher in collaboration with Jürgen Golte, Anneliese Mönnich y Heins-Jürgen Pinnow. Berlin: Iberoamericanisches Institut. Gebr. Mann, 1976.

Garibay K., Angel Maria, *Huehuetlatolli, Documento A*. Tlalocan, v. I (1943): 31–53, 81–107.

―――. *Historia de la Literatura Náhuatl*. Mexico City: Editorial Porrua, 1953–1954.

Garza, Mercedes de la. *La conciencia historica de los antiguos mayas*. Mexico: Universidad Nacional Autonoma de Mexico, Centro de Estudios Mayas, 1975.

―――.*El hombre en el pensamiento religioso maya y nahuatl*. Mexico, Universidad Nacional Autonoma de Mexico, Centro de Estudios Mayas, 1978.

Gillmor, Frances. *Flute of the Smoking Mirror: A Portrait of Nezahualcoyotl, Poet-King of the Aztecs*. Albuquerque: University of New Mexico Press, 1949.

Gossen, Gary H. *Chamula in the World of the Sun: Time and Space in a Maya Oral Tradition*. Cambridge: Harvard University Press, 1974.

Lehmann, Walter. "Die Bedeutung der altamerikanischen Hochkulturen für allgemeine Geschichte der Menscheit." *Ibero-Amerikanisches Archiv*, April–July, 1943, pp. 65–71.

León-Portilla, Miguel. *The Broken Spears: Aztec Account of the Conquest of Mexico*. Boston: Beacon Press, 1961, 1966.

―――. *Aztec Thought and Culture: A Study of the Ancient Nahuatl Mind*. Norman: University of Oklahoma Press, 1963.

―――. *Pre-Columbian Literatures of Mexico*. Norman: University of Oklahoma Press, 1968 and several reprints.

―――. *Time and Reality in the Thought of the Maya*. Boston: Beacon Press, 1972.

Morley, Sylvanus G. *The Ancient Maya*. Revised by George W. Brainerd. Stanford University Press, 1956.

BIBLIOGRAPHY

Porter Weaver, Muriel. *The Aztecs, Maya and their Predecessors: Archaeology of Mesoamerica.* New York: Seminar Press, 1962.

Sanders, William T., and Barbara J. Price. *Mesoamerica: The Evolution of a Civilization.* New York: Random House, 1968.

Seler, Eduard. *Gesammelte Abhandlungen zur Amerikanischen Sprach- und Altertumskunde.* 5 vols. Berline: Ascher and Co. and Behrend und Co., 1902–1923.

Soustelle, Jacques. *La Pensee Cosmologique des anciens mexicains.* Paris: Hermann et Cie., 1940.

Thompson, J. Eric S. *Maya Hieroglyphic Writing.* Norman: University of Oklahoma Press, 1960.

———. *A Catalog of Maya Hieroglyphs.* Norman: University of Oklahoma Press, 1962.

———. *Maya History and Religion.* Norman: University of Oklahoma Press, 1970.

Tozzer, Alfred M. *The Chilam Books and the Possibility of Their Translation.* Proceedings of the XIXth International Congress of Americanists. Washington, 1915, pp. 178–86.

———. *A Maya Grammar with Bibliography and Appraisement of the Words Noted.* Papers of the Peabody Museum, Harvard University, Vol. 9 (1921).

Zimmerman, Günter. *Die Hieroglyphen der Maya-Handschriften.* Universitat Hamburg Abhandlungen aus dem Gebiet der Auslandkunde, Vol, LXVII, Series B (1956).

Index to Preface,
Introduction and Notes

Acamapichtli, 23, 153.
Acolhuas, 217.
Adam and Eve, 126, 143; Nahuat counterparts, 143.
Afterlife, see also, Black and Red Inks, Death, *Mictlan, Quenonamican, Tlalocan*; 6, 14, 35, 42, 44, 72, 79, 80, 173, 178, 179, 181, 183, 185, 186, 195–196, 251; doubts regarding, xv, 43–44, 183, 185, 186, 251.
Ages, Cosmic, see Suns.
Agriculture, 3, 11, 13, 14, 15, 18, 22, 84, 154.
Ahuitzotl, 26.
Alvarado Tezozomoc, Fernando, 24, 36.
Amantla, 191.
Amecameca, 267.
Ancient Word (*Huehuetlatolli*), xvi, xvii, 6, 35–39, 46, 51, 53, 55, 63, 64, 68, 70, 71, 81, 84, 86, 102, 173.
Andean Area, 9, 20, 151.
Anderson, J.O. Arthur, 36, 55, 56, 72, 167, 178.
Anthropology, xvii, 9, 34.
Aquiauhtzin, 48, 52, 267.
Archaeology, xvii, 13, 15, 16, 17, 18, 33, 151, 216.
Aristocracy, see also, Eagle Knights, Tiger Knights; 15, 20, 23, 30, 64, 66, 77, 84, 87, 89, 92, 95, 173, 177, 178, 192, 270; Aztec military, 24–25, 76, 77.
Aristotle, 37.
Arizona, 12.
Art, xvii, xviii, 3, 11, 12, 17, 20, 50, 51, 52, 53, 204, 211, 213, 214.
Artists, 114, 208, 210, 211.
Astrology, 29, 113, 145, 175.
Astronomy, see also, Calendar; 17, 31.
Atheism, 5.

Atitlan, Lake, 102.
Austin, Tex., 57, 241, 242.
Axayacatl (Axayacatzin), 26, 51.
Ayapanco, 52, 267.
Ayocuan, 50, 52, 276.
Azcapotzalco, 23, 24, 25, 217, 248.
Aztecs, see also, Sun, People of; xv, 5, 6, 21–26, 38 39, 50, 51, 67, 76, 77, 96, 137, 152, 153, 155, 191, 192, 208, 215, 217, 220, 225, 226, 227, 228, 231, 259; art, xvii, xviii, 208; arrival in Mesoamerica, 21, 22, 197; conquests of, 25–26, 225; culture, 6, 39, 44, 55, 226; defeated by Spaniards, 226, 228, 270; geographical extension, 26; language of, see Nahuatl; mystic militarism, xvii, 6, 8, 24–25, 29, 44, 79, 137, 155, 179, 218, 219; official history, 25; official religion, 6, 8, 24–25, 27, 43–44, 45, 72, 173, 178, 215, 251; society, xvii, 24–26, 152; world-view, 27, 29, 44; writing, 31–32.

Barrera Vasquez, Alfredo, 58, 230.
Bautista, Fray Juan, O.F.M., 37.
Belize, 16.
Benson, Elizabeth P., 31.
Berlin, 55.
Bernal, Ignacio, 14.
Bible, xvi, 8, 112, 126, 127, 128, 157.
Black and Red Inks, 67, 154; Land of, 170.
Bonampak, 16, 17.
Book of Counsel, see *Popol Vuh*.

Cakchiquel, 20, 21.
Calendar, Mesoamerican, 3, 4, 6, 11, 12, 14, 17, 22, 26, 30, 31, 32, 95, 101, 102, 103, 105, 135, 137, 138, 145, 175, 233, 234; compared to

102, 105, 122, 143, 151, 216;
syncretised with Dual God, 201;
temple of, 15.
Quetzalcoatl, Priest and Sage, see
also, Uemac; xvi, 19, 20, 40,
42–43, 46, 96, 102, 151, 152, 153,
154, 155, 164, 166, 167, 168, 169,
170, 207, 216; self-immolation of,
167, 170; successors of, 21; title of
Aztec priests, 96, 97.
Quiche-Mayas, 21, 41, 43, 101, 102,
106, 110, 111, 113, 114, 127, 129,
131, 132, 136, 146.
Quiche Maya Language, see also,
Maya Language; xviii, 40, 41, 42,
43, 56, 101, 102, 105, 106, 122,
123, 133, 134; pronounciation,
xix-xx.
Quiche (Region), 20.
Quimixtlan, 50.
Quirigua, 16.

Rain God, see Tlaloc.
Recinos, Adrian, 56, 102.
Rio Grande, 12.
Rites, see Ceremonies.
Robertson, Donald, 33.
*Romances de los Señores de la Nueva
España*, 57, 186, 242, 243, 244, 245,
247, 249, 250, 252, 253, 255.
Rome, 9.
Roys, Ralph L., 58, 236, 237.

Sacrifice, see also, Penance; xv, 27,
86, 137; "arrow-sacrifice", 231;
human, 6, 25, 26, 29, 42, 44, 137,
178, 231; of the gods, 28, 29, 137,
142, 143, 215; of Quetzalcoatl,
167, 170; of slaves at funerals,
178.
Sages, 3, 6, 7, 8, 15, 17, 24, 29, 30,
33, 34, 35, 36, 42, 43, 44, 45, 47,
48, 49, 50, 51, 52, 53, 57, 58, 68,
79, 87, 92, 101, 102, 112, 151, 173,
183, 186, 200, 204, 219, 241, 257,
273.
Sahagún, Fray Bernardino de,
O.F.M., 34, 35, 36, 37, 42, 47, 55,

93, 151, 173.
San Lorenzo, 13.
San Luis Potosí, State of, 155.
Santa Fé, N.M., 56.
Schools, Ancient Mesoamerican, see
also *Calmecacs, Telpuchcalli*; 3, 4, 6,
15, 26, 30, 33, 34, 35, 36, 39, 45,
55.
Science, 5.
Seler, Eduard, xiv, 12.
Sinaloa River, 12.
Socrates, 37.
Soul, 4.
Sources, 55–59.
Spain, see also, Charles V, Mexico,
Spanish Conquest of, Philip II;
34, 38, 55.
Spirituality, 4–5, 35; Mesoamerican,
3, 4, 5, 6, 8, 19, 29, 33, 35, 44, 45,
49, 50, 53, 58, 59, 204, 214, 218,
231; Native American, 4–10;
Western, 3, 8, 10.
Sun, xvi, 8, 28, 29, 79, 130, 137, 143,
215, 220; People of, 6, 25, 29, 220.
"Sun of Movement", 27, 28–29, 40,
137, 215.
"Suns" (Cosmogonic Eras), 27–29,
40, 42, 56, 121, 130, 135, 137, 138,
143, 215.
Sun-God, see also, Kin, Tlaltecutli;
6, 8, 25, 29, 44, 73, 79, 179, 191;
identified with Huitzilopochtli,
191.
Supreme Being, 5.
Supreme God, see Dual God.
Symbolism, 5, 14, 18, 50, 51, 52, 53,
116, 211, 214, 237.
Syncretism, 191, 198, 201.

Tabasco, State of, 13.
Tamaulipas, Sierra de, 13.
Tamaulipas, State of, 155.
Tecamachalco, 50.
Tecayehuatzin, 51–53, 262, 276.
Telpuchcalli, 39, 84, 86, 90, 93, 94.
Tenochtitlan (Mexico City), 22, 23,
24, 25, 50, 51, 191, 192, 259;
building of, 23; development of,

Black and Red Inks, Ideograms, Pictograms; 3, 4, 11, 12, 14, 16, 17, 18, 22, 25, 26, 30–33, 67, 154; Aztec, 31–32; Maya, 18, 31; phonetic, 32.

Xayacamach, 52–53, 272.
Ximenez, Fray Francisco, 41.
Xiuhnel, 197.
Xiuhtecuhtli, 16, 198; temple of, 198.
Xochipilli, 16.
Xochiquetzal, xvii.
Xochitlan, 160.

Yaxchilan, 16.
Yohuallichan, 216.
Young, Thomas, xiv.
Yucatan Peninsula, 16, 20, 58, 233, 237; Toltequization of, 21.
Yucatán, State of, 58.
Yucatec Mayas, 43.
Yucatec Maya Language, see also, Maya Language; xviii, 43, 47, 58, 106, 230; literature, 58; pronounciation, xix-xx.

Zapotecs, 16, 17, 18, 145; decline of, 20.

Index to Texts

295

Mystery, place of, *Quenonamicam;*
181, 182, 183, 184, 200, 235, 242.
War, 90, 191–193, 259–261; death in,
79, 80, 179, 218; spirituality of,
218–219; spiritual futility of, 219,
276.
"Where-in-some-way-one-lives", see
Quenonamicam.
Wind Jaguar, 123, 125, 128, 133,
134.
Wind-of-Nine-Caverns, 146.
Wind-of-Nine-Snakes, 146.
Wisdom, see also Black and Red
Inks; 69, 87, 126, 127, 200, 207,
209, 243, 252, 253; City or Land
of, see Tollan-Tlapallan; loss of
by first men, 126–127.
Women, 63–71, 82, 83, 84, 92, 93,
94, 95, 175, 187, 260–261; creation

of, 127–128, 143; duties, 65, 66;
public, 67, 68, 254–255.
Writing, 200.

Xacayamach, 272–273.
Xicohtencatl, 262, 268.
Xippacoyan, 152.
Xiquipilco, 260.
Xiuhcoatl, 223.
Xiuhnel, 198.
Xochitlan, 160, 163.
Xohcotitlan, 260.
Xuchatlapan, 216.

Yaomanatzin, 275.
Yohuallichan, 216.
Yoyontzin, 250.

Zacatepec, Mt. (Zacatepetl), 157–158,
162.